D1078346

SOLO ROUND SCOTLAND

The first single-handed circumnavigation by boat and bike

ALAN RANKIN

Whittles Publishing

Published by
Whittles Publishing,
Dunbeath,
Caithness KW6 6EY,
Scotland, UK

www.whittlespublishing.com

Text and photos © 2010 Alan Rankin
Foreword © 2010 Sir Ranulph Fiennes

ISBN 978-184995-003-9

Printed by InPrint, Latvia

Solo Round Scotland route

Scotland has 6,200 miles of coastline and over 800 islands. The route taken by *Pegasus* totalled 998 nautical miles (1148 miles). The cycle route was 163 miles with 8,400 ft of ascent.

Total elapsed time: 18 days 2 hrs 5 mins

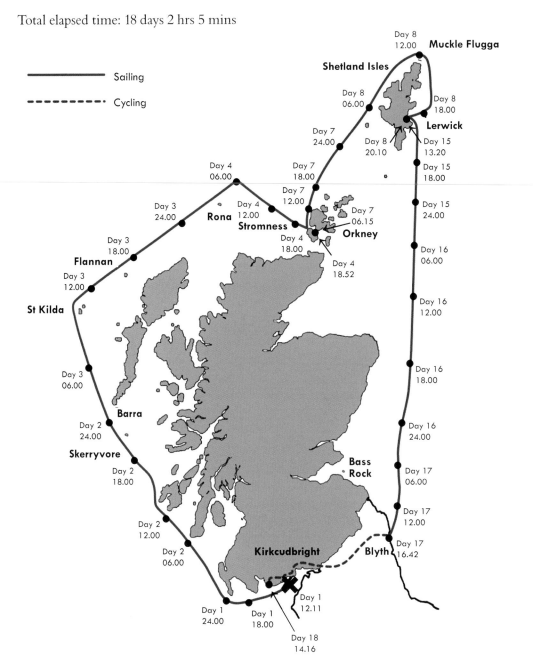

CONTENTS

FOREWORD

In April 2006 Alan Rankin set out from Kirkcudbright, on the Solway Firth, with three ambitions in mind: to raise funds for charity, to become the first person to sail and cycle around Scotland and to set a sailing world record in the process. Despite Alan's attempts to set a non-stop unsupported world record being thwarted by mechanical failure and further delays and frustration due to bad weather Alan battled on, to complete the solo voyage of some 1,000 miles. That done he did cycle back to his starting point at Kirkcudbright, and he did raise funds for charity. *Solo Round Scotland* is an account of an epic challenge, right here on our doorstep.

One of the major lessons I learnt during big polar challenges was that, in order not to be crushed by the very thought of all the difficulties and hazards of the task ahead, divide your target up into a number of much smaller goals and then think of them only one at a time. Alan describes the same principle in another manner: how do you eat an elephant? In bite-sized chunks.

The notion of sailing a 50-foot yacht single-handed round the entire coast of Scotland and its islands is daunting to most, if not all of us. But to then fully understand that achieving such a feat involves sailing out to the deep Atlantic waters off St Kilda and then on to the northern tip of our country round Muckle Flugga, a piece of land that is further north than Alaska, is hard for many to comprehend. Follow that with the long sail down the North Sea for the entire length of Scotland to Blyth on the north-east coast of England and you know you are on an adventure indeed. To pedal back to Kirkcudbright after two weeks, days of high drama, intense effort and no small amount of diversion and frustration is indeed an immense personal achievement. *Solo Round Scotland* gives us an insight of Alan and what drove him to pull off his vision of becoming the first person ever to single-handedly circumnavigate Scotland and its islands by boat and bike.

Successful adventures and challenges that are at the mercy of the elements and depend on human fortitude and determination do not come about as a matter of chance. Detailed planning and painstaking research of the environment you are entering is a bare minimum for a safe and successful outcome. Throughout this account of Solo Round Scotland it is clear that Alan held the elements and potential forces of nature in absolute regard. Having built an essential team of experienced people around him he minimised the risk as far as he could. But what is a challenge without risk? In today's society risk and personal danger is not an everyday experience. Alan shows how such risks can be managed. This is shown by the fact his passage plan had well researched 'bale out' points and by understanding the environment he was entering and even researching the number of merchant ships and tankers he was likely to meet in the busy shipping channels off the Pentland Firth. By putting in the groundwork with layer upon layer of careful planning the risks, so apparent and diverse in a challenge such as this, were mitigated. Solo Round Scotland may be an 'amateur' adventure in its truest sense but it is as professional and daring in its execution as many a large scale international expedition.

I was greatly impressed with Alan's work when he was director at Discovery Point Dundee, home of Scott's Royal Research ship *Discovery*. In 2001 Alan pulled together a year-long celebration programme and profile raising events to celebrate the centenary of the launch of RRS *Discovery*. I was fortunate to be involved and much enjoyed the Discovery Dinner, exactly 100 years to the day since the launch of the great ship. His creative approach to projects and focussed determination to get things done was a fair indication of the drive within the man. That approach to life had taken him to compete at international level in athletics and he was seven times Scottish Decathlon Champion, a feat never before achieved. That approach has taken his working career to senior positions in the Scottish tourism industry, an industry that fires an acute sense of pride and passion within him. His competitive sporting side still burns strongly and he is an ardent participator in the gruelling Scottish Islands Three Peaks Race and has over the years been on or near the podium on many occasions.

Alan had deep personal reasons for generating wider good from the Solo Round Scotland challenge. Parkinson's disease is a callous disease that had touched his own family with the loss of his father. It is a disease that can be eradicated as a result of bringing brains and cash together to find the cure. His second charity, Ocean Youth Trust Scotland, does a magnificent job in bringing forward our youth and in doing so helps many to grasp the real essence of life. OYTS is yet another organisation, vital to the fabric of our society that depends on the selfless giving of many volunteers. I commend Alan for raising money during the challenge and furthermore donating proceeds from the royalties from sales of *Solo Round Scotland* to these good and deserving causes.

Solo Round Scotland is a classic concept and is one of the last great adventures on and around our shores. It is a fascinating trip in the company of someone who had the determination and self-belief to get the job done. On the way Alan opens his soul to us and the experience he shares with us will be an inspiration to many.

Sir Ranulph Fiennes OBE

PREFACE

In April 2006 I set off from Kirkcudbright in a 50-foot yacht to become the first person to circumnavigate Scotland and its islands by boat and bike, set a world record and raise money for charities. The end result did not quite turn out the way it had been planned and *Solo Round Scotland* is an account of euphoric highs, mind-numbing lows, the elements in their rawest state, congested shipping lanes and, through cumulative fatigue, being reduced to tears on the hills within touching distance of my goal. More important than all of that, the two charities – The Parkinson's Disease Society and Ocean Youth Trust Scotland (OYTS) – gained vital funds and publicity. What was a meticulously planned and risk managed project came down to man and machine against the elements – and the elements came out on top.

The journey starts off in a Solway Firth gale and from that baptism of fire continues around Scotland and its islands before hitting the road across England and back to the starting point at Kirkcudbright. It is a journey around our coastline, a coastline that is ancient in its form, steeped in history but above all is presently in our hands for safekeeping. For what lies on the doorstep of Scotland is a resource that is often taken for granted but has in the past sustained us through bountiful provisions; in more recent times it has provided oil and gas, and, perhaps, will be the source of the clean energy of the future.

The one person I really wish could have sat down to read this book is my father who introduced me to sailing. Unfortunately, I will not have that nervous wait to hear his thoughts, comments and resulting conversation. Parkinson's disease took him from us before the trip came into being. I just hope the little I have done through the funds raised during the challenge and sales of this book will help in some way to find the cure so others are not cheated of such cherished moments. My other charity of choice is Ocean Youth Trust Scotland who carry out an amazing role in our society, offering youngsters the opportunity of realising the potential that lies within.

Solo Round Scotland, the book as opposed to the journey, came about as a result of detailed log book notes kept during the trip and the subsequent process of writing them up. That writing process started off simply to nail down some of the experiences behind the damp stained scribbled notes before they were lost to fading memory. In total it took over two years to complete and at times it felt like a journey almost as daunting as the trip itself. There are aspects within this book that I did not expect to write about at the outset. Inner thoughts and feelings experienced along the way tumbled out more than I ever would have expected. I hope *Solo Round Scotland* will appeal to not just sailing and outdoor enthusiasts so I have attempted, without too much dumbing down, to reduce technical jargon wherever possible. At times however, the language of the sea prevails, simply because of the immediacy and resonance of the vocabulary with the moment.

This is an account of my journey on a yacht and a bike round Scotland. Not a herculean challenge in comparison to global adventures, but it is one that took me to the absolute edge of my capabilities and from that I draw a massive level of satisfaction. In some way I hope this book might act as a prompt for a reader, just one reader to go and do something extraordinary that they might not have thought possible or beyond them.

Special thanks must go to my wife Shona who has weathered the full seasons of Solo Round Scotland. Not just my complete immersion through the months of preparation, my absence during the trip along with all of my ups and downs but, just when she thought it was all over, the hours at the keyboard. Thanks also to my dearest but long-suffering daughters Jennifer and Katrina for putting up with their old man's antics. Thanks also to my sister and brother, Helen and Ian, for seeing me in over the last few miles and cousin Derek for all the 'fixes' at Kirkcudbright. The trip and many family holiday experiences at sea and on far off west coast islands would not have been possible without the yacht *Pegasus* and for her I will forever be grateful to my good friend David Warnock. The quiet patience and guidance from the 'team' at Whittles Publishing has been much appreciated and a vital element in getting this challenge completed.

Alan Rankin
Carrbridge

1

HOW DO YOU SAIL AROUND SCOTLAND?

The plan was to sail and cycle round Scotland. It trips off the tongue, sail and cycle, by boat and bike, by wind and pedal power, take your pick. When you look at a map of Scotland, the course on the water is at first glance fairly straightforward. But then the options of hugging the mainland coast and sneaking round headlands or going for bust and taking in all of Scotland's islands has to be considered. Including the islands is another matter altogether as that follows a course well out into the Atlantic Ocean to St Kilda and then away to the far north, round the top of Unst at the Shetland Isles. Which way – clockwise or anticlockwise? What about the cycle route? Where is the starting point and, by definition for a circumnavigation, the finish point? Is it to be non-stop, unassisted or otherwise? Each combination loads even more questions, all needing answers.

So had Scotland been circumnavigated before? It seems a pretty basic question to which one would assume the answer to be 'yes'. Well, the answer is surprisingly a big 'no'. Having trawled the internet and the bookshelves I could find no mention of any attempt to truly circumnavigate Scotland. The fact that Scotland is not an island in its own right might have something to do with that. On closer study the claims to have paddled, cycled or walked around Scotland did not in my view 'do the whole job', certainly not in the entirety of Scotland, her coastline and the islands. There have been some great efforts to walk, kayak, cycle and sail but each of these attempts had been done in what I can best describe as 'bit part'. I am not trying to belittle what were brilliant efforts in conception or execution. Each heroic account was chased down on the Internet and bookshops with some books bought and avidly read, but all closely studied. Each were great efforts in their own way but each lacked that fundamental element; they did not go the whole way.

So my conclusion was that Scotland had never been truly circumnavigated. I suppose anyone who has sailed right round the UK could claim to have done so but where is the relevance to Scotland if the route takes you sailing down and around the Scilly Isles? Merchant ships had plied trade around our country for centuries but who had been from one corner of Scotland to the other corner and then joined the two corners together? Small boats had hopped around the coastline and could tick off the Scottish mainland but they fell well short when the islands were brought into the equation. Sea kayakers had flitted from bay to bay around our coastline with fortitude and stamina that defies belief but they had not been all the way round. One look at a chart or map of Scotland and it becomes pretty clear why it has not been done before. Places like St Kilda and Shetland come immediately to your attention as they lie away off in the open oceans that surround our shores. So the concept was established; to be the first person to truly circumnavigate the whole of Scotland. Now the onus was on 'person' so that, in my book, meant that it had to be single-handed. Such a challenge in the company of others would devalue its currency by so much to render it another of the also-rans that had gone before.

With the challenge established, some questions were fairly easy to answer, such as 'which way round'? I had decided that west to east, clockwise, would make best use of prevailing west to south-west winds that sweep in from the Atlantic. My attention therefore went straight to the Solway Firth for the start and Berwick-upon-Tweed for the end of the sailing leg. The subsequent bike leg of Berwick-upon-Tweed to Gretna looked good on a map and, for added value, carried with it two identifiable iconic border towns. But in sailing terms Gretna was totally impracticable due to the shallow tidal waters of the Solway Firth. What did appeal was the fact that Berwick-upon-Tweed to Gretna, on a bike, was not too long a trip. It was a narrow part of the country to cycle across and that put a smile back on my face.

The Solway Firth is a notorious piece of shallow water with tides that rip in and out, setting in general an east or west flow. Massive shifting sand banks are also a feature of the area and, as I had never sailed down there before, an amount of research would be needed. So if I was to circumnavigate Scotland and its islands, the course was pretty academic: Solway Firth, out past the most south-westerly corner of Scotland at the Mull of Galloway and then north-west, crossing the North Channel, the stretch of water that separates Northern Ireland from Scotland. The route would then skirt the Mull of Kintyre and head over to the southern shores of Islay, keeping out of the shipping lanes feeding the Clyde estuary. From there I would be out into open water, with the lighthouse at Skerryvore left to the north and on out to Barra Head at the most southerly tip of the archipelago that is the Outer Hebrides. From there my route would be a 60-mile sail into the open Atlantic waters to St Kilda, then north-east passing the Flannan Isles, Sula Sgeir and North Rona. The island of North Rona represented a 'corner' of the course at which I would be furthest away from mainland Scotland than at any time in the trip, over 80 miles from anything or anyone. From North Rona the heading is taken to the north-east and the 140 miles or so across open seas to Muckle Flugga, the most northerly outpost of Scotland and the UK, further north than St Petersburg, Bergen and, believe it or not, Anchorage in Alaska! Muckle Flugga is closer to the Arctic Circle than to Edinburgh, never mind to London. From there I could be facing a 350-mile beat into the wind to take me south and down the east shore of Shetland and Orkney before heading again into open water and the North Sea. My concerns at that point in such a voyage would be fatigue, potentially boat-breaking conditions plus heavy shipping traffic funnelling in towards the Pentland Firth. Once beyond that busy area of our coast, the route is almost dead due south passing some 40 miles or so off Aberdeen, Dundee and across the approaches to the Forth Estuary, then down to Berwick-upon-Tweed in Northumberland, just south of the Scottish border. Navigationally, the whole voyage is fairly straightforward but my main concerns lay with the busy shipping activities feeding the Clyde via the North Channel, the west and eastern approaches to the Pentland Firth, oil supply ships running in and out of Aberdeen and, last but not least, shipping entering or leaving the Forth. In a series of straight lines the route measured 985 nautical miles (1133 miles). If I could maintain a boat speed of, say 5 knots, the sailing leg could be done in just over 8 days. From there I would be on my bike and pedalling the 160 miles or so back to my starting point down on the Solway Coast. Do that, and I would be the first person to have circumnavigated Scotland by boat and bike.

So what lay behind such an idea, and what brought all of this together? I have been all my life a competitive sod and I fear until the day I cannot shuffle without a zimmer frame will continue to measure, time and test myself. Every game of golf is an attempt to beat my record score, every hill run is timed to compare it with my last run and every business challenge is one to be worked out, considered and aimed to bring about the very best outcome possible. To be cursed or blessed, depending on your viewpoint, with this outlook on life has many plus points associated with it but also some costs. This condition has formed my life in work and play and at times has cost me valuable time with my family.

Behind all of the thinking about such a challenge there also lay a very real desire to do some good out of my exploits, and that meant a contribution to charitable activities. The choice of charities to benefit was pretty straightforward and did not take as much thought as the route or direction in which to head. I lost my Dad, Tom Rankin, as a result of Parkinson's disease and I had never really done anything before or after his death to help the charity find the cure. A cure, I strongly believe, is out there. It is just a matter of time and money until it is found. Dad had been a keen sailor all his days. During the war he was posted to India and the first thing he set about in his free time was building a sailing dinghy. We have some grainy black and white photos of that first build, alongside a very satisfied young trainee officer. After that he was posted to Hiroshima in Japan, not long after the bomb had been dropped. I always had a sneaking question in the back of my mind that his posting to that horrible place had come back to haunt him and affected his health in later years. He never spoke of that time of his life, unlike his spell in India. I have on a bookshelf at home a piece of molten glass melted with sand, wood and metal;

a contorted souvenir of Hiroshima's history. Dad, for whatever reason and no one yet knows why, picked the short straw and contracted Parkinson's. It is a wicked, wicked disease that slowly takes your loved one away into a dark place; the person you knew is stolen from you and cheated of their own short time here on earth. Like many families we did not really discuss and dissect the situation to the 'nth degree'. It just took over and all of a sudden Dad was 'not with us', kidnapped from right under our noses. It was so strange because his long-term memory on selected matters was faultless. A case in point; he could recite with absolute precision passages of Shakespeare and poetry, along with his party piece of *Little Miss Muffet* in Urdu. Somehow these childhood and adolescent memory chips were unscathed, yet short-term and conversational memory slipped away ever faster by the day. He had the tremor or the 'shakes', as he would say but at times made light of it. On looking at photographs of one of my sailing trips, he quipped that he had better stop as with the shakes it might make him sea-sick. Near the end, which did come suddenly, thank goodness, he announced that he was going to stop seeing the doctors as every time they found something else was wrong. In the end Parkinson's disease marginalised the man and finally took him from us. By a strange irony, I was lying in my berth onboard *Pegasus* on the morning of the Scottish Islands Three Peaks Race, thinking about race tactics, when I took the call from my brother Ian that Dad had died during the night. There was no sailing and hill-running race for me that year but there was a race that morning to get home to say goodbye to my Dad before the men in black took him away from us all. After having made some tentative enquiries of the Parkinson's Disease Society, I found their staff to be very helpful and keen to know more of the project that was swilling around in my head. On a business trip to London, I made some time to visit the Society at their headquarters at Vauxhall Bridge. After that, there was no doubt in my mind that I could work with these people.

The second charity I selected was Ocean Youth Trust Scotland (OYTS). I was their Chairman at the time of the challenge and remain mightily impressed with the work they do. OYTS operates in Scotland as the leading sail training charity, each year taking over 1,000 youngsters aged between 16 and 24 to sea and quite literally changing lives in the process. Like so many charities, OYTS is totally dependent on staff who 'go the extra mile' and on dedicated volunteers who simply 'allow' the organisation to function. They also have the great good fortune of having two of the most generous patrons you could ever hope to meet in the shape of Barbara and Curly Mills. Through their generosity, OYTS operates a fleet of yachts that offers the charity a superb platform to deliver their vitally important youth work. At the time of writing OYTS has two ex-British Steel round the world 72-footers and a 70-foot Oyster ketch.

I had been aware of the work that OYTS did and was initially involved when Curly asked me to help with some fund-raising activities. That led to a successful Lottery bid that put in place an Education Officer. One thing led to another and I was on the Board of Trustees not long after. One defining moment, regarding the impact of their work, hit me one evening on the daily train commute from Edinburgh to Perth. Well into the journey and after the 'sardines', as I referred to the Fife commuters, had cleared the train I was conscious of a rather loudly-spoken individual a few seats behind me. He sounded like one of those poor unfortunate youngsters on whom drugs had taken their toll. His voice was slurred, loud, broad Glasgow and on occasion had elements of incoherency. He was engaged in conversation with the conductor about arrival times in Inverness and how the train was so busy he did not get a seat until after Kirkcaldy. He went on and on about this and, having lost patience with the one-way conversation, the conductor headed off up the front of the train. 'Hey pal, what do you think of that?' boomed the voice from two seats behind me. With my nose deep in a sailing magazine I took the easy option and ignored the lad. Undeterred he was up from his seat and standing over me. 'Is there a trolley on this train?' Taking a snap assessment of the lad who was in his mid-twenties but with a gaunt and thin presence, I jumped to the conclusion that the question was code for the booze trolley. I advised him that it might be further up the train and sought the safety of some inconsequential small ad in my magazine. Off he went. Without any success on the trolley front, he found the conductor and re-engaged him in a loud but not unpleasant conversation, one from which your natural tendency is to turn away. On his way back past my seat he muttered, 'There is nae pishing trolley on the train.' He sat down, soon followed down the aisle by a rather nervous-looking conductor. With my head still buried in the magazine, my worst fears came true for I was aware of the young lad now

The Oyster ketch Alba Venturer *under full sail – former round the world challenge yacht*

OYTS Alba Venturer *under full sail (courtesy OYTS)*

standing over my table seat and then, in an instant, in the seat opposite me. 'Dae ye sail?' I looked up and nodded, thinking frantically of escape routes and what-ifs. 'Yes I do,' I replied, not really wanting to know where this conversation might go. The following half hour to Perth Station has influenced my life, my approach to people and the recognition of the easy pitfall of jumping to conclusions. We exchanged sailing stories, he regaling me with the fact that he was on his way to Inverness to join a sail training boat, and how he had worked up so many 'brownie points' to get away for his third voyage. His conversation glowed with absolute pride as he described his first night at sea, taking the helm under the moonlit night skies and how he had learnt to flake rope in the correct fashion so as to avoid tangles and knots when it was needed in an emergency. His pride in being the best 'flaker' on board was clear. As we exchanged sailing stories, the conductor made many more trips through the carriage than I had ever seen on such a journey, each time nervously glancing in my direction. We were fine and it was a pity to leave this nameless lad as I got off at Perth. The hope and focus that sail training had brought to that young man's life was tangible and the veneer-thin consideration that I had for him was perhaps even more enlightening for me. From that evening I have never judged a person from an initial impression or by their appearance. Through my work with OYTS I was delighted to play just a small part in helping the organisation and people like the lad on the 17.42 Edinburgh–Inverness service.

Dad had introduced me to sailing at an early age, having built a Mirror dinghy in the dining room for us kids to sail. My Mother was fine about it as, after the event, she got a newly-decorated dining room. I can still vividly remember the dinghy being heaved out of the big bay window, varnish glinting and gleaming in the sunshine. The dinghy was to start my whole journey afloat and one for which I will always be grateful to Dad. My sailing started on Loch Ard where we competed most weekends in mixed fleet handicap dinghy races. I crewed and my brother Ian was helm; it was sort of natural selection really as he was bigger than me. I spent many a jittery cold wet Sunday afternoon down by the leeward gunwale with water splashing over me as Ian pressed me down there with his foot firmly wedged between my shoulder blades. I was mere ballast. To say we had our moments was an understatement as we were quite often at each other's throat by the time we reached shore at the end of the race. I can remember on one occasion being told off in no uncertain manner by a rather embarrassed and irate Mother who made it very clear to us that voices travel over water, especially raised vitriolic fraternal abuse. I suppose I should thank my brother Ian for his part in instilling a competitive streak in me; or was it beaten into me?

Having been lucky enough to be introduced to sailing at an early stage in life, I enjoyed a great relationship with boats throughout my childhood. As a family we holidayed at Carradale on the Kintyre Peninsula and each summer our sailing developed as we pushed our boundaries. Sailing around Port Righ Bay was followed by sneaking just out of the bay and then the huge leap of sailing out to the Kilbrannan Rock buoy off Carradale Bay. A solo crossing of the Kilbrannan Sound in our little Mirror dinghy met with disapproval from Dad, but it was not a real telling off. The Mirror progressed to a Kestrel dinghy, a boat that was to offer us great fun and enjoyment. I parted company with sailing in my late teens and twenties as I concentrated on athletics. It was when I heard that Dad was thinking of selling the family Kestrel that I bought her and, from then on, it has been boats, boats and more boats. My first keel boat was a Club 19, one that should come with a health warning. Fast, over-powered and exciting would sum it up best. She was first sailed on the Forth out of Port Edgar, the marina that sits right under the Forth Road Bridge, and then laterally at Loch Earn Sailing Club. On one annual Lochearnhead Race we had the dubious pleasure of capsizing the boat. Yes, she was a keel boat and they are not supposed to capsize, but she did. We gybed and lost the spinnaker and *Ookytoo*, as she was called, was pulled over by the now-uncontrolled sail. She just lay on her side with mast in the water and refused to come back to the upright. I was sailing with my cousin Ian Philp that day and, whilst I was wedged in the now vertical cockpit holding on to our panic-stricken, white-faced third crew member, Ian had neatly climbed onto the now horizontal side of the hull and was standing on the keel righting her like a dinghy! She was sold not long after this episode to my friend Gordon Jack, who was looking for a nice entry level safe-to-sail boat! I must have glossed over the capsizing issues prior to the sale. Anyway it did him no harm and he now enjoys his sailing on a 42-footer on the west coast of Scotland.

The Club 19 Okytoo *– the author's first keel boat*

Hot on the heels of *Ookytoo* came *Cloud Nine*, a Delta 25-foot. Now, she was a cracker and a boat that delivered in every way. I bought her in partnership with my cousin Ian. Between the two families we numbered nine so *Cloud Nine* aptly summed up the state of mind of the respective fathers when we were out sailing, and the head count of the Rankin–Philp tribe. *Cloud Nine* served her time on Loch Earn both racing and cruising. We also campaigned her on a couple of East Coast Sailing Week regattas and she just lapped it all up. In 1995 she was taken over to Dunstaffnage after the use of a mooring buoy was offered to me by John Leckie of Crieff, another man stricken with Parkinson's, and from that moment salt water has been in my blood. *Cloud Nine* took me off into another world and to places that I am sure very few people have seen and enjoyed, other than those lucky enough to have experienced the west coast by boat. Being a small boat with a lifting keel, I could sneak her into all sorts of corners and anchorages. *Cloud Nine* took me on my first 'real' solo voyage when in 1997 I did a single-handed sail round the island of Mull. It was a trip of 98 miles in some of the most sublime sailing waters imaginable, passing Iona, Staffa and the Treshnish Isles. She was also the very first boat that I skippered in the Scottish Islands Three Peaks Race. At 25 feet she was the smallest boat in the fleet but we acquitted ourselves very well. The SIPR, as it is known, is a great weekend of hard graft, the course being a 120-mile sail with hill running interludes roped in for good measure. The runs over three hills amount to 56 miles, with just over 14,000 feet of ascent. *Cloud Nine* did well but my crew complained at the end of the race that we had run out of water, beer and, because of the aging battery, electricity as well. Due to her size I was also accused of running out of headroom in the cabin and, because of the close proximity of five sweaty runners and sailors, 'fresh air' was also added to the list of onboard shortages. 'What a bunch of complaining whingers!'

In 1998 everything changed, and changed in a big way. My

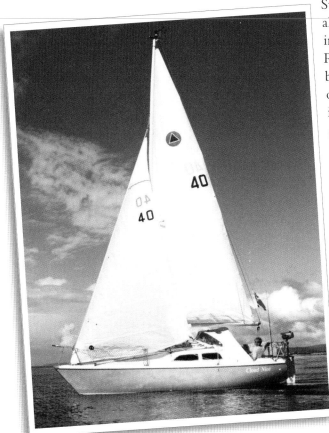

The Hunter Delta Cloud Nine *ghosting along on a sublime west coast day*

Pegasus undergoing sea trials off Mull, 2001
(courtesy Andi Robertson)

lifetime pal David Warnock joined me for a sail on *Cloud Nine* and was smitten by the whole experience of the west. Before we knew where we were, a brand new Bavaria 41 was on order. The jump from 25 feet to 41 feet was entirely due to David and the success he had carved out as a highly gifted fund manager. The Bavaria 41, *Ziggy*, took us up a level and opened up all sorts of opportunities as she had longer legs and could get much further afield than little *Cloud Nine*. Moving up from 25 feet to 41 feet also presented me, as skipper, with some boat handling challenges. On our first arrival at Dunstaffnage marina I proceeded to stuff her bow into the pontoon. It was an awfully long way away from the wheel! With *Ziggy* the glorious west coast of Scotland had been opened up and many a great weekend and family holiday was enjoyed aboard her. Then one fateful day a couple of years later, as we were sailing back to Dunstaffnage marina from Lismore, David casually threw into conversation the possibility of getting a larger boat. *Pegasus* was to follow and we were now operating at stratospheric levels compared with *Ookytoo* and *Cloud Nine*. Coming in at 50 feet and over 14 tonnes, *Pegasus*, a Beneteau 50, was just a sublime blue-water yacht and that is the only way to describe her. David never did anything in life by halves so *Pegasus* was kitted up to the highest standard.

She was a fantastic boat for family cruising as we had opted for the four-cabin option, each with en suite heads (toilets) so, for the ladies, *Pegasus* banished the hardships of 'normal' sailing weekends. Up top she had the taller sports mast and we rigged her with all lines running back to the cockpit for short-handed sailing. Everything about *Pegasus* was big. Her cockpit sported two steering wheels and all lines were heavy, with equally heavy-duty winches and tackle. *Pegasus* was a magnificent yacht and one that took groups of lads and families off for some classic weekend and holiday cruises on the beautiful and stunning west coast of Scotland. There are too many places to mention but three stand out: Loch Scavaig/Coruisk on Skye, Fingal's Cave on or, more to the point, in Staffa and Canna. Loch Scavaig is an awesome natural drama. This deep sea loch with cliff face and flowing fresh water lies on the south-west shore of Skye, right under the Cuillins. In 1814 Sir Walter Scott joined Robert Stevenson on the Northern Lighthouse Board Ship *Pharos* on a 6-week cruise, inspecting lights and potential new sites for lighthouses. No better description than Scott's matches the splendour of that place:

> *For all is rocks at random thrown,*
> *Black waves, bare crags, and banks of stone,*
> *As if were here denied*
> *The summer's sun, the spring's sweet dew,*
> *That clothe with many a varied hue*
> *The bleakest of mountain-side.*

Lord of the Isles
Walter Scott

Left: Sitting safe in Loch Scavaig under the brooding Black Cuillins of Skye

Right: Pegasus at anchor in the blue waters of Canna harbour, Canna

I mention the famous Fingal's Cave as, on one perfectly calm day when sailing was not on the cards, we rowed our rubber dinghy into its jaws and proceeded to punt our way to its very head, deep inside the basaltic columnar heart of that normally wave-dashed island. It was a truly memorable experience and I could go on but we have a country to navigate and such stories of heaven on earth are for another day. So from a start in a 14-foot Mirror dinghy, Dad sent me on a voyage neither of us knowing where it would take me. 'What it is to be given such an opportunity and opening to a lifetime of experience by my parents!' So Dad had started it all off and, if I managed to pull off this madcap idea, I reckoned that he might approve.

Now this idea of circumnavigating Scotland had started off in a totally different direction. In the dark nights of November and December 2004 I had religiously followed, online, the efforts and heroics of Ellen MacArthur as she screamed around the globe on *Kingfisher,* her hyper-tuned ocean-going trimaran speedster. It was fascinating to watch the drama unfold as day by day she raced her boat against the ever-ticking clock to eventually beat the record. Earlier in the same year Frenchman Francis Joyan had sailed round the world on his multi-hull in an astounding 72 days, taking 37 days off the previous record. Some observers had questioned whether it was worth Ellen, now Dame Ellen, even attempting the record. Better she maintain her air of greatness on matters achieved than take on what was an 'out of sight record'. To break the record would not only need cutting-edge technology, which she had, determination and skill, which she had in boatloads, but also luck, in the winds, in the state of the seas and the awesome battering that both could unleash on the boat. Undeterred she set off on her voyage around the world and it very soon became obvious that this was a challenge that meant business. *B&Q* went ahead of the schedule to beat the record and stayed there for days and days on end. It was only in the last quarter, as she crawled her way north through the doldrums off South America, that doubts started to creep in. *B&Q* picked up some unfavourable light winds and Ellen famously had to scale the mast to repair a 'showstopper' of a problem with the sails. She managed to break through the light airs, and the rest is history. She had recorded the fastest single-handed circumnavigation of 27,354 nautical miles (50,660 kilometres) at a stunning average speed of 15.9 knots. Her time of 71 days 14 hours 18 minutes 33 seconds beat Joyon's world record time by 1 day 8 hours 35 minutes 49 seconds. Clearly feeling miffed at the loss of his record, Joyon set off in *IDEC II* and on 20 January 2008 slaughtered the record in a Bob Beamon-like performance in a time of 57 days 13 hours 34 minutes 6 seconds, at an average speed of 19.8 knots. To poach a well-worn phrase from another warp factor ship, 'This is not sailing as we mortals know it ...'

As I sat glued to the computer screen through that winter, watching the live online data feed reporting Ellen's progress, my mind was working overtime and from there an idea was spawned that I had to do something myself, something grand and something challenging. I had an unfulfilled 'something' deep inside that I needed to exorcise. I wanted to do something big, something that would be a 'stand out' life moment. I wanted to set a world sailing record, but what world record? Behind all of the officially recognised world speed sailing records, be they windsurfers or indeed Ellen's round the world record, there is one body that oversees attempts, timing verification and listing for all to see. This defining authority is the World Speed Sailing Record Council (WSSRC). A quick look on their website revealed that the nearest record to home was the circumnavigation of Ireland, a passage of some 975 miles that stood at just over a not too daunting 11 days. The idea of making an attempt on the Irish route lingered for a few days and then started to dig into my thinking more and more. The passage was a realistic project for me to consider as it was close to home and the time was beatable.

Now all thoughts of taking on a serious sailing endeavour were possible as a result of David Warnock, for it was he who put our boat *Pegasus* in the water. She had the size and sea-worthiness to take on such a passage and, most importantly, keep me safe. However, a trip of such magnitude and challenge was no normal weekend jaunt, so a chat with David was required. He confirmed that he had no objection to me considering such a trip and was fully supportive of the concept, even if in his mind he thought it a touch mad. With David's OK, I knew I had the means to undertake a serious voyage and, deep inside, I knew I had the capability not to turn this whole passage into a 'Captain Calamity' affair. I had the will to do it and the good fortune in the shape of a solid ocean-going yacht. Putting all of that together, Solo Round Ireland was born.

The following spring, summer and autumn of 2005 saw detailed planning, contact with WSSRC, sponsors and the building of a project team, only for all these plans to be torn up and Plan B come into play. The record around Ireland of just over 11 days meant an average speed of 3.6 knots. In order to make the most of winds and forecast, the challenger had the choice of making the passage clockwise or anticlockwise, as long as it started from Dublin. I spent hours and hours passage planning the trip, estimating arrival times at the key tidal pressure points around the Irish coast and, like on any passage, throwing in a whole load of 'what-if' scenarios for good measure. As all of this frenzy of thinking and planning was underway, an Englishman pitched up in August 2005 and took the record down to just over 9 days, dealing the concept of my challenge a standing count, but not a knockout blow. The original record had stood for over 10 years and it was just

David Warnock at the wheel of a gleaming new Pegasus *in 2001*

12

my luck that, when I had turned my attention to the record, it was broken. But worse, much worse was to follow. Some 6 weeks later in October a Belgian, in an out-and-out racing yacht blasted round Ireland and took the record down to 4 days 1 hour 53 minutes 29 seconds. To do the trip in that time meant that an average boat speed of 7.2 knots would be required and that was simply just out of sight for *Pegasus*. The new record meant that my campaign was over. The possibility of breaking the record was gone and the notion of 'it's the taking part', which I have never really subscribed to, was not really an option. This was a real blow, 10 months of dreaming, planning and getting people to believe in the project had just gone up in smoke – Belgian smoke. I had raised money from sponsors, donators and had in-kind support lined up. I had a shore team and a boat insured to race but nowhere to go. It was a hammer blow and one that really did floor me for a few days.

I had put too much into this idea for it just to fade away and be forgotten. After a few days of feeling sorry for myself, Plan B came to me in a flash when running down a hill near Pitlochry. Sailing round Scotland is something I have not heard anyone talk about. Further down the hill I had refined the voyage to a sail from west to east, perhaps the Solway Firth to Berwick-upon-Tweed. I was convinced I had a plan and one that might have closer resonance with home. After all, why go and promote Ireland when we have such fantastic sailing waters around Scotland? By the end of the run I knew I had a plan to convert into reality. First purchase was a planning chart of Scotland – I set about plotting the course and the Solway to Berwick-upon-Tweed jumped off the page. The fact that it was a one-legged sail, albeit right around the Scotland and its islands, from A to B and not returning to A nagged away at me for a few days. It was on the commuter train the following week as we were pulling over the Forth Rail Bridge that it became blindingly obvious to me. Get off the boat at Berwick-upon-Tweed and run back to the starting point. A quick glance at the map in my pocket diary suggested the 'on land' route would be about 160 miles. That sobered me up very quickly. By the time I had reached Perth at the end of my train commute, 'on foot' had been developed into 'by bike'. It all seemed pretty clear and in a very quick jotting on a pad of paper the whole plan tumbled out: be the first ever person to circumnavigate Scotland by boat and bike. On getting home I went straight to the PC and found with relief that domain www.soloroundscotland.com was available. I bought it and the project was born or, to put it another way, 'soloroundireland' was reborn. A quick look in a sailing almanac indicated that Kirkcudbright was the main marina along the Solway shore so the Solway to Berwick-upon-Tweed was refined to Kirkcudbright to Berwick-upon-Tweed. I made telephone calls to everyone that had offered to help with the 'Irish project' to tell them Ireland was no longer on the cards and for Ireland, read Scotland! The bit about Scotland not being an island took a bit of explaining. No-one baulked at the idea and it did feel during the conversations that local home support was likely to be stronger for a Scottish passage than one around Ireland. With that support in hand, the Solo Round Ireland project management file was closed and Solo Round Scotland opened.

The World Sailing Speed Record Council (WSSRC) was established by the then International Yacht Racing Union in 1972. The object was to provide impartial results for increasing numbers of claims to high-speed sailing craft on water. Early on the decision was made to base such speed ratifications on a one-way leg of exactly 500 metres. Meetings were held throughout the year, often several meetings a year, in various places around the world as speeds climbed and interest in speed sailing and setting records increased. Following several controversial claims about the times and status of long voyages, WSSRC was asked in 1988 to take on the administration for offshore sailing records. Since 2001 the organisation has had a full-time Secretariat and hardly a day goes by without some form of activity in what is now a separate and increasingly specialised branch of the sport of sailing. The expert council draws members from Australia, France, Great Britain and the USA. Its most immediate duty is the ratification, or otherwise, of timed records, inshore and offshore, that have been achieved in accordance with the rules of WSSRC. Certificates are issued to record holders and their times are listed for all to see on the WSSRC website. WSSRC has a facility for issuing Performance Certificates to sailors who wish to be officially timed over accepted courses, but are not expecting to beat a record. The Performance Certificate is also issued to register the performance of a boat that has established a new route, or first attempt at a new route that has not yet been ratified as an official route. The route of Kirkcudbright to Berwick-upon-Tweed certainly did not figure as an official route. All of a sudden my trip round Scotland was not just an attempt to be the first to do it but had just added another layer to the whole challenge. 'Why not do it non-stop, register as an official passage and obtain a WSSRC Performance Certificate?' The idea rumbled around in my head for a few days until I had it all tied up. Solo Round Scotland: first; to circumnavigate Scotland non-stop with no external assistance; second, to make it a 'world record' in waiting; and third, to raise money for charity.

The WSSRC has a very efficient approach, with any candidate required to apply through the proper channels and complete the appropriate registration forms. I duly completed the paperwork and was helped along the way by their secretary, John Reed. He was sympathetic to the 'Irish situation' and moved seamlessly into supporting the round Scotland challenge. He was particularly intrigued by the boat and bike element and could not have been more helpful. He advised that the WSSRC would recognise a passage from the south-west corner of Scotland, out past St Kilda and Muckle Flugga, ending on the north-east coast of England. The WSSRC would require a timed start and timed finish, with an independent 'commissioner' to take the times. On checking his records, he confirmed there were no such commissioners in the Kirkcudbright or north-east areas so he would need to come up to inspect *Pegasus* and that I would need to have two 'respectable' individuals at either end to verify times. WSSRC was now aboard and the challenge had just become official. I must admit to being rather chuffed that such an august body as the WSSRC would consider a new 'official' passage dreamt up by me.

I had decided at the outset of the 'Irish plan' that my main communication tool was going to be web-based. Through work I had been introduced to Iain Taylor who runs the company E-zone Interactive. E-zone is in the content management system business, the platform on which to build a website. No sooner had I mentioned the challenge to Iain than he offered to provide a free licence to his content management system. In addition, he secured free web-hosting and e-mail support from Titan internet. I was in business, I had the domain www.soloroundscotland.com, I had an e-mail account and hosting and I had the shell of a website. The build of the website took a significant amount of time and there were evenings when my wife Shona must have been really tested. I would come back from work, hit the bike for an hour, grab supper and then vanish upstairs to the computer to work away on the website. As a by-product of the challenge I now have a good understanding of websites, their build and the issues surrounding getting them right. I do not profess to be an expert, perhaps proficient in a very easy-to-use web management tool in the shape of the WMS content management system. So in early December 2005 www.soloroundscotland.com went live. My project was now out there and I felt that there was no going back. This was no Irish false start; this time I had a live website and it was attracting interest and, more importantly, public donations to OYTS and PDS had started to trickle in. During the course of the challenge the website proved to be invaluable as a communications tool. At the time of the actual sail, over 1,000 visits were coming in each day. Through working on links and various other tricks, the site became very highly ranked on Google and MSN search engines. The website was building a history of latest news and cash barriers being broken by the donations fund. It carried images of *Pegasus* and, through the site, links to OYTS, PDS and the online donations pages. Iain poured more goodwill into the project by offering to manage a map page that would track my progress at sea and on land. So thanks to a mix of Iain's cunning and the brilliant resource of Google Earth, SRS was online, capable of taking money and a great communication platform.

So it was all falling into place. I had a boat that I knew would be safe to attempt such a trip, a website to generate publicity and take money, two good reasons to take money, a challenge that no-one had done before and a strengthening determination to make this my big one.

2

PREPARATION

The blue touch paper had been lit good and proper. Now, it was down to the real nitty-gritty of making sure I completed the whole adventure safe and sound. *Pegasus* was a hell of an expensive boat to stuff up the rocks and I had no ambition to turn into another statistic for air sea rescue or the RNLI. To help prevent any of these nightmares happening, or any other calamity, I defaulted back to an approach that had served me well back in my twenties when I was competing at international level in athletics. My chosen event, away back then in another lifetime, was the Decathlon, ten track and field events spread over two days. Some would say jack of all trades, master of none. To compete at a serious level and to have a modicum of competence in each of the 10 disciplines required an approach to training and preparation that was entirely dependent upon a methodical team-based approach and hard graft. I needed to run, jump and throw. As a result of my competitive nature I could go out and do the one-to-one stuff on the track, but the level of competence was only a product of working with a team of people, each specialists in their own field or, in this case, event. It worked; I represented Scotland and won the Scottish Decathlon title on seven occasions. With that approach applied to great effect, I simply put the same principle into play when it came to the challenge. So I set about building a team to help me with my personal challenge of sailing and cycling around Scotland. With some arm twisting and some chatting up, my team came together, and to each individual I will be eternally grateful for their interest, expertise, time and commitment to the challenge.

A Shore Manager was critical as the point of contact both for me and for family and friends when I was at sea. Much as I would have liked it, I did not want to have dribs and drabs of calls and contacts coming out to *Pegasus* when sailing. Because of the 24-hour nature of the trip, and the fact that this was going to be a non-stop attempt, the role was split in two. It fell to two really good pals to fill this pivotal function, Erik Archer and Gordon McGeorge. Erik, a great sailing mate, was one of the most reliable and enjoyable men I knew to sail with. He is 'steady-Eddie' personified, knowledgeable with a vast range of sailing experience, including a transatlantic and passage racing background. He was only too happy to help out where he could. Gordon was a multiple Scottish sailing dinghy champion and the competitive foil to Erik. Gordon's background is health and safety so he could and would look at issues and see their potential downside and problem. For that 'glass half empty' approach Gordon was a vital cog in the team. I would set up six-hourly safety contacts throughout the voyage with the guys so I could give them my position and allow them to relay weather forecasts and other information to me. My contact on the six-hourly routine was vital not only for good safety management but also for vital and much-needed connection with friendly voices. Gordon and Erik were to give so much time to the challenge by alternating the duty of manning a telephone every six hours, night and day. Each contact would confirm my position, course, speed and general well-being. They in turn could feed me any specific weather information and news and also keep an ear open to my mood and mental state.

I had the good fortune that my cousin Derek Collins lives in Kirkcudbright and he proved to be a fundamental lynch-pin in setting up arrangements in the area, both ashore and afloat. Derek brought into play Rab Thomson, the local Harbourmaster, along with Peter Roberts at the marina and John Aitken, who provided a support boat. Derek also pulled out of the hat Colin Warden, who agreed to act as official timekeeper on behalf of the WSSRC and Keith Newman, who would supply a boat on standby at the start to ferry the camera crew back to shore. At a stroke Derek had taken off my plate so many logistical arrangements – *Pegasus* had a berth, a local network and, most important of all, I had a known, trusted and friendly face in Kirkcudbright. With Derek aboard the team, Kirkcudbright was basically sorted!

Back on matters afloat, Nick Fleming, Chief Executive of Ocean Youth Trust Scotland, was up for the challenge and was a good sounding board on safety and a great 'weather eye' on the overall state of play. Nick had been a round the world yacht race skipper so my trip was but a small hop compared with what he had experienced. Although Nick did not get as far as hands on with the planning, he came up trumps with a portfolio of charts that covered the entire trip. I had in an instant a folder with over 30 passage planning and detailed local paper charts affording me a complete back-up set of charts from Kirkcudbright to Berwick-upon-Tweed. The cost of acquiring such a comprehensive portfolio would have been many hundreds of pounds. Nick also took from stores an Emergency Position Indicating Radio Beacon (EPIRB) to bolster safety equipment aboard *Pegasus*. If activated, the beacon would send out a unique distress signal that, when detected, would help search and rescue services locate *Pegasus* or, God forbid, my life raft. If I had a catastrophic incident forcing me to abandon ship, I had a grab bag stowed and ready to hand at the companionway to the cockpit. In the bright yellow waterproof bag I had stowed, each in a sealed plastic bag: water, food, hat and gloves, thermal survival bag, flares, handheld VHF radio, spare satellite phone, mini toolkit and a first aid kit. If it was 'curtains' and abandonment was the only and last option, the life raft could be deployed from the stern and my grab bag gathered in seconds. Not that I was planning to use either. Nick took on the not-inconsiderable task of making arrangements to get *Pegasus* sailed back from the east to the west coast after the challenge. To do this he lined up a crew of volunteers who would take charge of *Pegasus* at the east side finishing spot and sail her back to Oban via the Caledonian Canal. *Pegasus* would be in very safe hands as the crew would be qualified with RYA Yachtmaster certificates and thousands of sea miles under their belts. That was a huge worry off my mind.

One vital key factor for success was getting the right weather for the trip. April had been picked as it presented the optimum time, in my view, for wind predictability and average strengths. This assumption was reached having studied the average wind speeds over the past 30 years from both the Irish and UK inshore forecasts. The information pointed towards an April, late September or early October trip. Average wind speeds were high and each month fell just after or before the periods where there was a higher propensity for gales. I hit gold when I was introduced to Fiona Campbell, who is absolutely at the top of the tree when it comes to sailing weather forecasting. Fiona would be my insight to weather patterns and would ultimately give me the nod as to when it was the best time to set off. Fiona was at the time meteorologist for GBR Challenge and was also the meteorologist for the RYA Olympic sailing team. Growing up on the Isle of Skye and sailing around the Scottish Hebrides had instilled a passion for weather. A degree in Meteorology from Reading University and experience as an operational forecaster presented the opportunity to work as a freelance meteorologist specialising in marine meteorology. Her talents also took her to work as forecaster for *Spirit*, the Volvo 60 which won the 2003 ARC Race. Fiona's website – www.skyeweather.com – is well worth a visit. She was spot on with her predictions for the whole trip and, without her certainty on all matters meteorological, the trip would have been based considerably more on guess work as opposed to well-advised expert decisions.

The bike leg was more of a challenge as I had not really undertaken cycling over any distance, even as a youngster. Basically, I was not a cyclist. Somehow I had to fast-track into some cycling knowledge. A conversation with my good friends Chris and Maggie Creber at the Scottish Islands Three Peaks Race prize-giving dinner led me to Alasdair McKendrick of Perth City Cycles. Now Alastair is another of life's positive people and on my first visit to his shop in Perth he quickly cottoned onto what I was trying to do and set about getting me on the right bike for the job. His recommendation, taking into account my lack of cycling background and type of cycling I was to undertake, was a Trek Pilot 1.0. Moreover, he pulled in some sponsorship from Trek bikes and his shop, both of which had me on a set of wheels and kitted out with some really good gear. Bikes had moved on since my old Raleigh and Alastair brought me up to speed and face-to-face with the advanced technologies of modern bicycles. His grounding of information and help got me through the cycling leg. I was set up on a Trek road bike and, to really show his colours, Alastair gave me the loan of a pair of racing wheels that were light and fast. The difference they made to momentum almost defied belief. He also threw in a back-up bike on loan just in case I suffered some mechanical meltdown on the road. The spare bike was in a bike bag and, thankfully, it remained in the boot of the car, although there was one moment when it nearly came into play. On the day that I collected it from Alastair he gave me an overview of the bike and the kit bolted to it. During the handover Alastair stopped in mid-sentence and asked. 'Have you ever worn shoe/pedal clips before?' I had not. Alastair said without a moment's pause, 'Well, you will fall over a couple of times.' I thought he was pulling my leg but I did, just as he said.

On the second trip out on the bike I set off along Golf Course Road in Blairgowrie and arrived at the T-junction to the main Dundee road. Knowing I was still getting the hang of unclipping, I slowed and made ready to twist and lift my left foot out of the pedal clip to be able to stand free at the junction. I pulled to a halt and, as Alastair had predicted, I just could not get my foot free. Now stationary and still trying to twist my foot free, there was only one way to go and that was down. I tipped to the right and, thump, down I went like a sack of potatoes onto the white lines and tarmac. I was on my right side and lying in the middle of the road, both feet firmly secured to the bike. More of a worry though was that I was now closely studying the front number plate of a car that had turned right into the junction from the main road. 'What a lemon!' I was completely stuck, not able to wriggle myself free of the pedal clips and, with the bike stuck between my legs, unable to move or get up. The car in front of me was halfway out into the road and there was traffic halted, not able to swing round its tail end due to now queuing traffic coming the other way. A car had also come to a stop behind me and I felt a right prat. I managed to get my left foot free but that was on the upper side of the bike and no help at all in the situation. The driver behind me got of his car and offered a helping hand which I readily accepted. He took my arm and, with his help, I was levered up and onto my feet. I held on to his shoulder, twisted my right foot and 'click' my shoe was disconnected from the bike. Now free of my shackles, I stood red-faced and bloody-elbowed and thanked my knight of the road for his help. It was the last time I fell off the bike but it was a good one for starters.

Pegasus is a large 50-foot long cruising boat. She has a brilliant turn of speed and a lovely long waterline length that allows her to eat up the miles. Because the sailing leg was in effect a time trial I wanted to make her as competitive as possible. The Beneteau yard at Ardrossan offered to help with boat preparation and this was eagerly taken on by Chris Dodgson. Chris is a 'well-kent' face on the Clyde and is often seen working and playing hard on the Beneteau 47.7, *Playing FTSE*. Chris and the team at Sunbird Ardrossan were to help getting *Pegasus* race ready. Chris was particularly looking forward to seeing how much weight he could strip out of *Pegasus* and was also to look after tuning the rig for the challenge. The winter service and pre-voyage gear check was in their hands.

With the website in place I still had to make as much 'PR noise' as I could to raise awareness of the whole escapade in order to raise cash for the two charities. It was also a

*Pre-launch fit out at Ardrossan marina,
February 2006*

key element in sponsorship proposals. Again I struck gold when my friend Sue McKichan of Marketing Matters agreed to work on the project. I had met Sue some years back and she has a wealth of experience in marketing and PR in tourism, sport and outdoor activities. Sue proved to be invaluable in promoting awareness and PR matters for the challenge. Sue has the most incredible little black book with contact details of feature writers, journalists, editors and people in the know in sailing circles. She hooked the project into so many media streams, the scrap book bulges in testimony to her work and support. In addition to Sue's great work, Andrea Tofta, Senior Media Officer Parkinson's Disease Society, was the other driving force behind what became a very successful campaign of awareness raising for both OYTS and PDS. Andrea provided superb levels of support with press releases and media work and was always a positive voice at the end of the phone or by e-mail – again another of life's really positive people who did a huge amount of work and was a really great person to deal with. Andrea kindly made up a record book of all the PR exposure as a result of the challenge and it remains a lovely memento of the whole experience.

All of the shore-based support became fairly academic unless I could deliver out on the water and a very important element of that was my well-being. Again I struck a rich vein of specialist advice. Top of my list in this area was sleep management. I had done some initial research on the matter, mostly through the web and from reading everything I could get my hands on, about long-distance single-handed sailing voyages. I realised that purely desk-based research was fine but not as complete as I wanted it to be. I needed to find some local face-to-face advice on the subject as this one could be a deal-breaker if I got it wrong. I was lucky to find Dr Chris Idzikowski, Director of the Edinburgh Sleep Centre and a sleep consultant for British Airways aiming to help passengers beat the effects of jet-lag. Chris first started his work at Edinburgh University before moving on to Cambridge to study anxiety and fear. Since then he has been actively involved in research and helped set up the British Sleep Society and the Royal Society of Medicine Sleep Medicine Section (as founding Chairman). He also works as a consultant at the London Sleep Centre. I went to meet Chris at his Heriot Row clinic in Edinburgh and immediately took to him. In return I was lucky that he took to me and the project and was very keen to help. Chris is quite a character who comes over a bit like the nutty professor but he was to be a great help in confirming my research findings and taking my preparation for the trip up another level. He identified where on the planned route I would be starting to run into sleep debt and counselled me on managing such a situation and what to look out for in my performance. He also took me through my thinking processes and overall ability to cope with issues of the moment with the onset of sleep debt. Although a busy man he took time out to travel down to see *Pegasus* so he better understood my surroundings and environment. Out of our conversations Chris advised me that there is ongoing research looking into the links between the tremors associated with Parkinson's and the chemicals released into the brain to relax the body and brain activities when asleep. Chris also hooked the project in with Mike Purdy at Cambridge Neurotechnology Ltd. Mike and the team at CN agreed to supply the sleep monitoring equipment that was to record and assess my sleep patterns before and during the challenge. However due to user incompetence, i.e. me, and a computer incompatibility, the recording devices ended up in a drawer for the entire trip! CN is an independent company which supplies Actiwatch sleep monitoring equipment, Actiheart heart monitoring equipment and Tremorwatch used to detect Parkinsonian tremor.

Dr. Peter Copp of GP Plus in Edinburgh was kind enough to supply me with the appropriate medical kits and, along with Chris, provided a bag of pills, including the necessary high velocity pain killers should I come to grief and need some medical expediency to get me out of an unpleasant zone. Chris also set up contact with Dr Ewan Crawford of NHS Lothian who, as part of the medical team, would advise on health matters if called upon during the challenge.

Although I do not have 20/20 vision, I am fortunate enough to be able to wear contact lenses as sailing with glasses would have been an unpleasant and cumbersome handicap. I discussed the challenge with my optician at Black and Lizars, Davidson's Mains in Edinburgh and he promptly came up with some free trial pairs of Bausch and Lomb constant wear contact lenses. I could now sail and sleep without having to dig my contact lenses out of bloodshot eyes with salty, sore and hacked finger tips. Constant wear contact lenses are, in my book, the answer to every sailor's dream!

The engines of *Pegasus* were down to Chris Owen of Owen Sails. This company had supplied all the sails for *Pegasus* since her launch in 2001 and are Scotland's largest independent sail-maker. All the sail materials, including a new and heavily discounted GXG Carbon-based headsail specially made for the challenge, had been supplied by Dimension Polyant Sailcloth Technology. The wardrobe of sails that *Pegasus* carried gave me a great range of weapons to make the most of wind and sea conditions, from lightweight floaters to help her along in the merest of zephyrs, right through to some bullet-proof gear that could be carried in gale force conditions. Chris was contacted early on in the project to supply a new sail that David had agreed to fund. The sail that Chris came up with was a monster that was the most powerful and versatile headsail I have ever sailed with. Made from a carbon laminate, it was designed to create drive in anything from an 8-knot breeze right through to 18 to 20 knots of blow and across all of that wind range still retain its shape and drive. The sail shape and power was in perfect harmony with the mainsail and really did move *Pegasus* along. Since the challenge in 2006, Owen Sails have gone from strength to strength at their Oban loft, with Chris and the team supplying sails to the victorious 'three blondes in a boat' gold medallists at the 2008 Beijing Olympics.

So I had a team around me that ran well into double figures and helped immensely in getting me to the start line and through the whole challenge. All in all it was a fairly impressive line up that included an Olympic sailing weather forecaster, an Olympic sail-maker, a world-renowned sleep specialist, a multiple Scottish sailing champion and round the world yacht race skipper, a highly-qualified crew to look after *Pegasus* after the event and some serious PR skills and knowledge. All of the help was on a volunteer basis and for that I will always be very grateful. I look back on the support that they provided and know deep down that without them I would not have had the guts to sail off into the Solway Firth and beyond.

On many a trip I had sailed *Pegasus* on my own, despite there being others aboard, so I had complete confidence in myself being able to manage all lines and equipment. However, I needed to really test myself and see if I was up to overnight passages and time alone on a boat. At the tail end of the 2005 season I took a couple of single-handed trips to confirm if I was indeed capable. On a fine August evening I set out from Dunstaffnage marina to sail around Mull. This was a re-enactment of the trip done 10 years before in my little Hunter Delta. There was symmetry to the situation. Ten years had passed since my last single-handed sail round Mull and boat length had doubled from 25 feet to 50 feet! I set off clockwise and ghosted south on a dying evening breeze. I reached the south-east corner of Mull at McQuarie's Rock and then faced a beat along the south shore to Iona. It was a drastic night sail with light winds that made it hard work to keep *Pegasus* moving. It was one of those west coast nights where it did not really get totally black dark. The sunset left a warm glow in the sky that seemed to keep the darkness at bay. Then it was an early sun that brought fresh light to this delightful corner of Scotland. I reached up the Sound of Iona and skirted Staffa, on north to Calgary Point and round to Tobermory Bay. The sail down the Sound of Mull was slow and uneventful. *Pegasus* was back on her berth at 20.00, some 21 hours after we had slipped lines, not a record circumnavigation but a good shakedown and overnight sail. The second trip was a simple overnighter out beyond Mull, round Coll and Tiree, then back to Dunstaffnage. Again there was no challenge to my confidence, quite the reverse, and I was now convinced I could handle *Pegasus*. During that trip I had all sail options up and down and ran through some practice drills in setting sails, reducing sail, reefing and flying the big spinnaker. None of it caused me any problems but what I did need was a hard overnight passage with a big blow and seas to deal with. I did not have to wait long. In early September I set off early on a Friday morning, safe in the knowledge that the weekend was going to be a test. My plan was to sail down the west side of Jura and Islay and then over to Ireland and back. The wind blew up into a nasty Force 8 out of the south-east. Just south of Mull I took the decision to go outside Colonsay so I freed off and made a fast passage through the night to the west and in the lee of Colonsay. Emerging at the southernmost tip and from the shelter of the island, the wave height increased dramatically with some of 2 metres or so coming in from the south-east. I battered my way south and decided that it would not be smart to head away into the open sea to the north-west shore of Ireland. I held a long tack away out past Colonsay and then turned back onto a north-east heading taking me back between Islay and Colonsay. The wind was getting fresh and I decided that I needed to get out of it and into the shelter of Islay. There was no obvious anchorage to aim for so I elected to sail to the west side of Jura and anchor up at the mouth of Loch Tarbert for the remainder of the evening to let the wind blow through. It was a very fast reach back, I was shattered and totally wiped out. With a certain amount of trepidation I dropped the anchor, sat for 30 minutes to make sure it was holding and then hit the sack. The wind howled and howled through to 07.00 hours and then started to die down. Energised with some breakfast, I ran off north and back to Dunstaffnage, a little bruised but very happy that I had had to deal with hard sailing conditions, big wind conditions and had taken reefs in. I had baled out from the night sail, something I could not do halfway through the challenge, but my main concern that night was a breakage that could set my plans back. My last single-hander of the year was taking *Pegasus* from Oban to Ardrossan at the end of the sailing season. On 23rd September I set off and did the 145-mile passage to Ardrossan in pretty strong winds. The passage took me past Oban, down the Sound of Luing and to the east of Scarba, Jura and Islay. Rounding the Mull of Kintyre was fast as I caught a favourable tide and just screamed along the shore line. I opted to go outside the island of Sanda so as to maintain safe sea room from the Kintyre shore and then, with a following breeze, ran off north towards Ardrossan. The only real drama of that trip was landing at Ardrossan marina at 22.30 hours as at that time there was no-one about to take my lines. I motored *Pegasus* through the narrow harbour gate and found a sheltered berth right over in the top left-hand corner of the marina. There was nothing else available that had vacant space either side of a berth as I did not want to ding another boat in the process of getting alongside. The big downside was that the berth had an off-pontoon breeze, making a single-handed tie up that little more tricky. Having made three aborted attempts to get *Pegasus* manoeuvred into the right position, I ended up taking a major risk by bringing her up to a pontoon, stopping her dead with a blast of astern, then jumping with a midship breast line in my hand. No sooner had forward momentum stopped than *Pegasus* was moving off and away from the pontoon, entirely on her own with no crew aboard. I did a quick figure of eight over the pontoon cleat and she was secure. The only problem was that she was lying on the midships breast line and had by then been blown some 6 feet off the pontoon by the wind. What a job I had muscling her back in to the pontoon so I that could get back aboard. Anyway, trip done, this time with one and a half night sails, and confidence was growing in all the departments needed to get *Pegasus* around Scotland in one piece.

The whole project was growing arms and legs as the full scope and implications of such a trip were becoming clearer by the day. Sleep management was one of the unknown areas that the challenge was taking me into and I needed to take a risk management approach to it. After a cursory assessment, it was clearly the most dangerous of issues to manage. Apart from the blindingly obvious danger of running aground when asleep, or hitting another ship whilst in a deep stupor, fatigue accumulation would also eat into my strength and well-being. Initial research and the discussion with Dr. Chris indicated that the recognised approach to counter sleep deprivation over extended periods, and one that was successfully adopted by Ellen MacArthur and her peers on the high seas, was to grab catnaps each lasting 15–20 minutes. Sleep debt is cumulative and the only cure is sleep itself. On further study sleep debt could be managed and that was indeed essential in order to maintain adequate levels of safety. One potential show-stopper in all of this is contained in the International Collision at Sea Regulations (Colregs). They state that at all times a watch must be kept for all other shipping and hazards. Clearly it was impossible to maintain a full watch when sailing single-handed so, to undertake this passage, I would be committing a breach of Colregs. That indicated a risk that had to be mitigated through a robust management plan.

Prior to the 2000–2001 Vendée Globe, Ellen McArthur realised that a competitive advantage could be gained if she became a sleep specialist. That lady has undoubtedly had some pretty hi-tech boats to help her on her way, but it is the person who drives the boat who takes the decisions. With a well-planned sleep strategy, Ellen became the youngest person and first woman to win the 2000-mile transatlantic race and, the following year, the fastest yachtswoman to race around the world, finishing second in the Vendée Globe. In 2002 she won the Route de Rhum. Ellen's peak performance, however, was reserved for her epic solo round the world record on *B&Q* in the winter of 2004–2005 when she became the fastest human being to sail single-handedly around the world. If it was good enough for Ellen, then it was good enough for me. After all, it was Ellen who had got me into this lark as I had followed her round the globe during that awe-inspiring voyage on *B&Q*.

Sleep and being awake is not a simple binary state: on or off. Reading indicates that a night of sleep can be split into distinct phases, each of vital importance to our well-being. It should also be said that the length of time I was planning to be at sea did not take me anywhere near the territory of severe sleep debt, but it was still a matter that needed managing. On the flip side, the deep ocean sailors have thousands of miles of sea room to play with, where I had a shoreline and busy shipping lanes. My shortest distance around Scotland would, should I choose to, take me within spitting distance of rocky outcrops and shorelines. The overall time at sea was not as much of a challenge in itself when compared with the deep sea mariners. Where my challenges lay were the obstacles, shoreline and heavy shipping, so demanding higher levels of alertness and course control.

Phase One of sleep lasts for about 10 minutes; eyes are closed and, if woken, a person may not be aware that they had even fallen asleep. Phase Two lasts for about 20 minutes and results in muscles alternating from a relaxed state to tensioned; heart rate slows and body temperature drops. The body is now preparing to enter deep sleep. Phase Three prepares the body for deep sleep and is a transitional stage between light and deep sleep. Phase Four is where brain waves slow and is known as 'delta sleep' – a deep relaxed state that last for about 30 minutes. Phases 1–4 are known as non-REM (rapid eye movement) and in total last for about 90–120 min. It is also established that the sequence of sleep phases run 1, 2, 3, 4, 3, 2, and then REM – Phase 5. The REM phase is when the real action takes place; when heart rate and breathing become erratic and the face, fingers and limbs can twitch. This is when dreams can start and, with a more active brain, the body runs the danger of acting out the dreams. To counter this, the body subconsciously releases chemicals to enforce a partial paralysis, suppressing large muscle group movement and stopping an individual flailing about. This is the crossover between Parkinson's research and sleep research mentioned earlier; the answer is in there somewhere. It has been identified in the very early stages of Parkinson's that the REM stage of sleep can be interfered with and suppression of these involuntary movements are not as controlled as they should be. It is all so true – my Mother often made reference to my Dad suddenly and at times in a quite animated manner jumping or leaping in bed at night. It was as if he was re-enacting the moment of scoring a try. Was he innocently replaying his rugby days or was it the sinister prequel to his Parkinson's disease?

To waken during the REM phase results in a groggy feeling and one from which it is hard to recover. This can explain why some mornings it is more of a struggle to get up and get going. The recommended approach at sea, or if dealing with possible sleep deprivation, is to catch 20-minute naps so that Phases 1 and 2 are maximised but deep sleep, Phases 3–4 and REM 5 are avoided. It also appears that Phases 1–2 provide cerebral and cognitive recovery and recuperation, whereas Phases 3–5 support physical recovery. The length of my trip clearly was within any parameter that would take me into a physical recovery debt. However, alertness reduction for sleep debt was more of an issue for me. To avoid waking in a groggy state, sleep would need to be taken in 20-minute or 90-minute slugs. To waken at or around the 60-minute point would result in disorientation, grumpiness and general negative effect on my well-being. Clearly a 90-minute sleep was out of the question as a boat travelling at 10 knots could travel nearly 15 miles and hit something very hard in that period of time. So regular 20-minute naps were to be my strategy.

To cross reference the sleep target of 20 minutes with risk assessments and lookouts I had to square what 15–20 minutes asleep or off-watch meant in terms of a moving yacht at sea. If I was to sleep for 15 minutes, I needed to make sure that during the 15 minutes of sleep I was not going to hit anything or anything was going to hit me. This could be resolved by a simple equation around speed and time, using both speed of approaching vessel and my speed, resulting in a closing speed on other vessels under way, or on a stationary rock.

In a worst case scenario, *Pegasus* might be travelling at 10 knots and a ship approaching at 20 knots, a closing speed of 30 knots. This could equally be me at 8 knots and them at

22 knots, or 6 and 24, or 4 and 26, So a closing speed of 30 knots seemed appropriate. The calculation was simple: 30 nautical miles in one hour, 15 nautical miles in 30 minutes, 7.5 nautical miles in 15 minutes, and so on. If there was nothing within 7.5 nautical miles, I could sleep for 15 minutes before impact. Not wishing to trust the human eye and a tired brain, and to build in enough time to react to a danger in order to take the appropriate avoiding action, a broader safety margin was clearly required. The radar aboard *Pegasus* was to be my eyes into the distance. The modern radar has a feature where a guard zone can be set up around a boat. Once set, if anything breaks into the zone, the alarm is raised. Set the guard zone at 10 nautical miles and I had 20 minutes to react. Set it at 12 nautical miles and I had 24 minutes to get out of trouble. With a guard zone set at 12 nautical miles and a sleep time of 15 minutes, I had a further nine minutes to take avoiding action, or about a 5-mile gap between me and a problem, assuming a head-on closing speed of 30 knots. If I was travelling at an angle to an approaching vessel, the critical time from identification as a threat to impact was greatly increased as we would not have a head-to-head closing speed. In theory that all stacked up! If the closing speed was 20 knots, safety margins expanded accordingly, but the 30-knot closing speed rule formed the basis of my anti-collision strategy. The next element was to have a trustworthy alarm system to wake me after 15 minutes. The solution was simple; an electronic kitchen timer tagged to my jacket collar set to go off and pierce the night silence. It was loud and sure to get me on my feet. To bolster the standard issue inbuilt radar alarm, I fitted an amplified alarm buzzer that would, when triggered, waken the dead. Dr Chris advised me that it was unlikely I would sleep through these alarms, even in a deeply fatigued state, as they were key to my 'preservation of life' and I was tuned in to hear them. That was a relief!

The other fuel that was needed in addition to sleep to keep me going was of course food. Unlike the sleep management that was all new to me, food intake management and planning were familiar territory. Having 'fuelled' myself for the Scottish Islands Three Peaks Race, long hill runs and the years of track and field training, I knew exactly what my body needed to keep it on the go. My objective was to maintain energy levels whilst keeping some variety in the menu so as to keep the food interesting. One basic rule I was going to apply to my diet plan was not to go extreme in respect of all dried food but to have a good varied diet with fresh food that had high carbohydrate and sugar levels. *Pegasus* has a very well-equipped galley with fridge, freezer box and a microwave, so I was not slumming it and it would have been silly not to use the facilities. The overall diet plan was in effect to carbo-graze during the sailing leg, then carbo-load before the cycle leg, when energy demands would be entirely different to the sailing leg. Above all, hydration was one principle that was essential for both legs. Studies show that dehydration does more to empty you of energy than lack of food. Dehydration upsets fluid levels and a whole basket of chemicals and electrolytes that are essential for bodily functions and clear thinking.

I had two completely different physical challenges. The first was the long sailing legs that demanded extended periods of concentration, endurance and bursts of strength when tacking or sail changing. The second was the bike ride where higher aerobic effort was sustained over long periods. This would need to be powered by 'batteries' that might be running pretty low by that stage of the trip. In addition, my research suggested that large meals would interfere with my sleep strategy as they affect the ability to take short sleep naps. So carbo-grazing seemed to be confirmed as the best approach at sea. The bike ride requirements were clear to me: a long period of high sustained energy demand. To cope with this aspect I picked up a high performance cycling coaching book and zoomed in on the food intake chapter. Fluids, fluids and more fluids seemed to be the message, along with high carbohydrate pre-race loading. In short, the sailing leg was to have a menu of porridge, cereals, pasta, cake, coffee and hot chocolate. The bike leg would revolve around cramming

Plenty of carbohydrates on the provisions list

big meals of pasta before the transition, with on-the-road snacking on energy bars, energy drinks, cake, more energy drinks and water. Carrying appropriate food was not a problem as *Pegasus* was very capable of storing and keeping in good order any foodstuff selected for the sailing leg. My wife Shona would be acting as support car driver so all foods and fluids for the bike leg would be carried in the boot of the car. She was a source of constant amazement during the cycling leg as no matter what time of day, what conditions or requests, Shona could open a door or boot lid and put her hand on whatever was asked for. It was uncanny; juice, cake, sandwich, energy gel drink, jacket, Vaseline, spare wheel, sticking plaster, spanner, underpants, socks were all amazingly within quick and easy reach.

Pegasus was to be my means of getting around the sailing route in one piece. She is a solid sea boat and one in which I had total confidence. I had sailed her from Les Sables D'ollone in the Bay of Biscay when new and been out in F9 gales and in big seas and she had never worried me. She was most definitely capable, but was I? Now the 'engine' of the yacht was her sail wardrobe and, like anything on *Pegasus,* David had always been supportive in kitting her out very well indeed. The mainsail is the original and that was into its fifth season but still holding its shape superbly well. The fully battened sail has single line slab reefing which in effect means that the sail area can be reefed, i.e. reduced in area. We had *Pegasus* very well set up so that such a sail handling manoeuvre could be carried out from the safety of the cockpit. Reefing lines are led aft to the cockpit so, to reduce the area of the mainsail, the reefing line is loaded onto a winch and wound in; the bottom third of the sail is lowered and, bingo, job done. Due to the size of the sail there are metres upon metres of line to wind in before the tension comes in and pulls the sail down taut to the boom. Taking a reef in on *Pegasus* is an exhausting job on your own and one that takes about 10 minutes of hard graft. There is an awful lot of rope to move through the winches, all under some massive loads. All sails and ropes have to be wound in and let out, but as long as it is done in the correct sequence and the equipment used correctly, it was certainly not beyond me. For this trip I had three reefs rigged and, if pushed by conditions to pull in to the third reef, it would be storm conditions I was facing. The third reef really does leave only a small area of sail. Up front *Pegasus* has an impressive array of sails to maximise the weather and conditions. These range from a large and lightweight No 1 made of Pentex through to a storm jib, which is simply bullet-proof and made from heavy Dacron. New for the challenge was the hi-tech carbon-based foresail that would carry in winds from light airs right up to 25 knots plus. *Pegasus* was kitted with a rolling reefing arrangement that made foresail management very easy. The sail, when not in use, is rolled round and round the forestay on a revolving foil of aluminium. At the foot of the stay is a drum that can coil about 15 metres of rope from there and feed it back along the deck to the cockpit. When deployed the sail unrolls as it is pulled out by the sheets attached to its lower back corner, and the reefing line is pulled forward by the rotation of the unrolling sail. This action loads the drum with the 15 metres or so of reefing line rope. To reduce sail, the reefing line leading back to the cockpit is loaded on a winch and pulled in, so rotating the drum and the forestay foil in the opposite direction to when the sail was pulled out. The rotation rolls the sail away, so reducing sail area. It is a brilliant system that revolutionises sail handling for cruising boats and short-handed sailing. The bow can be a dangerous place in a blow and big sea so having the equipment to roll away the sail from the safety of behind the sprayhood in the cockpit is basically essential for safe sailing. The final piece in the armoury is a blade jib that is rigged off an inner forestay. The blade is an awesome weapon for going upwind in really foul weather. The sail is narrow and tall. Fully tightened in, the blade sail does not quite come as far back as the mast and is angled well inboard, so giving a really great set up for beating to windward in a big puff. The sail is impressively powerful and was one of the best pieces of work that Chris Owen did for *Pegasus*.

Pegasus has an asymmetric spinnaker which really does give her a turn of speed sailing on a downwind reach but is next to useless with the wind directly behind. Sailing dead downwind, the slowest course to the wind, is best dealt with by 'goose winging' the Genoa and mainsail. To do this the mainsail is set to one side of the boat and the Genoa is set out the other side, presenting the maximum area of sail to the following wind. At this angle to the wind the Genoa is unsupported and collapses easily, but it is a constant task to steer and change course and attitude to the wind in order to keep the sail filled. To avoid this the spinnaker pole comes into its own by holding the sail out and pinning it down, so reducing boat roll and subsequent sail collapse and loss of power. To do this the pole is secured to the mast at about head height; it sticks out over the side of the boat and so keeps the sail open and presented to the following wind.

Pegasus had all of the above gear but, for good measure for this trip, she was kitted up with more besides. One concern I did have was a failure of the boat's GPS system, which would render the main navigation systems useless. To counter that potential event I decided to carry not just one but two back-up independent GPS navigation systems. Even with really bad luck it was unlikely that three systems would fail during the voyage. I plotted a course that had a series of fairly conservative waypoints well off land or jutting headlands. Yes, this would add distance but, should I arrive at critical turning points in foul dark stormy weather at Islay, Barra Head, St Kilda or Muckle Flugga, I wanted to have some space between me and these very hard bits!

Owen Sails blade jib perfectly set

Boat speed is everything in sail racing. Consider the difference that an increase on boat speed of 0.1 knots would make over the course of sailing a 1000-mile passage. The Holy Grail of boat speed was the main reason for stripping out the forward berth of all dead weight. Bunks, doors, floorboards and doors were stripped out by the lads at the Sunbird Beneteau yard at Ardrossan. A conservative estimate of weight taken out of *Pegasus* ranged from 100–200 kilograms. Furthermore, the weight was taken out of the front of the boat, so keeping her lighter and higher at the all important entry point to the water. The average boat speed over the sailing time at sea turned out to be 5.7 knots over the 1000-mile passage, giving an elapsed time of 175.4 hours. Drop to 5.6 knots and the time taken increases to 178.6 hours, over three hours difference! Lift average boat speed from 5.7 knots to 6.0 knots, and that's just under nine hours taken off the total passage time. It is only when the impact of a small improvement in speed is applied over a decent length of passage that you can really comprehend the importance of shaving weight and undertaking endless hours of tweaking sails so that they are pulling at close to

100% of optimum. In a two-boat race over a 1000-mile passage, 6.0 knots on one boat against a boat doing 5.7 knots is a difference of 8 hours 50 minutes come the finish line or, to put it another way, a clear 53 miles ahead. One of the best sailing quotes I have heard was from a French round-the-world single-handed sailor when asked what was his favourite boat. He answered, 'It will be my lightest one.' That says it all really.

If Berwick-upon-Tweed on the east coast was my likely landing place, I needed to know where to go and what to look out for when entering these waters, especially when tired after a number of days at sea. As I had not sailed down that part of the country for many years, I took to studying the pilot books and also made a trip to check out the marinas and facilities. After a cursory check of the pilot books and charts, it was clear that the ports along that coast are tidal. The appeal of taking *Pegasus* into a tidal harbour such as Berwick-upon-Tweed that dried out at low tide waned very quickly. If I was approaching port, tired and in bad weather, the last thing I needed was the worry and complications of restricted access due to tides and shallow water. All I would be looking for at that stage would be a sound, deep and easily navigated harbour entrance. Berwick-upon-Tweed is a working port and, from the pilot book, it looked as if I would be taking our pristine and much-loved *Pegasus* into a harbour occupied by logging and coal boats. The tidal restrictions and likely company dealt Berwick-upon-Tweed a fatal blow. I looked further down the coast to Amble, next on the list to check out and, yes, they had good solid pontoons to tie up to but a worrisome tidal cill that could only be cleared two hours either side of high water. The retaining cill meant that, out of every 24-hour cycle of the high tide, 8 of them would be no good for getting in to the marina. That not-so-minor detail ruled out the port of Amble as the landing point. I looked further south again, scanning the charts and pilot books; Blyth was the obvious candidate. I had race-sailed there several years ago with Hugh Scott in the East Coast Week, a very social affair from what I recall.

Blyth is an all-tide port and marina, has an enormous sea wall to get tucked in behind and is well-lit with navigation marks. The wide open bay at Blyth can be a bit lumpy in a blow but it was the all-tide harbour and marina that sold me Blyth. I parked up and wandered around the marina and harbour area. It all looked just perfect for the job of bringing in *Pegasus* after a week or so at sea. Now hooked on the place, I set about walking the area in detail and taking pictures of the harbour entrance, sea wall and conspicuous buildings to help with sighting land and the way in from sea. The large wind turbines along the spine of the sea wall were each squeezing energy out of the light breeze coming in from the North Sea. As I wandered around, my mind went back to the sailing regatta all those years ago with Hugh and the team aboard his *Albin Express*. It was a happy time, with some of us bunked up in a caravan ashore and some in a B&B. The regatta had two great moments to savour, one afloat and one 'awash' ashore. Hugh was a bit of a crotchety sailor and had the habit of barking instructions at his crew. Now anyone who had been on a racing yacht and has the job of trimming the spinnaker will know that the art of good sail control is to have the luff edge of the sail just off the fold or collapse; that way the sail is set well and pulling to its best ability. If the sail is let loose just a fraction too much, the spinnaker edge curls in and, if the sheet rope is not tightened straight away, the sail collapses and speed drops. Another factor that comes into play is that when the sail does start to curl, human reactions are sequenced as follows: eye registers edge curl, signals to brain to pull rope, brain sends message to muscles, muscles react and rope is pulled, sail reacts to rope and resets. However, in between brain receiving and issuing instruction to muscles to pull, anyone who is a bit 'gobby' can get in before the pull command with, 'Sheet, sheet!' (usually shouted). Such an interjection is OK perhaps three or four times a race, but to have this constantly shrieked in your ear from an old bugger sat on his backside at the helm can be wearing. Suffice to say Hugh overstepped the mark that day and, at one close and fraught contest with another yacht, Hugh barked 'Sheet, sheet!' just once too often. Ally Summers, who was on the sheet, had reached his tipping point and turned to Hugh, blasted a few oaths at him, threw the tensioned rope at him and said if he could do any better to do it himself. Needless to say the sheet, now free from restraint, ran off like a banshee and the spinnaker flew out from the masthead and flogged in the wind. We managed to get the sail back under control but the boat was very quiet for the rest of the afternoon. The second moment that sticks with me from that tour was being thrown out of a Chinese restaurant. We smart lads put our pints on the rotating tray in the centre of the table and gave it a good spin, being too drunk to appreciate that centrifugal force would then see the six pints of lager slosh their contents all over the table, our laps and the floor. Unsurprisingly, it obliged and proved the physics. We did not even get our starter! I was content I had my sea passage: Kirkcudbright to Blyth, via St Kilda and Muckle Flugga.

Having chosen Blyth, I then set about replanning the cycle route and, to my absolute delight, the route back to Kirkcudbright was actually 15 miles shorter than from Berwick-upon-Tweed. As far as humanly possible, I would be circumnavigating Scotland, sailing outside its islands and cycling across northern England before crossing the Scottish border at Gretna. To define my start point I thought I needed to start sailing from the most easterly point possible in the Solway Firth. To navigate a boat the size of *Pegasus* would require at least 3 metres depth of water at all states of the tide. In the Solway that prerequisite takes you well to the west to find such depths. Close scrutiny of charts and pilot books pointed to just off Balcary Point some 7 miles or so east of Kirkcudbright. I also needed a base for *Pegasus*. The local pilot books confirmed that the marina at Kirkcudbright could, at a push, take *Pegasus* and her 2.3 metre draught.

My ambition was to sail round Scotland and her islands. I wondered if starting from Balcary would leave any islands outside my course and have the potential to invalidate that claim? Careful study of the Solway charts highlighted that the most easterly all-tides island in the Solway was Ross Island which sits at the mouth of the River Dee at Kirkcudbright. So that was another tick. It was all pointing towards Balcary Point as the start point. Plotting the key waypoints to allow me to take in all the islands of Scotland meant the sailing route looked like this:

- Start—Balcary Point, Kirkcudbright
- Mull of Galloway
- Mull of Kintyre
- Rhinns of Islay
- Barra Head
- St Kilda
- Rona
- Muckle Flugga, Shetland
- Kinnaird Head, by Fraserburgh
- Farne Islands
- Blyth marina—End

On the matter of sailing around Scotland and her islands, the vexed issue of Rockall was raised by my friend Gordon Jack. He maintained that I should change my project to 'Solo round Scotland except Rockall'. This comment was treated as a wind-up until I received an e-mail from a clearly very pernickety type of person who commented that I was not sailing around Scotland and its islands if Rockall was not included. I turned to the text book for my defence and established that Rockall is a rock and not an island, according to the 1695 census of Scotland! It defines an island as a piece of land that can support one man and two sheep for one year. Ask John Ridgway, intrepid explorer, adventurer and all-round hard man about the potential of that inhospitable rock supporting life; he would be quite clear on that matter. Now in no extreme of imagination could Rockall support one man and two sheep, so I was not going to sail around Rockall – case closed.

The cycle leg needed to be fully mapped and routed. My good pal Willie Gibson, with whom I do the Three Peaks Race, came up trumps with a piece of software that worked out a route between Blyth and Kirkcudbright and, hey presto, a set of maps popped through the letter box marked with a red line showing the route. After a couple of discussions over the phone and some further tweaks, we had the chosen route. The next thing was to drive it and see what the computer had offered. So one evening after a Friday appointment in Glasgow I headed south to Kirkcudbright to do a reconnoitre of the area and the road route between the two coasts. Now my cousin Derek and his wife Mairi, who live in Kirkcudbright, will kill me for this but I slipped into Kirkcudbright and stayed overnight in a B&B rather than appearing on their doorstep. The next morning I was out the door by eight o'clock and heading for the marina to have a good look at the facilities and layout. Kirkcudbright marina sits in the River Dee and that morning I coincided with low tide. The river was dripping through the middle channel, hemmed in by grey, claggy mud banks. My heart sank. How on earth would I get *Pegasus* in here with her 2.3-metre keel? The pilot books advised that there was berthing for a 3-metre draught, so clearly there must be some regular dredging done to maintain such a berth. The main pontoon was sound and very well-appointed so, depth allowing, *Pegasus* could sit safe and well-secured to the pontoons as the river flowed by on its way out to sea.

Pre-voyage visit on a rather uninspiring morning at Kirkcudbright marina

That done I then drove off to find Balcary Point. Parking at the back of the Balcary Hotel, I took the 10-minute walk down the rocky outcrop and identified the start position for my long voyage with my hand-held GPS. I was happy that a start line of 180 degrees, due south from that point could be established. I jumped back in the car and followed, in reverse, the cycle route along the Solway coastal tourist trail through Dumfries and on over to Gretna. All the way over I carefully took notes of key landmarks at junctions and wrote down signposts, knowing that when I transcribed all of the detail my lefts should be rights and my rights should be lefts! The value of that long drive was immeasurable. I immediately found that the computer had done exactly what it had been asked to do; avoid A roads wherever possible. However, the end result, whilst looking fine on a map, took a tortuous route down small country lanes devoid of signposts and, in the main, between hedgerows that did not offer any feeling of place, heading or orientation. The chances of a missed turn, or of heading off in the wrong direction were too high so the computer was thanked for its route suggestion and I turned around and headed back to replan the route from Gretna.

After the test drive, and with further consultation with Willie, the cross country cycle route was decided upon:

- Start—Blyth marina
- Blyth town centre
- A193 Bedlington
- A192 Morpeth

- B6524 Sun Inn / Whalton / Belsay
- A696 (north-west)
- B6309 Stanfordham / Harlow Hill
- B6318 (west along Hadrian's Wall) Once Brewed / Greenhead / Gilsland / Nickies Hill
- Unclassified road Walton / Newton
- A6071 Longtown (north of Carlisle)/ Gretna (back in Scotland)
- B721 Rigg / Dornock / Annan
- B724 Solway Coastal Route / Bankhead
- B725 Shearington / Dumfries
- A710 New Abbey / Kirkbean / Drumburn / Colvend / Dalbeattie
- A711 Palnackie / Bankhead / Auchencairn / Dundrennan / Kirkcudbright

In total the route was 163 miles but, more alarmingly, there was a full 8,400 feet of climb. That shocked me. It was a concern which meant that the training on the bike had to be upped with more miles on the saddle needed.

So the challenge that now lay before me was a 1,000-mile sailing passage into some of the most exposed water around our country. After that it was a cycle of 163 miles and a climb of 8,400 ft, all in all a trip that was quite daunting. I needed to parcel it up into bite-sized chunks or the scale of the challenge could overwhelm me. So, as the saying goes; 'How do you eat an elephant?' The answer is 'In bite-sized chunks'. I needed to split the whole challenge up into chunks, each one a goal and, when achieved, a mental reward. I sat down with my planning chart and pinpointed key locations or legs that made up the trip, parcelling the whole distance into 12 legs, each one to be a big physiological win as it was ticked off. They were:

- Islay—Solway, North Channel and Mull of Kintyre
- Barra Head—Open water between Islay and the Outer Hebrides and Skerryvore
- St Kilda—Most westerly point of the voyage, key landmark before turning northwest
- Muckle Flugga—Big sailing leg of 140 miles into potentially wild and open water at the top of Scotland
- Aberdeen abeam—Open ocean water all behind, now a coastal course south to Blyth
- Blyth—Job done

On the bike the following were identified as the last few chunks of my elephant:

- Morpeth—Only a few hours out, but so important for setting the rhythm for the rest of the cycle

- Milecastle Reservoir—West onto the B6318, my companion for 28 more miles
- Greenhead—The moorland and Hadrian's Wall done and dusted, now heading into rural Carlisle district
- Gretna—Back in Scotland, so much behind me and not far to go
- Dumfries—Last main town before Kirkcudbright, with only the last few hills to worry about
- Kirkcudbright—Job done

The physical build-up during the winter before the challenge did not turn out exactly as planned. Having identified that April was the month to make the most of a higher percentage of 'good wind days', I had two trips to the operating theatre in the intervening period, one planned and one most definitely not planned. For some years I had been carrying what I had identified as a slight hernia and had simply lived with a problem which caused me little or no worries. However, in Spring 2005 I was becoming more and more conscious of there being an 'issue'. A trip to the doctor confirmed the obvious and I was off to see a surgeon, who took no more than 15 seconds to say that I needed an operation. Not wanting to miss the sailing season, I asked if I could go on the slab at the end of the summer. The consultant agreed and I thought no more about it. However, time ran on and it was not until late October that I received the call-up papers to go under the knife. The operation was simple and straightforward and I had a nice little piece of metallic gauze stitched into my abdominal wall. It was a really neat job and, whilst taking it easy, I recovered over the months of November and December. It did put a dent in my preparations, especially in the gym, as sit-ups and weights were definitely off the cards for a few weeks.

The second trip to the slab was not planned and it was one that really did put the skids on a number of issues. On 16th December, a date etched in my training diary, I came in from an hour-long run in the woods feeling just great. I had been running on toes and that night the heavier plods of early December were now just a memory. The next day, however, I could feel a slight pain on the inside of my left knee and, as the day wore on, the pain became an ache. By day 3 my knee was no better and, to make matters worse, I could detect a distinct clunk when walking. By day 7 I had sharp pains in my upper calf, inner and back of the knee. By then it was holiday time and I could not get a physio appointment so spent Christmas on RICE (rest, ice, compression and elevation). Deep down I knew there was something up and time spent on the web doing some e-diagnosis indicated that I had a cartilage problem. Immediately after the festive break I saw James, my physio, at the Space Clinic in Edinburgh. Having manipulated my knee, he confirmed my fears that the meniscal cartilage felt very dodgy indeed. James arranged an appointment with the consultant, who took no more than a couple of minutes to confirm that I had a meniscal cartilage tear in the left knee. One week later I was in a gown and on the slab again, but this time with two portholes in my left knee. I was watching the inside of my knee on a colour monitor as Gordon McKay rummaged around to find the offending tear. With an eerie tug that I could feel and see, the pincer snipped off a barb of cartilage, which was then withdrawn from my knee. The floor flooded with fluid that had been pumped in to open up the joint and, like a breathless mother, I was presented with my first born, a small lump of creamy white cartilage tissue.

I left the clinic on crutches, with my head down and worried. Mind you, I had no time to think about it as, an hour later, I was chairing a tourism workshop with 50 eager delegates keen to hear all about effective web-based marketing. This was a real example of how my sporting and working lives collide. Ever since my days as a young sales rep who bunked off work to go training at Meadowbank athletics track, work and pleasure have sat stiffly together. Year after year as my career developed, I have yearned to throw it all in, opt out and follow my natural instinct to go and play, if only it would pay the bills. To have been on the operating table and then, within an hour, be leaning on a crutch addressing paid-up delegates really did neither the delegates nor me any justice. The operation was a success and three days later I took a very tentative cycle down the driveway at home and along the street. Later the following week I did it again, with no adverse reaction. What a mess my knee was in; badly swollen and discoloured and, while I could pretend I could cycle, I still had no weight bearing or faith in my left leg. The following weeks turned in to a rehab plan with a series of exercises and mobility stretches. I had a good range of movement but still little or no strength, even on a slight knee bend squat. What I could do was cycle as the injury did not present any form of restriction in pedalling and building miles. Little did I know at the time that the majority of the workload on the bike was being done by my right leg. After two or three weeks, leg muscle bulk difference between my left and right thighs was becoming clearly discernible and it only got worse and worse as time and miles went in. No matter how hard I tried to push on my left leg, my body's self-monitoring systems maintained an upper hand and protected the weak side by sending more work to my right leg. My thighs were a picture to behold, the right one beefed up and looking in good shape, solid and strong, while my left leg was very much thinner and had no real power in anything past a few degrees of crouch or squat. I recall making myself really depressed when climbing stairs and feeling no push and lift coming from my weak friend. Squats, stretching and lots and lots of knee flexes, pulling and pushing against a elastic strap, helped build some stability before the start. By the time of the off I had reasonable mobility and strength and, most importantly, enough agility to move around the boat. I was no spring lamb but I could get freely around a moving deck and that was all that counted, although I was certainly a long way off being able to do a deep squat on my left leg. The detour to the knee clinic meant that I had lost some training so I was not as fit as I had planned to be. On the back of having lost a number of weeks with the hernia, it meant the original plan to deliver myself to the boat fit and strong was not fully achieved. I was going to have to really watch how I took on heavy physical tasks, sail changes and any hard labour that came my way. I was, however, fit enough to get on and do the job in hand, and what was more important, in a good frame of mind that the job was most definitely achievable.

My plan was to get *Pegasus* down to Kirkcudbright and leave her there, ready and primed so that, when the right weather came in, I could make a quick start. Erik, Gordon and I sailed the boat south to Kirkcudbright from Ardrossan, where she had wintered. In the weeks prior to departure she came under the hand of the Beneteau team for the pre-season servicing and weight-stripping exercise; more than that, she was polished, gleaming and race-fit. We had a great sail down from Ardrossan and *Pegasus* just galloped south. On the way past Ailsa Craig I gave an interview to John Beattie's BBC Radio Scotland Saturday morning *Sports Weekly* show. I must have sounded like an excited schoolboy as I gabbled out on air all of the excitement that was building inside me. The trip was the first time we had *Pegasus* really honking along in her stripped-out state and, boy, she was chomping south. We made such good time, and with the weather forecast good for the Sunday, we decided that a detour and overnight stop in Northern Ireland would be in order. So we did just that, enjoyed a few pints of Guinness, and set off for Kirkcudbright early the next morning. The sail across to the Mull of Galloway was electric and *Pegasus* had us back over to the Scottish shoreline in just a few hours. We were averaging 8 knots for long periods of time and the thought of getting this rampant horse out into long-legged offshore gallops was just mouth-watering. Mid-afternoon we entered the River Dee and made our way up the channel to Kirkcudbright marina. There was not really much water below the keel as we tickled the throttle upstream. We made our way in between all the green and red poles and navigation marks and, after one last check of the pilot book, took her into the narrow area of the river at the marina and slotted her onto the pontoon. We had pole position on the long walkway, and the gap that Rab Thomson had advised when I called him before we set off was, as promised, vacant and welcoming. I had phoned ahead when we came into the river to let my cousin Derek know we were coming up the river and he was there on the pontoon with Rab to take lines. After welcoming them aboard, doing 'the tour' and happy that all was well, we headed off into town for a well-earned meal and a pint. The next day we busied about some jobs and, that done, Derek gave us all a lift back to our cars we had left at Ardrossan. *Pegasus* was right on the starting grid, ready and waiting for the off but, most important of all, she was under the watchful eye of Derek and Rab. Now it was a time of waiting for the right weather window. Fiona was keeping an eye on the weather patterns that were coming in from the Atlantic and forward planning their development. As she was away at the Olympic training camp in Spain, our communications were by e-mail.

Correspondence continued with the WSSRC, John Reed now accepting that the guy up in Scotland was actually serious about setting a new course and really did mean to do it. I sent the £1,500 registration, expense and management fee cheque to WSSRC and was logged as an official attempt to set a new route that would, after my initial attempt, be open to all as an official registered passage. I was in the system and the system kicked in. John advised me that the rules required that the boat should be inspected and that disclaimers and paperwork needed signing. We agreed to meet in Kirkcudbright and a date was set. On meeting John my initial view of the man being a true gent was confirmed. A consummate professional, he took a close and detailed look around *Pegasus*. We settled in the saloon to go through the paperwork and I signed various documents required by the WSSRC. Being an engaging type, we soon had a good chat running and I asked why he needed to look and, in his words, identify the boat in such detail. The answer was somewhat surprising. In an attempt on an established record, some character had started a route, dodged round into an anchorage and then caught a flight to near the finish line, boarded an almost identical boat and sailed in to take the world record. Needless to say, this hare-brained and devious scam was uncovered and the scoundrel sent packing. Now I knew why John took notes of particular features and blemishes on *Pegasus*. Satisfied that all was well and that I was not a 'chancer', John signed off the challenge and 'Balcary Point to Blyth' as a legitimate and recognised route. The gem of an idea that pinged into my head halfway down that hill was now so real it was almost within touching distance and getting quite serious indeed.

Fundraising was also coming along. We had broken through the £4,000 barrier and, to help matters along, Peter Lederer, the MD at Gleneagles, agreed to support a prize draw on the website with a weekend break at Gleneagles. Website traffic went up and so did online donations. Boyd Tunnock of Tunnock Tea Cake and Wafers fame stepped up to the plate with a donation. Barbara and Curly Mills tipped in a cheque, as did Mark Tyndal at Artemis Fund Managers. Mark, whom I had known for a number of years, as he had bought *Cloud Nine* when David and I had moved up to *Ziggy* (a Bavaria 41) ended up in the real big time with his Artemis Round the World Vendée Globe campaign in 2009. In no time the £5,000 barrier was broken and we were halfway to my target of £10,000. The online site at www.justgiving.com was bringing in a huge range of donations, from a single pound up to £100 from an old friend I had not seen since I walked out of the school gates aged 17 in 1976. Through the contacts of 'PR Sue', APP Broadcasting, who produce the Seamaster Sailing Series, agreed to supply me with an onboard camera to record the challenge and to make a video diary for possible use in a future programme. It was all coming together and time was ticking towards my April target.

It was March and I was absolutely flat out at work. At that time I was Chief Executive of the Scottish Tourism Forum, the independent trade body that represents the interests of the Scottish tourism and hospitality industry. It was a role that carried high expectations from the industry, on what were fairly meagre resources. Tourism in my view is Scotland's most sustainable industry and will be here long after oil has run out and any last remnants of industrial wealth generation have been exported offshore. Work was always full-on and at a frenetic pace but March 2006 was a particularly busy period as it coincided with the launch of the first Scottish Tourism Week, a week of political pressing the flesh, meetings and conferences all about raising the profile of the tourism industry. The week has now established itself as a major event in the tourism calendar with politicians and power brokers recognising that it is good to talk. During the week I chaired conferences, sat on panels, gave media interviews, both live and recorded. Scottish Tourism Week made headlines in the business pages and achieved its objectives. On the Thursday of Tourism Week, I was at a reception at Holyrood addressing the great and the good of our industry, MSPs and ministers on matters of taxation, legislation, industry training and funding. The following Monday I was a million miles away on a yacht, smashing its way out to the Atlantic in a vicious hail squall. Tourism Week drew to a successful close and a mind filled with a lobbyist's key messages and radio sound-bites was switched off. Etched in my mind instead were sleep management plans, dietary plans, exit and storm escape plans. It was an extreme change and one that really needed separation between the two mindsets. This personality split really did ram it home to me how 'amateur' the challenge was; not amateur in detail of preparation, boat support or determination to succeed but amateur in the fact that within less than one week, two such different worlds could be inhabited with any sort of performance expectations in mind.

With just perfect timing as Scottish Tourism Week closed, Fiona called me and announced that approaching weather out in the Atlantic looked promising. It was 'amber to go'. That was all I needed. The stores, food and bike gear that were all ready and neatly piled up in the dining room were packed into the car and, the following day, Shona and I were off to Kirkcudbright. As we drove down the M74, I was still deep in work mode, making calls, speaking to press and closing off what had been a very successful week of lifting the profile of tourism with the political masters of the day and with the media. The last call was made, I sat back in the passenger seat and heaved a heavy tired sigh. I was exhausted, fraught and stressed as a result of the week and in no real state of mind to be looking at the challenge that lay ahead. Shona was a star and went with all the calls until they were done and then quietly told me to switch off my phone, I did that and sank into the seat and had a kip, totally exhausted. We arrived in Kirkcudbright and very quickly we were unpacked and all the food, gear and bike was onboard. All too quickly it was time for Shona to head home as she had work the next day but, as she pulled my leg, the more important task of feeding her chickens. After a long tight hug she was away and I was on my own. But that was not for long as Derek came down to the boat and we headed back to his house for an evening meal and chat. It was good to get some 'clear time' before it all kicked off the next day. I slept overnight at Derek and Mairi's and after breakfast headed down to *Pegasus* via the shops for rolls and some fresh bread, a strong coffee and the papers.

Erik and Gordon arrived later that morning and we set about the final tweaks and adjustments to *Pegasus*. A further conversation with Fiona confirmed the weather patterns approaching from the Atlantic were holding as predicted. The weather was good so 'amber' changed to 'green' to go! It was all very close now. After all that time of planning the Irish trip, then the round Scotland jaunt, along with all the cranking up of the media coverage, it was almost time to do it. I had a nervous twist in my stomach. The lads saw this and rather than sitting aboard worrying about what lay ahead we headed off to the pub for a good meal and a pint. That did the trick of calming me down and after a good nosh we set off to wander back to the boat. We took a detour and stuck our heads in to meet the RNLI crew who were in their training room. They set me going again with their view on how lumpy the Solway Firth would be the following day. They also confirmed that if there was no 'shout', they would be on standby the next day and see us down the river.

The three of us returned to *Pegasus*, had a dram and turned in. It was all getting very exciting!

3

KIRKCUDBRIGHT TO ST KILDA

I woke at 06.30 and there was no hope of just lying in bed thinking about the adventure ahead. I got up to make a cup of tea which brought Erik and Gordon from their berths. Although months had gone by with all the time in the world to prepare for this very morning, I felt slightly panicked by the thought that today I would be setting off to sail round Scotland on my own and sailing into waters that could and more than likely would be pushing me, if not the boat, to the absolute limit. We shared breakfast which offered the chance for a good easy chat with Erik who calmed me down. It was the first example of his steadying influence. By the time breakfast was done I was ready for the job in hand. I just wanted to get on with it. I knew the boat was as ready as she could be, bar the two jobs the lads had to do. Erik was busy up front stitching the ends of the batten pockets closed and Gordon was at the stern stitching closed the lifeline loop that ran along the length of the cockpit. They were busy; but I was moving things from one place to another and then putting them back; I needed to get going. The morning slipped by and soon Derek, my Uncle Charlie and Aunt Harriet and others were on the pontoon to see me off. I did an interview with Border TV and, just having done that, the BBC arrived. The BBC reporter Willie Johnston was coming down the river aboard *Pegasus* and his stepping aboard with his cameraman put the wind up me. It was time to go. The last two hours had shot by and it was time to slip lines and get on with the job.

The river was skooshing past the pontoons and, after a debate over which line was to be slipped first and which line last, we were ready to go. Supervised by Harbourmaster Rab Thomson, *Pegasus* slid off the pontoon and I edged her stern out into the river. With Erik, Gordon and the BBC crew aboard, we did a 180-degree turn and were now

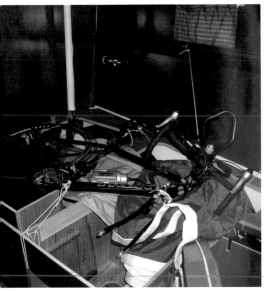

Trek bike lashed down in the stripped-out forecabin about to go for a sail round Scotland

Harbourmaster Rab Thomson oversees slipping lines at Kirkcudbright marina

Pegasus flying Ocean Youth Trust Scotland battle flag

pointing south and down the river. We motored with total respect for the shallows of the mud banks at the end of the pontoons and soon had Rab pulling ahead of us in his harbour pilot boat. 'Follow that boat' was the order of the day. To stuff *Pegasus* on the mud would be a bit embarrassing so attention was directed to Rab and his course. We were leaving right on the edge of the tide so we would not have much depth to play with. We tagged along behind Rab and as we headed down river the local Ministry of Defence range boat and the RNLI inshore boat joined in. 'Hey', I thought, 'this is feeling almost real with all these support boats accompanying *Pegasus* down the river'. We followed Rab's course between the navigation cans, perches and poles until the river opened up. By now the wind was picking up and it was clear that a reef in the mainsail was needed, along with the already rigged blade jib. Gordon, Erik and I set about reefing the main which was done quietly and efficiently. Willie did an

Left: Following the harbour pilot boat along the narrow channel down the river Dee

Below: BBC TV reporter Willie Johnstone heads to the start to get the story for the national news

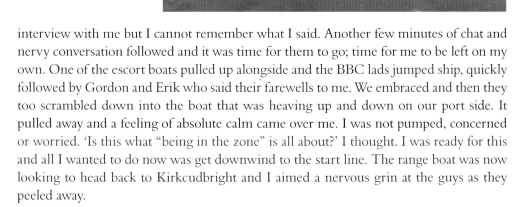

Above: Erik takes the helm on the way to the start

Right: RNLI inshore boat returns to Kirkcudbright after escorting Pegasus *to open water*

interview with me but I cannot remember what I said. Another few minutes of chat and nervy conversation followed and it was time for them to go; time for me to be left on my own. One of the escort boats pulled up alongside and the BBC lads jumped ship, quickly followed by Gordon and Erik who said their farewells to me. We embraced and then they too scrambled down into the boat that was heaving up and down on our port side. It pulled away and a feeling of absolute calm came over me. I was not pumped, concerned or worried. 'Is this what "being in the zone" is all about?' I thought. I was ready for this and all I wanted to do now was get downwind to the start line. The range boat was now looking to head back to Kirkcudbright and I aimed a nervous grin at the guys as they peeled away.

I had 7 miles to run eastwards to get down to my starting point so, with the engine roaring, I set off down the waves, touching 9 knots plus in an attempt to make up what I felt was about an hour of lost time. The last support boat pulled back and turned for the flat water of the river mouth. I gave them a wave and turned to focus on sailing to Blyth. My next task was to make contact with the coastguard to advise them of my whereabouts, course and intentions. This was a really neat moment and one that I cherished. The VHF radio conversation went:

'Liverpool Coastguard, Liverpool Coastguard this is yacht *Pegasus* with routine traffic.'

LCG: '*Pegasus* this is Liverpool Coastguard go Channel 67.'

Pegasus: 'Liverpool Coastguard this is yacht *Pegasus* going 67 and standing by.'

LCG: '*Pegasus* this is Liverpool, please give us your RT.'

Pegasus: 'Liverpool this is yacht *Pegasus*, one adult aboard. I am leaving Kirkcudbright, about to head due west from Balcary Point bound for Blyth via St Kilda, and Muckle Flugga, with an ETA which is very hard to advise. Over.'

Silence…

LCG: '*Pegasus* understood. Please check-in with Belfast CG at Mull of Galloway…'

So I had opened my safety traffic and over the coming days I would check in with Belfast, Clyde, Stornoway, Shetland, Aberdeen, Forth and Northumberland Coastguard stations. Closing my safety traffic at Blyth with Northumberland CG some 17 days later drew a huge sigh of relief from me after one hell of an adventure.

I dodged down to the chart plotter at the navigation table in the saloon to check my position and when close to the start line I called Derek on the mobile. Derek was positioned down at the line, with transit poles set up to define the start line as due south of Balcary Point. He had a visual on me and I then picked up the two bright orange shapes on the cliff face that signified position of the transit line. I popped the hand-bearing compass up to my eye and took a bearing; all I wanted was for the bearing to be less than 360 degrees, then I would know I was behind the line. The compass swung and swivelled and settled at 350 degrees. That was enough; I was due east of the 180 degrees due south start line from Balcary Point. I was behind and east of the line and all I had to do now was turn *Pegasus*, stop the engine, tighten sheets and go west. This was it; it was really time to go and do this thing that had consumed me for 18 months. I was ready; the boat was ready. It was strange as I now felt rushed into getting to the line and getting on with the whole trip. Months and months of preparation, visualising and managing issues, work, family, safety, boat, media, provisions, logistics and lots more and here I was at the starting line facing a beat to windward and I was being rushed into starting. I was on the water on my own, tense and nervy and the closest people were on the shore beyond sight but over there, close to the orange Day-Glo spots that were now my constant. It was me and two orange spots on the shore which was all that mattered right now. Derek confirmed again by mobile phone that I was behind the start line so it was now or never.

I rounded *Pegasus* up to the wind and cut the engine, bore away to gain speed and set myself to tack the boat across the imaginary line. I pulled the wheel down and she rounded to port; with a crack the jib and main set on the port side and *Pegasus* dipped her shoulder to the sea and gathered speed. I glanced over to the shore and in no more than a couple of minutes the shapes were on a bearing of 360° and I was away. I glanced at my watch and saw it was 12.11 hours so I started the stopwatch, hoping also that the important watch on the shore had been clicked into action to record the official time. I hardened up to the wind and realised that I could have positioned myself a little better for the beat to the Mull of Galloway. I should been a little further south to get a better slant and speed to the west against the prevailing south-westerly breeze. I was now on my way to Blyth and although I had a hard day's beat to the west ahead of me I was content to get on my way. But I was stressed and the elastic band inside me was wound up good and tight. Blyth was only 160 miles or so behind me but I was taking the long way round to get there.

The wind was blowing a good F6 with some gusts clearly at F7. I muttered, 'Bloody hell Fiona, you did say that we would have a beat to deal with?' This was going to be some beat. It was 48 miles to the Mull of Galloway. Beat to the Mull and then to reach north was the plan and I was in for a test before the sails were to be eased off at the Mull. I settled in behind the sprayhood, content that the autopilot could take this bit of the trip. It was lashing with rain now and the wind was blowing up hard. I sat in the shelter of the canvas sprayhood and thought to myself that it was going to be a long, hard and cold day.

Day 1

Thursday 13th, 12.11 hrs – Balcary Point

0 nm run – 998 nm to Blyth

Sleep in last 24 hrs: 6 hr 25 min

After two hours of battering into the Solway, we were hit by a vicious squall which built and built until, at its peak, it touched 42 knots. That was too much for the wind instruments and, ping, they were gone. Two hours in and I had my first piece of gear failure to contend with. The Raymarine Windex at the top of the mast looked to be in one piece but the read-out screens in the cockpit were spinning 360 degrees and reading a wind speed of 5 knots in a wind that was now howling very hard. This was not a showstopper, but a full trip with no wind instruments to monitor direction and strength would severely curtail my reading of conditions and sail plan management. To lose wind speed data so early on was a big handicap as it was the main means of reading backing or veering movement in wind direction trends, along with strength. The squall was accompanied by piercing hail that rattled the deck and crackled against the taut sail cloth. The cockpit floor was crunchy underfoot with hail and, apart from being wet and cold, I was not feeling at all well. I had absolutely no

Pegasus *ships water blasting to windward*

appetite and felt dreadful. Was this a combination of settling into the ways of the sea and the high levels of apprehension as to what I was taking on? I was stressed and felt cold and shivery, with cold hands and a splitting headache. Fiona, Erik and Gordon knew that the first day would be hard in order to battle out west before heading north. Timing was vital if I was to connect with the forecast south-westerlies. Right now the seas and wind were punishing me and the boat perhaps more than I would have preferred. I was intact but the boat had just taken its first blow, not quite a standing count but she was hurt.

We took a battering that afternoon. The sea was short and steep causing *Pegasus* to slam into the chop. The wind was whipping some spray off the wave tops which made looking forward painful and cold. I nipped down below and pulled from the cabin the ski goggles borrowed from my friend Ranald. I was fully togged up under layers, fleeces, waterproofs, gloves and now goggles and balaclava. I was only a few hours out and I was in a maelstrom that I would have expected off St Kilda and not in the Solway Firth. The sky was a stunning tumble of clouds scudding overhead with breaks of blue that allowed stabbing shafts of light down onto the green sea. The county of Galloway lay over to the north, just a slim line of dark shore reminding me of my main objective, reach the Mull and, zoom, we would be reaching off north-west. I decided to take longish tacks out into open water before tacking back to the shore. I did not want to lose ground to the north so kept my tacks on starboard to the south conservative. My sail plan was two reefs in the main and a blade jib upfront. The blade jib was just immense in powering to windward without putting excessive heel on the boat. The sail was board-tight, flat, hard in and had a sheeting position well inboard. All of these provided a great high aspect ratio powerful sail that allowed for a good angle of attack to the prevailing headwind. It was also an easy sail to tack. My bulletproof friend from Owen Sails was performing well. With the blade banged in hard, I was sailing the boat with a billowing and backing mainsail that was being slid up and down the traveller to depower the sail. It spilled wind from the mainsail to reduce the heel and leeway but, most important of all, it maintained boat speed. All this was exhausting and draining me of energy. I felt seasick and could not face even a cup of tea. Mind you, to make a brew in this bucking bronco would be fun, if not dangerous. I had not even had the presence of mind before the start to make myself a flask of tea to have ready for a quick swig of warmth. It was all symptomatic of the frenzy at the start. If ever there was a lesson, it was to cover every single detail in preparing for a major trip. With everything going on I needed a detailed list that would even tell me to make a flask of tea; that's what it takes to get it absolutely right. I laughed to myself, 'Perhaps Ellen had a list manager to ensure nothing was left off or forgotten on B&Q!'

> Day 1
>
> Thursday 13th, 18.00 hrs - Luce Bay
>
> 31 nm run - 967 nm to Blyth
>
> 6 hr run - 31 nm average speed 5.2 knots
>
> Sleep in last 24 hrs: 6 hr 40 min

It was 18.00, time for my first call to the Shore Managers. The check-in with Erik was a chance to unload some of the tension that had built up over the afternoon. He took it all and let me sound off about the wind and sea state, the wind instruments and my decidedly dickey state of health. What must I have sounded like to him? It must have turned him pale thinking that I was going to whine and moan like that every six hours. The job of noting the statistics or 'numbers' as we called them was not too onerous and, with some quick checks on the instruments down at the navigation table, I had all the information required. I was not impressed with boat speed. An average of only 5.2 knots in all this wind meant that I had been sailing too close to the wind. I needed to relax a bit and sail a freer course to get some more speed under the keel. The six-hourly check-in was a good routine to keep and it ensured that I had a written log for WSSRC verification, as well as the electronic log recording on the ship's plotter. The call done, I settled back into sessions at the wheel or tucked under the protection of the sprayhood. We had a good couple of hours; with an easier heading to the wind, *Pegasus* was much more comfortable in the sea way and speed was good. As the evening wore on, the wind started to drop but I held on to the blade jib, determined not be caught out being over canvassed so early on. Boat speed was suffering and I was now underpowered. To make matters worse, the waves were still fetching in and, with lack of power up front, *Pegasus* was not making good enough headway into the chop. My plan was to sail what I called percentage sailing. Golfers play percentage shots, i.e. reduce the risks and play for the heart of the green rather than go for the pin close to the edge of the green close to a menacing bunker. That was my plan, avoid the bunkers. At about 20.00 hours I unrolled about 50% of the Genoa from the forestay and dropped the blade jib. My strong little hero that had smashed us west across the Solway Firth was dropped to the deck and strapped to the guardrail, not well enough as it transpired a few hours later. Immediately boat speed picked up and, with some more power up front, *Pegasus* started to punch her way through the waves that the winds had bequeathed to the early evening. With things more settled I went down below and managed to grab my first 15-minute nap. It was not a deep sleep but it was rest and

*Late afternoon light off Luce Bay, Solway Firth
after hailstorm on day one*

some shuteye. I am not sure what good it did but it was the first of the napping sessions that were to become so much of the routine over the coming days.

By 22.00 hours the wind had dropped right off and the No.1 Genoa, now fully unfurled, was pulling nicely and keeping a good drive through the waves. The big problem I now faced was tacking the boat. To tack the Genoa round the outside of the inner forestay that rigged the blade meant that the Genoa needed to be rolled away by almost 75% before it would slip through the narrow gap between the inner and outer forestays. Fine, if you have crew and a decent wind but I had neither. So in Luce Bay we entered the next phase of the trip where light touch and ghosting tacks were needed to keep us heading west. Now down to less than 4 knots of boat speed, I would urge *Pegasus* forward and then set about furling away the Genoa for the tack. With the sail eased I frantically wound the winch to roll the sail away on the forestay. When the sail was released to roll away, speed was lost instantaneously and *Pegasus* became heavy and slow to respond. Pushing her through the tack was a nightmare as often the sail would catch between the forestays, lose the drive up front, stall and then not allow her to tack through the wind. When this happened she was set back and, worse still, with sails and a keel that were now stalled and next to useless, we just ground to a halt. Once a tack had failed I had to bear way back onto the original heading, unfurl the Genoa, build up boat speed and try the whole process again. It was soul destroying and energy sapping. The tide was also against me and that added to the block of our momentum. With our way halted by the tide it was inevitable that the tack would stall. Even if the tack was made it felt at times that I was going through 180 degrees and heading back down the course from which I had just come. Each tack seemed to lose height to the wind and it took what seemed like ages to pass the Big Scares, a set of rocks that jag out of the middle of Luce Bay. What was even worse was that each tack and all the effort it entailed was draining me of energy, energy that was going to be further sapped later that evening.

At about 23.00 hrs new wind came in and, having taken a tack well offshore, I had what I hoped was an angle to get round the Mull of Galloway when I turned back to the shore. *Pegasus* sails at about 40 degrees either side of the wind so when calculating when to make a tack to starboard (to the right) I add 90 degrees to the current heading. With that number in mind a quick glance with a compass at where the new course will take you allows an estimate to be made if a headland can be sailed past or not. I held on for a few more minutes as I wanted to make sure I could clear the Mull. Tide was still going to push me east so I needed to have some spare for the effects of the tide. *Pegasus* was on the move again and the wind was filling in nicely. Judging I could now get round the Mull of Galloway on my next tack, I turned back to shore and held the tack as long as I could. It was not to be and I realised that I had been a little too eager and was now very close to the shore. I was forced to turn back out to open sea. It was pitch dark and the sweeping Mull of Galloway Lighthouse was a fixation now, a fixation at which my every thought was directed. The tide was stronger than I thought and it had swept me back too far east so my next attempt to clear the headland was going to be a 'banker'. I had put in 15 tacks to come 40 miles but in the following 960 miles I would tack only four more times.

It was time for my check-in. It was midnight, so I set about collecting my numbers for Gordon. I had a signal so I called him on the mobile; he was quick to answer as he was clearly sitting by his phone waiting for the call. This was my first night-time check-in and it gave me a sense of the event. A midnight check-in had a certain aura about it; I had never done this sort of thing before and I enjoyed the moment. I gave Gordon the stats and position information and he responded, 'Is that all you have covered, I thought you would be miles further on.' I was deflated and angry with his comments. I recall being curt in my response. I completed the call and promptly settled into a wee huff for the next 15 minutes. The check-in felt like a kick in the guts and it got to me. It was midnight; the Mull of Galloway light was abeam on the starboard side and I was tired, fractious, cold and had no appetite.

Day 1

Thursday 13th, 24.00 hrs - Mull of Galloway

62 nm run - 936 nm to Blyth

6hr run - 30 nm - average speed 5.2 knots

Sleep in last 24 hrs: 7 hr 10 min

49

If ever there was a moment when an innocuous comment that, under normal conditions would be laughed off or kick-start some banter, could be taken so wrongly, that was it. It was irrational on my behalf but equally pretty straight line stuff from Gordon. I sat in the saloon quietly stewing in my own juices for about 10 minutes. 'Bloody hell man, get a grip', I told myself. I had lost the plot and had blown Gordon's comments way out of proportion but, no sooner had I rationalised the situation, than the nip of self-pity and injustice got me going again and I launched a few oaths in Gordon's direction. Gordon had unknowingly got me just at the wrong moment and I was not dealing with my situation at all well. Thankfully, I could see the red mist descending over the boat and I snapped out of it just as quickly as the call had plunged me into the little strop. I downed a can of tonic water, belched the gas and went up on deck to sail the boat hard, so that when we checked in again the chat would be of a different slant. I was now convinced that I had enough sea-room between me and the Mull so we tacked again and, yes, the heading was sweet as a nut. The Mull light was now under my sails; we had a heading that would take us up the Galloway shore and away from this place that had slowed progress. I eased the sheets and took an estimate as to the course to take and sat at the wheel for about 15 minutes or so just to make sure we were on a good heading. Content that all was well, I popped on the autopilot and went down to the galley for a brew.

Once down below I put the kettle on and topped up the water bottle I kept in my jacket pocket. This top up system reminded me of a fateful night on *Pegasus*'s delivery trip from France to Oban. Crossing the Bay of Biscay it was decidedly choppy and I had succumbed to a bout of the sickies. To keep myself hydrated I had been sipping from a 500 ml water bottle that was an easy size to keep in my jacket pocket. My little friend was empty and I had to get a refill. Checking that the helmsman was OK to be on his own, I went down below to replenish the bottle. The saloon was dark and quiet and, me being a nice sort of guy, thought that I would not put the cabin light on for two reasons: one, to save the night vision of my mate Richard on the helm and two, so as not to disturb the off-watch Ken who was doing a great impression of Rip van Winkle on the saloon berth. I felt my way along the galley to the sink where the larger bottle of water was stowed in amongst the dirty cups and kettle. I felt for a plastic bottle and flipped open my small bottle to top up. Knowing no-one could see me, I decided to take a swig from the big bottle first. I gulped it down and immediately thought that the water tasted funny and put it down to my general feeling of 'mal de mer'. I gagged and realised the liquid over the back of my throat was not quite what I was expecting. I blipped on my head torch to see I had the bottle of cooking oil in my hand. I bolted for the cockpit and spent the next 20 minutes conversing with the Bay of Biscay over the side of *Pegasus*. The following 24 hours were interesting to say the least. I made sure my Galloway brew was made from fresh water, but I still did not have any appetite.

I clambered up into the cockpit and surveyed the scene: sails pulling well, tell-tales flying, very little weather helm on the wheel, 7.5 knots of speed, on a heading of north-north-west. Then I noticed there was no light coming from the navigation lights on the bow; the next little problem was the loss of my navigation lights. I was not going to go into the busy North Channel without navigation lights. With screwdriver in hand I went forward to fix what had been a perfectly good working light the previous night when I had checked for one last time all the electrics and navigation systems. I had a good idea it was the contacts and, sure enough, once disassembled the light housing revealed that one contact had sprung off the lamp base. The fix took half an hour crouched over the pulpit rail, all the time dreading that I would drop a screw or, even worse, the red and green plastic light housing into the sea. What would that do to my confidence when entering shipping lanes and with all the night sailing ahead? No navigation light was a potential showstopper that had to be dealt with and there was no room for any error. After some choice words and a sliced open knuckle, which bled profusely onto the deck and my oilskin trousers, the lamp was working, beaming bright red and green for all ships to see – job done. I was relieved to be back in the cockpit with a bright navigation light gleaming up front.

Speed was really picking up with a good south-westerly wind blowing up behind us and in addition to the wind we had a helping following tide. At last we had assistance from the tide and it was not a battle with this force of nature. With wind and tide pushing in the same direction, gone was the lumpy sea; now flat water speed was the main objective of the night. This was what I had signed up for, night sailing at its best. It was me, the sea, the wind and just how much I wanted to push things. I was heading into very familiar waters and as high as a kite. What a mood swing from only a couple of hours ago! The lights of Portpatrick passed to starboard. By now we were really tramping north with white water being sent spraying out from under the hull. Speeds in excess of 7 knots were being held for long periods and, with the push of helpful waves, 8 and 9 knots came quite easily. This was what we were looking for, straight line sailing with wind, tide and wave. Fiona had changed from villain to hero in the space of three painful hours and Gordon was again my pal. In fact the whole world was my pal right at that moment.

I was pulling away from the Galloway shore and offering a course out into the North Channel. At this point only 12 miles separates Scotland from Northern Ireland and it is a bottleneck for shipping heading to Belfast or the Clyde. I had expected to encounter shipping in these waters but thankfully there was only one set of lights showing and they were away to the north-east up the Clyde estuary. After a good hour or so of fast sailing, I felt that the boat was chocking and a gut feeling told me something was just not right. I checked the sheets and, yes, they were nice and free. A quick blip of a torch confirmed the sails were set well with tell-tale tapes flying, those little strands of wool or tape attached to the sail that advise on wind flow over the surface. But speed and feel were not right and the helm was pulling to starboard. I flashed my head torch to the forward deck and to my absolute horror I could see the blade jib, that had been dropped and tied to the foredeck, was through the guardrail, half over the side and trailing in the water. I stabbed the autopilot on, clipped my safety harness to the deck line and carefully edged my way up the higher windward side deck to the bow. Once steadied, I slid down onto my backside and carefully moved myself down and across the foredeck that was at about a 30-degree tilt. I wedged my feet in against the toe rail that sits proud of the deck at the join to the hull and settled myself in readiness to haul the errant sail back aboard. It was trailing in the sea and clearly dragging under considerable pressure. To make matters worse, the sail had managed to twist itself through and between the deck and the lower guardrail and, under the drag of the passing sea, had pulled masses of sail cloth through the narrow gap. To compound matters even more, two sail stiffener battens had passed through the gap and were now jammed hard against the hull just above the rushing water. The weight of drag was immense. A guardrail stanchion had given way under the load and was buckled, bent double and hanging kinked over the side of the boat. There was no way of recovering the sail whilst underway so I reluctantly went back to the cockpit to depower the mainsail and the big ravenous pulling Genoa. I freed off the main and furled away the Genoa and speed dropped from a sexy and exhilarating 9 knots to just over 4 knots. I went forward again, but still the load on the dragging sail was too much to haul back aboard. A return trip to the cockpit brought boat speed down to just over 2 knots, which allowed me the upper hand on my deep sea trawling activities. All of the effort and hard work on the foredeck was also ramming home to me that, whilst my knee was fine for general movement around the boat, crouching and kneeling on a moving deck, hauling and pulling on rope and sail was another matter. The twist of sail round the stanchion was a nightmare to untangle and it took over 40 minutes of hard graft to fully recover the sail. Once I had the sail back on the foredeck, I stuffed it down into the forward cabin through the deck hatch. I was dreading that my work-horse sail was injured and that my ammo for later battles was spent.

This was the first real mistake and it was costing me dear. Having not made the sail secure on the foredeck was really basic stuff and I was now paying heavily with lost speed, a damaged boat and one of the key sails also potentially damaged. Worst of all was the fact that I had created a situation, through carelessness, that had not just had me up on the foredeck, the most dangerous place on a yacht, but had sapped me of huge amounts of energy, a resource that was not in large supply right then. It had also revealed the shortcoming of my fitness in respect of my left knee when it came down to hard work on deck. It was a wake up call in many ways. 'Don't screw up', was the clear message. Silly mistakes in basics can lead to major problems. Accidents at sea in most cases are a result of a series of events initiated by an innocuous situation or lack of preparation. Start the chain of events, issues multiply and, when combined, create a dangerous end situation. Play it safe, do not make rash decisions, check and double check actions and above all stick to the overall plan. It had been worked on for weeks and weeks and was based on a basic risk management approach. If this elephant was going to get eaten, the bite-sized chunks each had to be sized up, taken and digested in full without any hangover or make-do that would come back and give me serious indigestion later in the trip. It was fast flat water out there and I had just wasted an hour of good boat speed. At this point of the trip I also needed to keep an eye on the dark Clyde estuary to the north-east, in full expectation of seeing the lights of large merchant tankers heading south. The one that I had spotted earlier on had not moved so in my mind he was out of my life. I was tired, very tired, and sore with the effort of manhandling the sail back aboard, wet with sweat and now chilling as I cooled down. I was 14 hours into the trip and not in good shape.

The remainder of the fast night sail was done without any real event or worry. I had boat speed back up to good levels, the sea was kind and I had not encountered any real worries with any of the fishing boats moving to and from the Clyde. I snatched short dozes down below but never really got off to sleep; I had absolutely no appetite and I was depleting my batteries bit by bit.

I was delighted with my average speed and at 06.00 hrs had a good chat with Erik, who was impressed with progress. Things were looking up. I was in familiar waters and starting to recover from the previous night's exertions. The sail past the Mull of Kintyre was uneventful and, after snatching some more snoozes, daybreak of day 2 dawned. The next lump to bite off my elephant was the Rhinns of Islay and then on out to Skerryvore. I was now in the open stretch of water between the Mull of Kintyre and Islay. To the south, the shore line of Northern Ireland was close at hand and I could make out the shape of Rathlin Island. Out to the south-west was the open Atlantic Ocean and then ahead and on the bow was Islay, with Jura

Day 2 –

Friday 14th, 06.00 hrs – 3 miles south-west of Mull of Kintyre

100 nm run – 898 nm to Blyth

6 hr run – 38 nm – average speed 6.3 knots

Sleep in last 24 hrs: 2 hr 45 min

further on to the north. I could make out the Paps of Jura standing bolt upright in the morning light some 20 miles or so to the north. Take a right here and carry on up the Sound of Jura, through the Sound of Luing and a little further and I could be home in Dunstaffnage marina at Oban before the day was out. Instead I was going to sail away from well-known waters and put *Pegasus* just about as far away from her berth at Dunstaffnage as I possibly could.

By 10.00 hours the wind was starting to drop away as Fiona had forecast and I now had 100% of the Genoa pulling, with boat speed still well above 6 knots. The wind continued to drop as we headed to Islay. A glance over the stern revealed the Mull of Kintyre disappearing behind us. The wind took a shift to the north and it ended up a beat to get past Oa Head at the south-east corner of Islay. That little stretch of 15 miles or so forced me to use up two of my remaining tacks of the whole trip to get round the obstinate headland. It was a brilliant sunny morning and I was soon on a lovely course along the south side of Islay, close-hauled and heading for the Rhinns with tide under us pushing us north-west. I had the music system cranked right up blaring out Razorlite and U2 anthems. *Pegasus* was flying and I was Mr. Happy with a big cheesy grin, the worries of the previous night slotted away into the used and not-to-be-worried about file.

The south shore of Islay was a spectacle and the sheer cliffs of Oa ran down to the entrance of Laggan Bay. Islay sat there like a big wedge of fruitcake steeped in millions and millions of years of history, evidence that we have been here but for such a short time. To sail along the south shoreline of Islay is like being on a conveyor belt through the millennia. The high eastern cliffs at Oa Head are 600 million years old, the Dalradian remnants of shallow ocean floors that have been moulded by the earth's crust. Move on westwards and the lower mid ground of Islay is 900 million years old, Torridonian sedimentary rock from floodplains, rivers and shallow sea beds. At the far western end sit the Rhinns of Islay with the metamorphosed ancient rock aged at a staggering 3,000 million years. This is Lewisian gneiss, remnants of ancient earth's crust. To sail round our coastline can have a sobering effect making you realise our time here on earth is but a blink of an eye. However, man's impact and behaviour on this earth since we took up residence is fairly stark and, as if to remind me of that, standing high on the Mull of Oa was the monument erected by the American Red Cross to commemorate the 266 American servicemen drowned when their ship HMS *Tuscania* was torpedoed off the coast of Islay in 1918.

The midday check-in passed with Gordon – we were best of buddies again, last night was history. By now the sky was brilliant blue and the conditions fabulous as we sped onwards and to the west. I picked up with the binoculars some white water away in the distance, clearly some breaking waves in the tidal confusion off the Rhinns Lighthouse. Minutes later I could see breaking waves ahead caused by the tide pushing against the remnants of the wind and sea coming in from the south-west. I had tide under me pushing along with the favourable wind on a close reach; combined, they had us up to 11 knots.

Day 2

Friday 14th, 12.00 hrs – Off Oa, Islay

136 nm run – 862 nm to Blyth

6 hr run – 36 nm – average speed 6.0 knots

24 hr run – 136 nm – average speed 5.7 knots

Sleep in last 24 hrs: 3 hr 0 min

It was not long before *Pegasus* was in amongst steep breaking waves, some standing easily 8–10 feet in height. *Pegasus* banged and slammed into the commotion of waves, rising up and up on some of them, so steep it caused me to hold tightly to the wheel to save falling backwards. I dreaded the loss of wind and ran the risk of losing steerage and, sure enough with all the tidal melee going on, wind speed dropped and we were at the behest of the sea. *Pegasus* almost tacked herself off the back of one wave and I had thoughts for the sake of the boat to reach for the engine, a move that would have negated the efforts of everyone involved so far, all because of my stupidity at coming this far north and too close to the Rhinns. I should have taken the longer but less hazardous outer route clear of the tidal races. We were right in the middle of it and my greed to take the direct and shortest line had put us in a dangerous situation and one for which I was cursing myself. The tidal forces were immense and they controlled *Pegasus*. We slewed from side to side as we were caught by boiling swirls of turbulent water. The enormity of tidal power can be frightening at such close quarters. In amongst the waves, large tennis court-sized areas took on an eerie flat appearance and then, from deep within the centre, a whirlpool formed and moved off like a submerged hydrodynamic tornado. *Pegasus* was caught in a few of these twisters and she lurched off on a different heading, dragged by the greater forces.

The tide was now sweeping me north away from my course and there was nothing I could do to stop it. I tried to keep boat speed to make some way across the tide but each minute we were being taken way above the lay line for Skerryvore and away to the north towards Colonsay. After some 20 minutes the water started to calm and as the waves became less aggressive, confused and daunting, *Pegasus* started to make her way back to a sensible course. The boiling water started to cool and the whirlpools softened to mere eddies and spirals of surface water. We were slowly released from the clutches of the tidal flow. The wind was picking up again and soon I was back on a course for the waypoint south of Skerryvore. The tide had been vicious. For periods we were out of control and I had been moments away from turning the engine on and blowing the whole deal. However, that was behind me, just as last night was behind me and my focus was now on Barra Head. I thought that I should call Shona before I was out of mobile phone signal as it might be a few days before I could make contact without the fuss and expense of the satellite phone. We had a good chat; she was at work tucked away in a little office under the stairs at Kinloch House Hotel. Here was I with the Western Isles laid out before me, with infinity above my head and an open horizon to the west to gaze at. I felt sorry for her and promised to call again soon.

The day wore on fairly uneventfully with us on a close reach and concentrating on boat speed. The moment was all about keeping optimum sail-setting to the course and the variable winds that seemed to fill in and then slacken off. The wind direction stayed constant for most of the time but strength did come and go so it was not a relaxing day by any stretch of the imagination. It turned into a long bright day under a blue sky that was followed by a great sunset and mellow evening light, a perfect west coast sailing day. The glories of Islay and Jura to the north along with Colonsay, Mull and, away to the north-west, Coll and Tiree were each laid out to view. There can be no place on this earth in my mind that can compete with the west coast on days like this. From my perspective at sea I always like to consider that the view has not changed for millions of years. Only an instant ago, a few centuries back, early settlers, Irish nomads, Columba himself, Norse warriors, the Lords of the Isles and working fishermen will have gazed on exactly what I was seeing right now. Not a mark of human presence was impacting on the coastline and islands. Where else in Scotland is this the case? Certainly on the mainland generations of deforestation, sheep, deer, geometric square reforestation, impact of gaming estates, conservation of what we believe to be the past, intense farming and, of course, the odd pylon

Day 2

Friday 14th, 18.00 hrs – 10 miles
south-west of Skerryvore Lighthouse

162 nm run – 836 nm to Blyth

6 hr run – 26 nm – average speed
4.3 knots

24 hr run – 131 nm – average speed
5.5 knots

Sleep in last 24 hrs: 3 hr 33 min

A chill evening sets in south of Skerryvore
heading for Barra Head

The open Atlantic lies ahead as the sun sets on the second day at sea

thrown in for good measure have changed our landscape beyond its natural state. Yes, there will be pockets of hillside and forest that have not come under the axe or grazing of forced husbandry but out here it is unmarked and unchanged as far as the eye can see. Go sailing on the west coast and it is a voyage in a time machine; just bring your imagination and a total respect for the elements and your surroundings.

We were down to some desperately low numbers, and a paltry 4.3-knot average over the last six hours was demoralising to say the least. The last session had dropped my 24-hour average down to a pretty meagre

Heavily layered for a cold night ahead

5.5 knots that was nothing to write home about. I needed that south-westerly that Fiona had promised. The evening wore on and we were treated to one of those magical west coast experiences as the sun set on an uninterrupted horizon in a glow of deep red and orange with a vanilla sky rising and rising to the neutral greyness of the outer heavens. We were heading west and the swell rolled in from the open south-west Atlantic. Temperatures were dropping; it was chilling and a damp dew formed on the decks. It was going to be an interesting night, with an increasing wind forecast and a skipper aboard a boat that was ready and willing to head out into the open Atlantic.

I spent a fair amount of time at the wheel rather than using the autopilot as I wanted to savour the moment. There is a zone of absolute peace that I seem to transport myself to when sailing into the late evening and this evening was offering every condition for some relaxed peace with boat and sea. The designers who had created a Beneteau 50 had obliged with a great set up in the fibreglass mouldings and shapes near and around the steering positions. They offer some perfect contoured spots to sit in total comfort when at the wheel. Snuggled into one of those places, I was again 'in the zone' and just loving it all. My mind drifted to what my old man would think about all of this. I hoped my Mum was not worrying about me. Both Mum and Dad have always gone with me in all that I have done and I could not recall any moment in my life when they said, 'No, don't do that', or 'No, best you do not try that'; they were always there to support me. Well, Dad was not there now and I wondered what he would think about this trip. My mind wandered off wondering also what my Uncle Charlie would be thinking. He had seen me off at Kirkcudbright and that was special to me. Uncle Charlie, my Dad's brother-in-law, was also a big influence on my sailing. Way back on a distant day when we all visited the relations in Stranraer, Uncle Charlie took the 'men' out in his beloved yacht. She was a small sloop he sailed out of Loch Ryan. Off the boys went, Uncle Charlie, Dad, brother Ian and my late cousin Peter, and I think my cousin Derek was also aboard that day. It was my first ever sail on the sea and most definitely the first time in a keel boat. The day is crystal clear in my mind although it is some 40 odd years ago. The feeling of the boat heeling and digging her deck rail in to the water and speeding back and forth over Loch Ryan was just awesome to that small boy. I distinctly remember sitting down by the lower rail mesmerised by the rushing white water as it sped past, inches from me. It was hypnotic and, having understood that the boat was not going to tip over and the heeling angle was meant to be, I just lapped it all up. Another clear memory is also etched in my mind from that trip.

Sneaking down below to the saloon, I rummaged around the cupboards, exploring and searching around this new world. Tucked in a drawer I found a bottle of rum and, not being able to resist the moment, took a sip. My mouth exploded with the rasping burn of neat rum and I spat it out to get rid of the stuff. The bottle was put back and I went back up on deck feeling green and somewhat guilty. At the age of nine or 10, that day made a big impression and I have since spent many an hour down by the rail with white water rushing past, content and at one with the sea.

At 22.00 hours I was relieved to see the Skerryvore Lighthouse off to starboard; we were now due south of Tiree and about to hop across the open water to Barra Head. Skerryvore, like its sister, Dubh Artach, is a sentinel to the shipping channel taking ships north and south on the west coast. Dozens upon dozens of ships had foundered on the notorious sprawling Torran Rocks south of Mull and Skerryvore (Gaelic *skerry mhor* – big rock), a reef that slices through the storm-tossed surface of the Atlantic for a torturous 8 miles. In 1804 the Northern Lighthouse Board sent Robert Stevenson to survey the barren reef and in 1844 the NLB announced that as from 1st February that year 'a light shall shine from the rock'. The tall tower has carried out this task for 165 years with its massive light some 42 metres above the dashing waves. It is a shaft of light that has saved countless hundreds of lives. In 1814 Alan Stevenson invited Sir Walter Scott to join him aboard the NLB ship *Pharos*. The trip was to undertake inspections of the lights and to survey possible new sites. Each great man developed a sense of respect for the other. The granite engineer and the wordsmith struck up a relationship and when asked to sign a visitors' book, Scott hesitated and then penned:

> *Far in the bosom of the deep,*
> *O'er these wild shelves my watch I keep;*
> *A ruddy gem of changeful light,*
> *Bound on the dusky brow of night,*
> *The seaman bids my lustre hail,*
> *And scorns to strike his timorous sail.*

Pharos Loquitur
Walter Scott

Skerryvore light

In 1872, David and Thomas Stevenson, sons of the founder of the 'Lighthouse' Stevenson dynasty, built Dubh Artach and in one stroke the nearby Torran Rocks were likewise neutered. The little island of Erriad that sits off the south-west corner of Mull was home and headquarters for the build of Dubh Atrach. It is an island that I have visited many times when enjoying leisurely cruising weekends. On the island there is an old viewing shelter and just in front of it a stout iron bar with an eye at the top, like a giant needle stabbed into the mound of granite that protrudes from the thin topsoil. Sit in the viewing shelter, and with a little care, the unmistakable shape of the tower of Dubh Atrach, built of that self same granite, can be spied through the eye of the needle standing out on the horizon. It is truly a magical island, one that I have enjoyed pottering around in a dinghy and also run over and around with my running mate Ken Daly. It is a place of such natural beauty that Robert Louis, another famous son of the Stevenson dynasty, who was more skilled with the pen than the set square, was inspired to write *Kidnapped*. Beholden to the genius of the Stevenson dynasty, another mariner was being safely guided onwards.

With the sheets now eased and the sails pulling in the breeze, *Pegasus* and I were now cantering north-west in full flight. It is difficult to explain but there was an air of expectancy and excitement aboard. The wind started to fill in and the next couple of hours were fast; by midnight we were only 18 miles south of Barra, the second big bite of the elephant. It was Barra Head next, the southernmost tip of the outer Hebridean archipelago. Beyond that St Kilda, if you get your navigation right, if not then Newfoundland. Barra Head was the next big chunk of the elephant. The last time I was out there was on a cruise and had anchored up and enjoyed a run up to the top of McPhee's Hill on the neighbouring island of Mingulay. That had been a great day, when the breeze caused the machair flowers to dance and shimmer in the gusts. After our run and exploration of the supposedly uninhabited island, our crew of Gordon, Richard and I took a skinny dip in the sea and a chittery swim around *Pegasus*. Back aboard we dried off and got dressed and settled down to a hot coffee. No sooner had we settled than our eyes were out on stalks as we watched a completely naked and very buxom female saunter down to the water's edge. It was a great show, some 100 yards away from our floating front row seats. Our chat was feverish. 'Yes, she knew we could see her. What a come on!' Our mermaid slipped into the water, swam a couple of circuits and then, lingeringly and with an expert tease in our view, towelled herself off and wandered out of sight. We were dumbstruck and mightily impressed with what we had seen. We could only surmise that she was staying in the only habitable cottage on the island and was enjoying nature to the fullest. The island has only crumbling remains as proof of a once thriving community similar to that of its more famous sister island, St Kilda. Like so many west coast islands, it is a simply a wondrous place and one that should be kept just as it is right now.

The night sail was stunning and one that will live with me until I am pushing up daisies. With a silvery mercury moon illuminating the decks and sails, we scorched north at speeds regularly touching 9.5 knots and never really anything under 7.5 knots. The light was extraordinary and the speed was spectacular, all of this with a very kindly following sea. This was a sea that I could offer the aft port quarter of the boat to and, if timed right, have us lifted by the approaching wave, resulting in a glorious surfing motion as we seared north. On and on we would race sitting on a wave until we lost the momentum and the wave passed through and beneath us. Speed dropped and then after a short lull another wave would roll up from behind and push *Pegasus* onwards. This was open sea sailing and it was just great fun. Speed was the objective right now and I compromised on sleep to keep the boat going as fast as she could.

Darkness came in and we entered the ghostly realm of white head-torch light on white decks and sails. The white chemical light created by the modern head-torch creates a unique glow on a sailing yacht. The only comparable effect that I have experienced is in deep snow in the dead of night when a similar reflective glow is created by the surroundings. The white decks and sails reflect the light so the release of a single bulb is amplified by the surroundings. All this makes for a sort of ghostly glow that is a soft and almost warm light with no harshness at all. It is best described as a monochrome world. After a while you can be fooled into thinking you have lost colour vision. The sea and sky are black and the deck and sails white, and shapes and shadows on the boat are tints of grey and dark blacks in the inner recesses of the saloon. Glance upwards to the sail and the head-torch beam follows your tilt and the whole sail is illuminated, with the immediate reaction being that such a glowing beacon must be visible for miles and miles. To see a yacht's sails lit up by a head-torch is a regular view in night passage racing as crews attempt to eke out every last ounce of drive from their sails. In close proximity to another boat, tension rises and if one boat starts to pull away the invariable response from the slower boat is to check sails and the all important tell-tales. To see these needs light. Blip, the head-torches come on and are directed up and into the sails. Then follows the ratcheting of a winch and again a further blip of light to the tell-tales. Wait a couple of seconds and then you hear the squeak of easing rope over a winch drum as the over-tensioned rope is loosened off back to its original position. The light is back on, then it is off and the crew resume original positions. It is great to watch this ritual and also enjoyable to think that your boat speed has caused so much consternation and need for tweaking on board one of your competitors.

That night sail was really something to treasure, not just for the light effects but also at the business end of things. I had a single reef in the main and a full Genoa; the boat was very well-balanced, I was relaxed and everything seemed to be in control. Having played with the sea and felt that we had come out evens, I knew it was time to take the foot off the gas and get some sleep. The boat was feeling relaxed, as was I, and *Pegasus* was truly in her element. At last, after a lifetime of cruising in the inner waters of the west coast, she was now out in the open ocean, chasing down the miles and showing me what she was made of. I needed some attention now and that attention was sleep. I needed to start the all-important task of building up some sleep credits. I found a comfortable perch down below propped up in the corner of the settee at the saloon table. Arms outstretched either side of me along the top of the back rests and with one foot up on the opposite couch, I dropped off quite easily. From here, still in full waterproofs and with boots on, I could be up on deck in seconds. I had my kitchen timer clipped to my jacket lapel with a 15-minute countdown set to 'bleep' me out of my slumber and was surprised how easily I dropped off into the land of nod. So comfortable was the position, the overall state of play and so well set was *Pegasus* that I could take a 15-minute nap, waken, check radar and do a quick 360-degree lookout on deck and nip down below for another 15 minutes. The night passed and it was a good one. A good night for the miles covered, a good night for *Pegasus* and a good night for me. The team was on form and absolutely devouring the miles. After one of the naps I took a session at the wheel and, to help celebrate the moment, turned the CD player up to full volume and blasted out Pink Floyd's *Dark Side of The Moon*, shouting out the lyrics imprinted in my brain since my teens. What a life!

I checked in at midnight but now I was out of VHF radio signal and most definitely beyond any mobile signal so the satellite phone was called upon to establish contact. It had been my best six-hour run of the trip so far, with an impressive average speed of 6.7 knots. Average speed over the last 24 hours was 5.8 knots but I was so positive and in a good frame of mind I just wanted to press on and on to St Kilda.

I had been really impressed with the pulling power of the new Genoa throughout the night sail. The sail had been made by Owen Sails who supplied all the sails on *Pegasus*. Not cheap and made from a carbon-based laminate, the sail had been designed to offer a performance across a wide range of wind strengths. It is a big sail at 140% but carries the lightness, shape and strength to fly in anything from light zephyrs to 18 knots before needing to reduce sail area. Even par-

Day 2

Friday 14th, 24.00 hrs – 14 miles south of Barra Head

202 nm run – 796 nm to Blyth

6 hr run – 40 nm – average speed 6.7 knots

24 hr run – 140 nm – average speed 5.8 knots

Sleep in last 24 hrs: 4 hr 15 min

tially reefed, the new sail seemed to hold its shape and still offer a good low down area for drive and centre of effort and, although the foot is cut fairly low, there is still reasonable visibility under the sail. The evening before in the North Channel had seen the sail perform well, cracked off on a broad reach and pulling like a train. Now the second evening had seen the sail deliver beyond expectations, pulling and driving the boat fast enough to maintain occasional surfing speeds. The dark and horrible cold morning hours of 3 a.m. to 6 a.m. slipped by as we careered northwards. This was top drawer stuff and what made it even more of a treat was that *Pegasus* and I were borrowing this piece of sea for the moment, for, as soon as we moved on, our presence was forgotten forever. The sea moved aside for us, we passed through and it filled in behind us again. We left no trace, absolutely no imprint on this world other than turbulence in the water and a vortex of air as it slipped off the back edge of the sail. In a minute both effects would be gone, dissipated, and it would be as if we had never been there or had not existed. The sea would be left to roll, swell, break, foam and live on for all time, right here in this spot, as it had done for millennia before we came along. *Pegasus* and I were merely a big commotion in our own little world and the sea was letting us through one time portal to another.

The sails were eased and *Pegasus* sat level in the water as we reached north into the pitch dark. We were completely on our own out here, no one bothering us and we were not annoying another soul. This was completely new water to me; I had never been out here before and it was just great to be scorching along. We were 30 miles west of the Hebrides. A further 30 miles to the west of our position, the Atlantic Ocean shelves off to depths of over 2,000 metres (6,500 feet), deeper down by far than any part of Scotland is above the water. I scoured the chart for the deepest point and there it was, 2,936 metres (9,600 feet) of dark crushing depths beyond comprehension. My interest remained firmly up here on the surface, a surface that was white with foam. The white stern light shone out into the dark night. The water that had been disturbed by us folded and churned as if in a massive mixer, full of air, just like when a tap is turned on full into a basin or bath. *Pegasus*'s hull had pressed pockets and bubbles under the surface and they gasped for air in a foaming hiss, not an angry hiss but a releasing 'sssss' as they surfaced and returned back to their position in the natural order of this place. The texture of the water was soft and aerated, topped with delicate foam that gently dispersed as it moved off into the blackness. It was hypnotic and yet a comfort that water passing by us in such form and movement meant that we were not fighting forwards or competing with the elements for this space, and all was well. We surged onwards as the grey light of morning overtook the darkness and we were in a new day.

Another record had just tumbled and I had managed to keep boat speed to a very respectable average of 7.8 knots and, more importantly, lifted the amount of sleep over the last 24 hours. What a perfect sector and one that had propelled us closer to St Kilda. The morning moved in and brought with it a grey day. I still did not have any appetite and all I managed was a couple of mugs of tea for my breakfast. The sky was grey and the sea was grey. We were still tramping north; it was a noisy sail with the sound of the water whooshing out from under the stern as it tumbled off behind us. My attention was now totally focussed on picking out St Kilda over to the north. The electronic chart plotter told me it was over there; I just needed to see it for myself.

Dawn gave way to morning and it remained grey but still we cracked on northwards. It was my first morning of 360-degree sea. To have light come in at dawn and to be at sea away from any sign of land is one of the immense pleasures of sailing, and to be doing it on your own is just one of those 'pinch me' moments. I was not excited but I was full of anticipation that the next couple of days would be some of the best and most challenging sailing in my life.

Day 3

Saturday 15th, 06.00 hrs –
34 miles south of St Kilda

249 nm run – 749 nm to Blyth

6 hr run – 47 nm – average speed
7.8 knots

24 hr run – 149 nm – average
speed 6.2 knots

Sleep in last 24 hrs: 5 hr 15 min

A 'night out' on Pegasus

Dawn of day three – Pegasus at full speed west of the Hebrides heading to St Kilda

Left: Powering northwards to St Kilda – 14 tons and 50 feet of boat rush northwards

Right: Land ahoy! St Kilda comes into view in a running sea

10.15 hours: 'St Kilda, Yes!' St Kilda was in view and in less than 48 hrs. What speed, what progress! The islands loomed out of the grey morning and it spooked me. It was wild and awesome, really just as the books depict. I was at St Kilda, the fabled islands that I had read about, dreamed about and had at times even considered to be beyond me and the possible reason for calling off the whole challenge. I shaped a very respectful course around the collection of magnificent rock that rose sheer out of the sea. St Kilda is a massive lump of volcanic rock that juts out of the Atlantic. The islands of the St Kilda archipelago are the residual cooled magma that lay deep beneath an ancient volcano some 100 million years ago. They are the northernmost end of a string of volcanoes that stretched from Arran through Mull, Ardnamurchan, Rum and Skye, skipping the ancient Hebrides, ending at St Kilda. All the massive bedrock of the upper reaches of the terrain and volcano itself are long gone and the hard igneous interior of these volcanoes is all that is left. St Kilda is just a young scamp when one considers the neighbouring Lewisian gneiss of the Hebrides that comes in at a staggering 3,000 million years old and is some of the oldest rock in the world. The remnants of what had been soaring mountains and massive volcanoes worn away by millennia of wind, weather, sea and movement of the earth's crust had left a cluster of stark, rocky islands that make up the archipelago. My interest in the geology of our coastline had been sparked by my friend Ranald who had studied geology and ended up as a directional driller. Ranald has in his time drilled some mighty deep holes in most corners of the world. On sailing trips his enthusiasm for life and rocks is infectious. I was either worn down by his incessant geological pontificating and observations of the scenery around us or his imaginative descriptions of geological time lines. Either way I was hooked. To sail the west coast waters without a modicum of an understanding of the magnificent surroundings denies a large amount of the pleasure and appreciation of the place and experience. The names are ancient and befit the rock they represent; Stac an Armin, Stac Lee, Sgarbhstac, Boreray, Soay, Dun, Stac Levenish and the largest of them all, St Kilda (or Hirta). This was a very special place to sail and one with a human history and saga that beggars belief to us modern cosseted softies. My mind was stacked with the history and stories of the fabled islands soaked up from all my reading and flicking through web pages and leaflets over the years. The people who lived there defied the elements and what some might say rational civilised life. The customs and way of life seemed self-inflicted hardship. But yet, who are we to comment with our current civilised society of the 21st century? Of all the reading that I had done about St Kilda, one ancient habit struck me as really quite hard to fathom. Infant mortality accounted for more than half of all the deaths on the island. In 1838 a survey reported that eight out of every ten babies born on St Kilda died in their first few weeks, the cause being tetanus. The resident 'Men of God' claimed the deaths were of God's calling as it was his hand who took the infants. The cause of this catastrophic death toll was clear and blindingly obvious when a trained medical eye was cast over tradition and custom. At the moment of birth, the traditional 'bean-ghluine' or knee-woman took over as self-appointed, misguided and completely untrained midwife. She applied a poultice of fulmar oil and dung to the severed umbilical cord wound. Needless to say, with such a cocktail of filth and dirt applied to an open navel wound, the little innocents had little or no chance. It was the hand of the 'bean-ghluine' and not God that was doing the damage. Such practices had long gone when population numbers on the islands at the time of evacuation in 1930 ended up a pathetic struggling group of 36 humans. The population had reached a peak of 180 in 1697 when the first ever tourist and social observer Martin Martin visited. Legend has it that the people of Harris and Uist both laid claim to the islands and that the way to settle the claim was to race to the island; first man to lay a hand on the island was to take it in all perpetuity. The race was closely fought and, as the boats drew close, one of the Harris men, realising that all could be lost, drew out his sword, cut off his hand and threw it onto the shore; a grand story and one that is identical to the one that secured the island of Lismore off Mull. Perhaps it is folklore but a damn good story all the same. Scotland has an estimated 800 islands around its shores and of them all perhaps St Kilda holds the most fascination for us 'mainlanders'.

Back aboard *Pegasus* in the here and now I stared at the majesty of the black gabbro cliffs and sea birds that circled and rode on the turbulence of my sails. Large gulls and fulmars swooped around me. In the water some puffins, stuffed so full of fish they could not take off, frantically swam away from the bow wave of the ever-advancing *Pegasus*. St Kilda is the 'Holy Grail' to many sailors and represents a challenging voyage away from the comforts of shore. It takes you some 60 miles out into the North Atlantic. Here was I heading towards St Kilda, relaxed, in control and at speed. I was now at least half a day ahead of pace and not even two full days into the trip. It was just stunning to be away out here and viewing the islands. The archipelago of St Kilda was immense, not just to the eye as the perspective of the islands changed as I sailed round the 'dark side', but also immense in their presence. Cliffs broke clear of the water and rose sheer out of the sea and on up into the grey morning clouds that shrouded their tops and kept them secret from my prying eyes. It really did seem a special place. This was no cruise or history tour of the Western Isles. There was a job to be done so the romanticism of St Kilda and its folk had to wait for another day. I was at the most westerly extremity of my trip and I needed to shape a course away from here.

The sea was building and many of the waves now had white foam breaking off their tops which looked bright against the moving grey mass. *Pegasus* was taking the sea in her stride and still there was no feeling of this being too much for me and the boat. Yes, day 1 had been a nightmare but night 2 had been an adventure and one that had brought me out of the glorious moonlit night to a grey morning at St Kilda. This was the first point in the trip that really felt I was on an adventure, on a voyage to circumnavigate Scotland by boat and bike. This is what it takes to sail round Scotland, days and nights like this. I was a single-handed sailor getting to grips with being on my own, tired but still looking for boat speed.

Having rounded St Kilda, thoughts focused on the next leg of the adventure. This was the big one: St Kilda to Muckle Flugga. Wow, even writing that sends shivers down my neck. Look at any map and the enormity of the leg is clear. Sailing north-east, the direct line would take me to a position over 80 miles away from any land. The course would take me outside the infamous landmark of the Flannan Isles and near neighbours Sula Sgeir and Rona before cutting the 140 miles across open Atlantic to the very northern tip of Scotland at Muckle Flugga off the island of Unst. St Kilda was one mighty big chunk of the elephant despatched. The next bite was going to be even more challenging and quite a chew.

St Kilda is left behind as attention turns to Muckle Flugga

4

St Kilda to Stromness

As I left St Kilda behind me, the dark shapes slipped into the grey horizon just as they had appeared out of the grey dawn light a few hours before. I was back into 360-degree sea and it was a good feeling. The wind was still holding from the south-west. Such a wind direction meant that, with my north-east heading to Muckle Flugga, *Pegasus* would be on a dead run downwind, which really did not suit me at all. With the wind directly behind, it was not great for boat speed, general well-being and comfort. In addition the following sea was building and it had all the makings of an uncomfortable rolling sail northwards. The notion of reaching off further north, providing a more comfortable angle to the sea and wind, did not appeal as it would add far too many miles to the direct line to the next turning point some 140 miles off at Muckle Flugga. I could not gybe over to a more easterly course as I had to clear the Flannan Isles and Rona over to starboard, islands that would be met in the dead of night. Reviewing all the options, a straight downwind run it was to be then. I set the Genoa to the opposite side to the mainsail on a 'goose wing' and sailed a course to fill the sails and to keep the big Genoa pulling.

St Kilda was now well out of sight and we had returned to being alone at sea. I had views of rolling grey waves with the odd white top and only a few inquisitive seabirds for company. The sky was so nondescript, with no character or shape and perspective to it at all; it was just grey. It was time to take my numbers down and radio them to Erik, who would be sitting waiting in the warmth of his lounge for my six-hour check-in call. I went down below and gathered the figures, noted them all down in the log book and made the sat-phone call. Erik was his usual cheery and positive self and we exchanged some good banter, not really caring that each minute on the phone was costing me a fortune. The call ended with the latest forecast update relayed from Fiona which soon took the smile off my face. It was going to blow up in 24 hours to a Force 7 or Force 8 so, all in all, it was going to be an interesting couple of days ahead of us in this vast expanse of sea.

After I had read the numbers to Erik I sat back and thought, 'what a stunning set of results'; an average boat speed of 8.2 knots and a brilliant 162 miles run in the last 24 hours. Sleep was holding at a respectable 5 hours over the last 24 so, all in all, things were going very well and the check-in reflected my mood. However, outside things were starting to brew. The uncomfortable rolling action of the boat in a following sea had the sail regularly filling and collapsing. The constant attention needed to keeping the sail filled was making me tense and creating general sail wear and tear. I had to get the sail pulling to increase power but also needed to pin the boat down and make her steadier in the sea. I decided to pole out the Genoa, a technique that holds the sail supported by the spinnaker pole boomed out from the mast. Now this is a major task on a 50-foot boat as the spinnaker pole is quite simply a monster to handle on your own. In essence the task involved getting a length of aluminium the size and girth of a cross bar of a set of goal posts down from its storage position up the front of the mast, and end up with it rigged at 90 degrees to the mast, protruding well outboard so as to present the sail to the following wind. I went forward and set about rigging the pole with all the necessary lines: up-haul, down-haul and guy ropes. With all the control lines secured up-front and made off back in the cockpit, the pole was slipped down its mast track. Without too much problem and with the help of gravity the pole was soon down on the foredeck. I furled away the Genoa, then went forward and snapped the loose sheet into the spring-loaded jaws at the end of the pole. From back in the cockpit the pole was winched and hauled up into position and set to the required 90 degrees to the mast, pointing out over the side of the boat. I thought at the time that the thing was vaguely pointing to the North Pole. With everything in place, three-quarters of the Genoa was unfurled and sheeted in to trim the sail to provide drive. *Pegasus* immediately surged ahead and we had at least another knot of boat speed but, more to the point, she sat firm and steady in the water. We now had a fraction of the roll suffered earlier on. 'A fine job done, now let's have a kip', I thought to myself.

After two hours of catnapping, swilling tea and keeping a look-out it was clear that I was laying a course that was too far to the east; I had to head further north. This was not just for the straight and direct line to Muckle Flugga; I was thinking of the following

Day 3

Saturday 15th, 12.00 hrs - 20 miles north of St Kilda

298 nm run - 700 nm to Blyth

6 hr run - 49 nm - average speed 8.2 knots

24 hr run - 162 nm - average speed 6.8 knots

Sleep in last 24 hrs: 5 hr 00 min

night when I would be passing the islands of Sula Sgeir and North Rona. I wanted to have plenty of sea room to the east of me when passing these 'hard bits' in the dead of night.

Away over to my right lay the Flannan Isles which also had to be avoided. The Flannan Isles are also known as the Seven Hunters. Hunters indeed as they had claimed the lives of many seamen over the centuries. The teeth of the Hunters were blunted in 1899 when yet another Stevenson lighthouse was commissioned and shone its light out to sea. The light is one of the remotest lights in the world, but it is the night in 1900 when all three keepers disappeared into thin air that cements its place in history. Was there any skulduggery, or was it just a tragic accident? The story of the three men has attracted a great deal of fanciful writing over the years, none more than that of Wilfred Wilson Gibson's 1910 account *Flannan Isle*. That single poem fuelled many of the conspiracy theories that are associated with the island. All the emotional tosh that is written over the fate of the three men is rather perfunctorily dealt with in the report of the Northern Lighthouse Board Superintendent which reads:

Goose-winged sails with the spinnaker pole presenting the Genoa to the following wind

On receipt of Captain Harvie's telegram on 26 December 1900 reporting that the three keepers on Flannan Islands, viz James Ducat, Principal, Thomas Marshall, second Assistant, and Donald McArthur, Occasional Keeper (doing duty for William Ross, first Assistant, on sick leave), had disappeared and that they must have been blown over the cliffs or drowned.

All I wanted to see that night was the illuminating signature of yet another Stevenson-built light of two white flashes every 30 seconds. The lighthouse has a range of 20 miles so tonight I could pass well north of it and not even see the light counselling *Pegasus* that all was well with her course. As it worked out, boat speed was good so a night-time passing was not on the cards. The afternoon had gone and Flannan slipped behind me without the two of us becoming acquainted, and that just suited me fine. There would be no sightseeing opportunity today; no time to bear way off course and seek out the remarkable needle-sharp 100-foot high stack of Brona Cleit at the western end of the string of isles. We were sitting under a very comfortable sail configuration with all canvas presented to the breeze. *Pegasus* was really happy and so was I. The afternoon was behind us and early evening started to come in. It was time to check-in, this time with Gordon, who reconfirmed that the weather was to worsen and, what's more, the dead run downwind had done some real damage to my six-hour averages, but my 24-hour average speed now stood at a stunning 7.3 knots and 174 miles run. The thought of maintaining an average of over 7 knots was the very reason that the Irish trip was binned and here I was with superior numbers written in the log book. 'Perhaps Ireland could be the next job, but best to keep focussed on the job in hand', I thought.

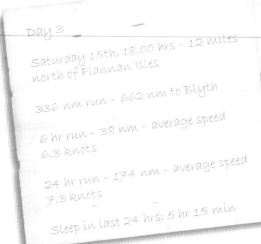

Day 3

Saturday 15th, 18.00 hrs – 12 miles
north of Flannan Isles

336 nm run – 662 nm to Blyth

6 hr run – 38 nm – average speed
6.3 knots

24 hr run – 174 nm – average speed
7.3 knots

Sleep in last 24 hrs: 5 hr 15 min

*Alan at the helm with a building sea
chasing* Pegasus *onwards*

Rain was forecast so it would be an inky black night. The barometer had dropped from 1003 to 999 in the last six hours and I knew we were in for a big wind. That sort of drop in pressure meant business. The wind had now shifted a few degrees to the north so it was time to drop the pole and get back onto a port reach. I also wanted to get the big pole stowed and on deck before dark. The Genoa was furled away and the pole readied for the drop. To drop a pole of that weight is a bit of a task and requires ropes to be pulled, released and managed in a particular sequence so as to keep the three-metre lump of aluminium under control. With the up-haul rope eased, the outboard end of the pole dropped to the foredeck. The inboard end of the pole was still high up the track it slides up and down at the front of the mast. The pole was now propped up at about 45 degrees to the deck, with the lower end resting on the deck. I went to the foot of the mast to haul the rope that would lift the inboard higher end further up the mast and, by so doing, would allow the outboard end to slide in and back across the foredeck. As I pulled and inched the top end higher, the lower end crept inwards and across the foredeck until it came to rest against the raised leading edge of the forecabin roof. One heave and it would lift and clear this 12-inch hurdle. Putting my weight to the rope I lost my footing and slipped, still clinging to the rope, with a crunch to my knees. As I hit the deck, I glanced up to see the pole, now pulled that bit higher and free of the deck surface, swinging like a pendulum towards me. Bang! The pole hit me square on the flat of my forehead. The impact knocked me back onto my heels and I let go of the lifting rope. The pole immediately dropped and dunted heavily, end first onto the deck. I had the presence of mind to grab the boat, any part of the boat as, although dazed from the impact, instinct kicked in to say I was going backwards and the edge of the boat was right behind me. In a flash of self-preservation I gathered my wits, regained my balance and dropped forward onto my hands and knees. There was a loud whooshing noise in my ears and the deck between my knees was black. The teak deck reappeared into focus and I was still onboard. I continued to stare at the deck and saw there was no dripping blood – I was OK. The pole was not secure so I needed to get the thing locked away on its mounting bracket as quickly as possible. I gathered my thoughts and ran through a mental checklist of risks associated with the securing of the pole to the bracket at the foot of the mast. Noting the potential finger jams, rope tensions and other possible problems, I set about securing the pole.

The notion of rehearsing moves and visualising step by step moves was my way of minimising risk. In the months before the challenge I had rehearsed sail changes and possible scenarios whilst standing on the commuter train as I trundled out of Edinburgh. Many a dark evening I would transport myself from my standing position in the jam-packed aisle on the 17.42 out of Haymarket, to a crashing deck, or a mental rehearsal of putting in a reef, un-jamming ropes, hoisting sails, halyards or other scenarios required when sailing a 50-foot boat on my own. At no time did I work out a plan for a wallop on the head from a spinnaker pole! Sure that no damage had been done from the impact of aluminium to forehead I had secured and stowed the pole and all its ropes and running rigging within a few minutes. All was well; I made my way back to the cockpit, sat down and cursed myself for allowing the accident to happen. We were on course for Muckle Flugga at the very top end of Scotland and that was what really mattered.

All the commotion with the pole and high levels of activity brought on my first real pang of hunger and I suddenly felt ravenous. I just wanted to eat. The first hours of the trip in the Solway Firth had been high stress in lumpy seas and a general feeling of 'mal de mer' had set in and stayed with me. But now 55 hours into the voyage I suddenly had my appetite back. I went down below and, care of the microwave, had prepared in no time at all a steaming bowl of chilli and rice and, boy, did it go down well. The feeding machine back up and running, through the evening I grazed the food lockers, drank gallons of tea, had bowls of cereal, cake, biscuits and more tea, and felt great for it.

The evening moved on into the night and it was black, as I had thought it might be. Now back into the groove, *Pegasus* gathered speed as we reached north. Over to my right

Ominous sky building from the west

lay Sula Sgeir, somewhere over there in the jet black night. Sula Sgeir is, in fact, no more than a rock with outliers, each with very little topsoil; just enough perhaps for the two sheep and a man demanded by census, but an island all the same. So heading clockwise around Scotland, it had to be on the starboard side of our course. Tradition has it that Sula Sgeir was once used as a place of incarceration for sheep stealers. It was time on the rock or the gallows back on Lewis as sheep stealing was punishable by death. In later times the islands were shown no respect as they were used as target practice by the navy before the Second World War. In 1965 Sula Sgeir and its neighbour Rona were accorded a little more respect when both were made a national nature reserve and, due to their inaccessibility, are now a peaceful haven for our wildlife of the west. Tucked in behind and to the north-east of Sula Sgeir is North Rona and that lump of rock was the corner where my course would change from north-east to north-northeast. North Rona had been a peaceful settlement since the eighth century with the islanders keeping to themselves and not affected by the outside world. That, however, all changed according to Martin Martin who visited in 1680. Up to that point the islanders occasionally travelled over to Lewis and had little or no interest in material wealth, preferring to use barter as an effective method of maintaining equilibrium of the island economy. They were simple folk according to Martin's account. He described two men having great interest in one of the very few women living on the island. She made her mind up and the jilted chap lived in torment as there was no other match for him on the island. Undeterred, he asked the minister if he could support his idea that the men should share the poor woman every other year 'so we both may have issue with her'. The reverend did not chide the man but told him to be patient and that he would procure a good woman for him from Lewis. Another island man, hearing about the offer to bring a wife to the island, gave the minister a shilling he had been given by a passing sailor. True to his word, the following year a woman was provided for the shilling. There is nothing said about the outcome for the poor love-struck man who made the initial proposition. The islanders' fortunes took a turn for the worse when a swarm of rats invaded and ate all the stored corn causing great hunger. On the back of this hardship thieves landed and stole the only bull; within a year the population of Rona had all but expired. A few years later the island was repopulated but, in truth, it never recovered. If I could get beyond North Rona I could relax and set course across the wide open seas for Muckle Flugga. I would be free of any isolated islands or rock for a couple of days, free to sail straight and direct to the top of Scotland.

Wow, 180 miles in 24 hours! I was pumped with excitement when I called in the numbers. We had just averaged 7.5 knots for the whole of the previous day and night. I was, however, brought back to earth with a bump. The midnight check-in went to plan and, having relayed yet another set of record numbers, the reward was a weather forecast that was worse than had been expected. The barometer had dropped another one point to 998. The wind was to continue to rise and in the next 24 hours I would be in gale force conditions in the most isolated stretch of the whole course. It was going to be an interesting day. The check-in completed, I sat down and thought through a few scenarios in an effort to acclimatise my mind to what might lie ahead in the coming hours: reefing down the sails, hoving to in the sea if conditions became too much, trailing warps or deploying the

> Day 3
>
> Saturday 15th, 24.00 hrs -
> 25 miles due west of Rona
>
> 382 nm run - 616 nm to Blyth
>
> 6 hr run - 46 nm - average
> speed 7.7 knots
>
> 24 hr run - 180 nm - average
> speed 7.5 knots
>
> Sleep in last 24 hrs: 5 hr 15 min

drogue astern to slow us down in a big following sea, being clipped on to the boat at all times, having emergency rations to hand, ensuring the survival grab bag was to hand and so on. There was a slight nervousness aboard *Pegasus* right at this time but I was very much enjoying the whole experience. I set about preparing *Pegasus* for the onslaught of the elements and ticked off each precautionary item. I was ready for battle.

As I moved on northeastwards, preparing myself for the challenge that lay ahead, it was also my first experience of the shipping traffic heading to and from the Pentland Firth. Thank goodness my bow light was now working after my North Channel repairs. At 00.30 hours ship's lights appeared over to the east and steamed on past and well behind. Another white glow appeared over the horizon to the right and with alarming speed that leviathan of the seas passed well ahead of us, going straight across my bows and on out to the open Atlantic Ocean. Over the next hour, two other monster ships came and went, much further off and were of no real worry or concern. Each ship was a bright green blip on the radar screen, each blip a thundering mass of metal and God knows what cargo. Alongside the innocuous little green blip, a data box displayed the heading, speed, distance and ETA of any potential collision with the 'acquired' target. A simple piece of geometry allowed the radar to advise me of hard fact, rather than what I might surmise from my observations. The night wore on with me sticking to the night-time strategy of catching 15-minute naps and 30-minute watches. I was confident that my collision avoidance parameters stacked up when considering closing speeds and, with the radar alarm set as my wing-man for the hours to follow, I felt prepared. At 02.30 hours lights appeared over to the left and well ahead over to the north-west. I trained the binoculars on the white glow and could make out two white lights and a red. The light formation indicated a ship under power, over 50 metres in length and passing to my left and behind. I picked up a hand-bearing compass fix on the lights and also saw her on the radar screen. The radar indicated all was well with my visitor and she was due to pass behind in about 30 minutes. I went down to make a cup of coffee, intent on watching this one steam by. Then I took another compass fix on her and the bearing was still the same, meaning the two of us were on a collision course. I started to worry. Whether she had altered course or I had slowed down I did not know but soon the lights were quite clear and she was closer than I really fancied. The radar alarm went off to confirm she was now within 6 miles of *Pegasus* but the good news was that the data box indicated that she would pass astern. I felt that needed some further insurance so I grabbed the big million candle power hand searchlight and, having closed my eyes so as not to ruin my night vision, beamed the light up onto the mainsail. This forlorn action was done in the hope that any dozing night-watch on the approaching ship's bridge might have visual on top of a radar fix. That done, I settled down and watched the big merchant ship pass astern of *Pegasus* but, as she came level with my stern, one mile off as the radar had predicted, a bright search lamp beamed out from high up in her infrastructure and picked us out. We had passed port to port as the text book advises, how much in control on my part I don't know, but it was not a close call in my book. It also struck me that it must have been a hell of a bright searchlight on board the ship, or else I was not one mile away as the Raymarine radar had suggested. I pondered that for a while, shrugged my shoulders and decided to put the radar exclusion zone out to an eight-mile radius.

I have been asked if at any time during the voyage I was scared or frightened. The answer is 'no', other than on one occasion. I can put my hand on my heart and say that the boat, wind or sea did not cause me any deep worry at any point. At all times *Pegasus* stood sound to the wind and waves and took all that was being thrown at her, more than could be said of her skipper, or indeed some of the equipment that had been fitted and screwed onto her.

During that night I heard strange noises which took on the form of voices to my tired mind. The mainsheet at the point of contact with the pulley blocks is, at times, under considerable loads and the ropes can groan or creak. It is little wonder as the ropes control the massive mainsail that drives 14 tonnes of boat. These noises would come over to me as cries or shouts but, even worse, cries from what sounded like a young girl. To compound the situation, they would appear to be coming from over the side, which would add to my alarm. When this happened, I would turn quickly to the noise, realise what was up and sometimes reply saying 'Hello!' to my visiting imaginary mermaid friend. It was very disconcerting to say the least; the groans were really taking on human proportions – a sign of the gathering effects of cumulative sleep deprivation and fatigue.

I mentioned that I was never scared or fearful of the sailing element of the challenge. However, there was one moment of deep gut fear that came in the early hours of day 4. Tired and hungry I came down to get some food and check charts and my position. I did my business at the chart table and then moved across the saloon to take a double check on the paper chart on the saloon table. I was jumpy and tired, having been spooked by my mermaid friend shouting to me from over the side and my 'close encounter' with the merchant ship. Suddenly a bright white light shone in through the cabin window and illuminated the saloon. 'Shit!' I screamed, immediately thinking that I was about to get run over by a ship and they had their spotlight on me. I was up the steps to the cockpit in a bound and turned to the light, expecting the worse. To my immense relief it was only the moon, bright, full and round, beaming down from a break in the clouds. I needed some sleep and I needed it quick.

Having survived my phantom knock-down, I went back down below to get the sleep that was clearly needed. I removed my balaclava and pulled off my outer jacket. Just at that point, I caught in the corner of my eye a movement in the forward cabin. I screamed at the top of my voice, 'No, get off!' I recall feeling an instant of surprise that I had reacted so strongly and what a bloody stupid thing to shout to this stowaway aboard *Pegasus*. The shape moved across my line of sight through the forward cabin door again and then again. A shiver of absolute fear shot down to the pit of my stomach and into my groin, so uncomfortable that I felt sick. The shape moved again and I realised in a blinding moment of logical thought that the apparition up front was not a pirate ghost of the sea, but a set of waterproofs swinging on a coat hanger from a roof hatch handle. It swung back again and I crudely cursed it with a string of disgusting and foul profanities that turned the air a deep blue. Bloody thing had near scared me to death; it was not a ghostly boarder, the only thing that had come aboard that night was fatigue. The thought of sleep did not now appeal, so I made myself a triple whammy strong coffee, cut a large wedge of fruitcake and went up to keep that big bright moon company. An hour later, after a session on the wheel and having brought some logical reason to the happenings that had spooked me, I came down and had a really good series of 15-minute naps.

The remainder of the night sail was uneventful with a building sea coming in from the aft starboard quarter. The seas that night were noisy, breaking and folding around *Pegasus*. The black night produced white-topped foaming water that came out of the darkness and was only revealed when picked out by the white stern navigation light. *Pegasus* was also contributing to the white water in her own way. At boat speeds of 8 and 9 knots water was forced out from under the stern and mixed with the chasing breaking waves. The mix of water and white foam shone in the night as it rushed away, disappearing into the now inky dark night. This was sublime sailing in my book, a tad tired, a little on edge but on a boat that was balanced and absolutely in her element. We were flying and, more importantly, in the right direction. The wind was also lifting, as Fiona had forecast, and in preparation for the blow I put in a second reef back into the mainsail and furled in the Genoa right down to a small patch of sail. The sail plan provided me with a well-balanced boat but one that was now working hard in the gathering following seas. We were totally focussed on boat speed and at 03.05 *Pegasus* touched 13.7 knots off the top of a wave. We were rocking, literally, and had Jimi Hendrix's *All Along The Watchtower* booming out across the seething rushing magic carpet. By 03.45 hours the wind was howling in the rigging and I was seriously thinking of dropping the main altogether and sailing under jib alone. Being without wind instruments was of course not really helping. At 04.15 hours a massive hail squall passed through that shook *Pegasus* and her skipper to the core. The wind built and built and with it came piercing hail that left the deck crunchy with white pellets. Salt spray was being mixed into the maelstrom around me; it was impossible to look astern as the hail shattered down on me and the decks. The seas were confused so to take some strain off the autohelm I took the wheel, but standing out in the weather was awesome. As the hail cracked off my hood, the noise was deafening. The illuminated water around *Pegasus* lost its jagged edges as the hail intensified and battered the surface flat. The hail stopped quite suddenly and almost instantaneously was replaced by the shrieking noise of the wind. I just stood there and held on to the wheel, dripping with water from the peak of my hood and from the finger tips of the gloves still clenched tight to the wheel. I can only estimate the wind speed at the height of the squall, but it could have been in excess of 45-50 knots, or even more. I have once experienced 65 knots of wind and it was not far off that, but again it might have been amplified in my mind in the middle of a very dark and cold night. The following hour was a battle as *Pegasus* surged down waves and screwed through troughs and over crests. The two reefs in the main had saved the day. I was not struggling with the wheel but it was a hard job to keep her true to the course. After a while things were starting to quieten down and I dabbed on the autohelm and took stock of the situation. We were still in one piece, with no damage to boat or crew; we had good boat speed and *Pegasus* was coping, I seemed to be coping too and we had seen off the hail. The cockpit was layered with hail so I grabbed the video camera and took a quick shot of snowball throwing on *Pegasus*. Well, it was hail slushball throwing, but it was white and the moment deserved to be caught on film.

I took the helm off and on from 05.00 to just before 06.00 hours; we were coming out of a long and tiring night. As it was time for my check-in, I engaged the autopilot and sat for a minute to check that the course was being held. I had the boat set up just to ride the weather, allowing the wind and waves to pass through and under us. Despite this we were still holding speeds of round about 8 knots and more. The morning light was now breaking through the darkness and day 4 was upon us. Content that all was well, I went down below to gather the numbers for the 06.00 hours check-in with Erik.

No sooner had I put pen to paper than *Pegasus* suddenly and violently rounded up to the wind and now, being broadside, sped up as she reached up the side of an approaching wave. *Pegasus* was flung well over on to her side and down below I held on at the navigation table to stop myself falling across the saloon that was now below me and not beside me. I steadied myself and then heaved my way to the companionway and up into the cockpit. *Pegasus* was now coming off the top of a wave at speed and she crashed downwards and deep into the following trough, battering hard into the chasing wave. The collision with the solid wall of water sent a sickening shudder throughout the boat. The wave broke and washed over the bow, cascading hundreds of gallons of water back along her decks. The sea water rushed aft and poured around the sprayhood and into the cockpit. In amongst it all, I grabbed the wheel and found myself up to my shins in water that was now streaming through and out the back of the cockpit. The cockpit was awash with white foaming sea. But more of a worry was that I was completely disorientated by our new heading and attitude to the approaching seas. We rose up on an approaching wave and crashed down into the base of the following wave, again shaking *Pegasus* to her keel bolts and sending a second torrent of water over the decks and out through the cockpit. Now cottoned on to our heading, I pulled on the wheel and struggled her round on to a heading with wind and wave astern. There was absolutely nothing out there to orientate direction, all was

Above: Remnants of the violent hail squall

Right: Heavy weather night sailing takes its toll on the skipper's looks

Day 4

Sunday 16th, 06.00 hrs
– 65 miles north of Cape Wrath

425 nm run – 573 nm to Blyth

6 hr run – 43 nm – average speed 7.2 knots

24 hr run – 178 nm – average speed 7.3 knots

Sleep in last 24 hrs: 4 hr 0 min

pitch dark with only the roll of the sea and feel of the wind on my face to understand which way was up.

What had happened? Why had the autohelm failed? I was frantically pressing buttons, trying to take it all in. With all this distraction, fatigue and stress I let *Pegasus* wander into a dead run with the wind directly behind us. A wave picked her up and pushed her stern up and up and slew it over to starboard. Before I could do anything about it we started into a gybe. A flash of realisation came to me but it was too late; I held my breath as she rounded her stern to wind and we rose higher up the wave. This wave was an angry breaker and folding white water rose above the stern. The stern of *Pegasus* went through the wind, the mainsail folded over with the leech and back edge now caught by the wind on the other side of the sail, and we gybed. It sounds corny, but I could swear it went quiet and in unstoppable slow motion the sail filled with the wind and hesitated for a second. I dropped on all fours to the cockpit floor in an attempt get myself down as low and as deep inside the boat as I could. The sail now filled and powered up, with the wind bringing the boom scything across the deck. It came to an abrupt and violent crashing halt, stopped dead by the mainsail control lines. The boom held by the mainsheet ropes had come to a very abrupt and devastating smashing stop against the tensioned port support runner jump stay that ran from the aft quarter upwards to half way up the mast. With power now on the sail, and with the wave at its peak behind us, we careered off down the steep face. *Pegasus's* bow was way down below me and the whole boat had an attitude that I had not experienced before. The hull vibrated as we sped down the wave; we were sailing and falling down the face of the wave and I was not sure which one had control. I had to take the wheel and control this breakneck charge. I held my breath and came upright from my crouched position from the cockpit floor. I held our course and the big wave passed under us. With the tension off for a few seconds in the slight wallowing effect after we had parted company with the brute, I was able to take stock. Sails were flogging, ropes were lashing about and the wind was howling in the mast and rigging. The mast was still standing and I was still in the boat. The following wave broke under our quarter and *Pegasus* rose over the crest and allowed the big powerful mass of water to course on and under us. My eyes darted around seeking out signs of damage. Yes, the mast was still there, as was the boom and everything on deck seemed to be OK.

I pressed 'auto' to engage the autopilot so I could fully assess what damage had been done, but the pilot was dead and the autopilot would not hold a course. The display read 'drive-stop'. I frantically pressed the autopilot engage button again and again, but nothing. 'Shit, the autopilot has gone. Shit, shit, shit!' I screamed. My mind raced. 'I cannot carry on, the record is gone, the attempt is over, the whole show is over'. I looked up again to the mast to take further stock of the situation and saw that the mainsail had parted company with the mast just above the boom. Two or three of the running cars that affix the sail to the back edge of the mast had burst. Worse still and to my horror, I could see that the boom was bent and creased about three quarters the way to the back end. My foot crunched on something on the cockpit floor. Looking down, I could make out it was not hail but the grey plastic sheathing, or part of it anyway, of a main pulley block. Be it the mainsheet or runner stay, I did not know.

Within a few seconds I had come face to face with the only obvious option open to me. No self-steering and a damaged mainsail in the teeth of a gale and in a big breaking sea – no go. I remain surprised but also quite pleased with myself that with all the emotions, levels of fatigue and chaos around me I managed to think straight and come up with the right decision in pretty short order. I hesitated for a moment. Could I continue? If I needed to sleep, I could lash the wheel and drop sail, ride out the weather for half an hour and then get going again. 'Yes, I could do that and nurse my way down to Blyth', yelled my aggressive inner self. 'No, I can't even think about that. How am I even going to get to Muckle Flugga with no sleep?' shouted Mr Sensible from over the other shoulder. The questions flooded my mind and each one was quickly answered. To continue would have been nonsense, nonsense that would have probably led to some real problems later in the trip. I had to draw a line under the situation. There was no way I could carry on and that was final! With that decision reached my mind then searched for where I should head. I knew that I was at almost the worst possible place for this to happen, some 80 miles north of Stornoway and 80 miles easily from Cape Wrath, not that that hulk of land offered any comfort to me right now, and again some 80 miles north-west of Stromness on Orkney.

Stromness lay way downwind and that would be the place to head for. It was one of the pre-determined bail-out points around the coastline that had been identified on the dining room table the previous winter as an emergency bolthole. Without any further thought I went for the engine start and kicked the 100 horsepower diesel into life. The engine started up and I looked over the stern and the sides to ensure that there were no trailing ropes in the water. Happy that all was clear, I put my hand on the throttle. With a sense of relief that I could still get out of the predicament, I pushed the lever forward and engaged 'ahead'. Prop wash appeared from under the stern and a quiet finality settled over the boat the second I pushed the engaged throttle forwards. That was it. My dream was over. After all the planning, all the effort by so many and all the hype at the start – the bloody game was over. 'Perhaps I could carry on, stop the engine and tough it out?' 'No!' came the answer almost in an automatic self-preservation response. 'No, the game is over, don't even try it'.

I checked the cockpit plotter and could see the course to lay was 150 degrees to Stromness, some 80 miles off to the south-east. The angle to waves was not too bad; *Pegasus* was coping well with the sea state. With the engine in control I returned my attention to the sails and the rehearsal as to how to drop a mainsail on my own, in a Force 8 gale with no autopilot. Any more pressure on the mainsail could rip the other remaining cars from the mast. I decided I must get the mainsail down and quickly.

I knocked the engine into very low revs to keep some directional control, lashed the wheel to offer some stability of course and went forward in the cockpit to flake out the main halyard. The last thing I needed was a tangle in the rope as I pulled down the mainsail. I threw off the main halyard jammer and the mainsail crumpled against the

Dawn after the wipe-out with the elements winning the day – Pegasus *lies*
broadside to the approaching waves as the author gets the damaged sails down

rigging. With the main ready to run down the mast track, I moved back to the wheel and prepared *Pegasus* to turn more to the wind in order to take pressure off the sail, so making it easier to haul it down the mast. This change in course brought her beam on to the seas and she rolled wildly from side to side, the motion exaggerated by the massive range of movement covered by the top of the mast some 16 metres above the deck. With the pressure now off the sail, it slipped further down the mast track. I clipped on and went forward to hand it down further. It was a process of back and forward on my hands and knees from the mast to the wheel to drop a bit of sail and then back to correct the course. On the third of these round trips the horror of horrors happened.

Somehow the Genoa furling line jammer, that holds the tensioned rope in place, was flipped open and I stared in disbelief as the Genoa streaked out and unfurled itself from the fast revolving forestay. The 15 metres or so of reefing line was stowed in one of the halyard bags in the cockpit and, in what I thought was a safe place, I had tucked my satellite phone into the accommodating and shock-proof coil of rope. As the Genoa unwound itself, the reefing line whizzed through the jammer and streaked out of the halyard bag. As it did so the satellite phone was, before my very eyes, catapulted up into the air. It took one bounce on the cockpit combing, while its second bounce was a splash as it neatly jumped ship and took up residence in Davey Jones's locker. 'Bloody hell, that's just cost me 1,300 quid!' I squirmed with surprising but clear recall the terms of hire and my reluctance to tick the exorbitant opt-in insurance box. To this day I will never know how the reefing line managed to run so free. Ninety-nine times out of 100 that situation would result in a twist in the rope clogging up the exit route through the jammer and bringing the rope to a jolting stop, but not this time. Damage done, my attention was dragged back to the sail as it flogged violently in the gale. The sheets wrapped themselves around each other and then the leeward sheet streamed out from the cockpit and ran off to flail and whip on the surface of the water like an angry and demented sea snake some 20 metres or so away from the boat. The noise of flogging crisp new sail material was excruciating and I knew damage was inevitable. I had a decision to make as to which sail to drop first, the main or the Genoa. The main was not flogging but was certainly still driving the boat. It was the sail that kept bringing *Pegasus* up to the wind, but the pressure was off the cars so no further damage was likely. So under lashed wheel and crumpled main I set about winding the Genoa in. With the unchecked speed that the sail had unrolled, the reefing line had jumped out of the reefing drum at the foot of the sail and wound and snarled itself around the top of the drum. The line was bar tight and going nowhere. The only solution was to go forward to the foredeck and prise open the jam of rope and metal. I grabbed a screwdriver out of the tool box and slithered my way forwards. The rope was wound hard and tight and, with the screwdriver hammered in between the rope, I managed to unlock the tangle of rope. Meanwhile the sail flogged and flailed off to the side of the boat and I knew we were in the shit, more than we had been a few minutes ago. The Genoa sheets slammed and slapped on the deck, energised to dangerous levels by the wild flailing sail. The sheets were 16 mm rope and I took several lashes on the back from the heavy wet rope for good measure. I could see a tear starting to appear on the back edge of the sail and there was nothing I could do. After what must have been about 10 minutes of reloading the reefing line, I made my way back to the cockpit and wound the sail in as fast as I could. I could see the tear, now grown in length, along with the tatters of expensive sail material streaming out from the gaping hole. A sailing horror movie was being played out and *Pegasus* and I had starring roles. After a great deal of effort and hard winding on the winch, the sail was eventually rolled up round the forestay in a messy, crumpled, twisted, ugly mess. The jammer lever was secured and the reefing line also left secure on the winch as double insurance against a repeat episode.

Totally exhausted I returned to the back and forward circuit between mainsail and wheel until I had the mainsail down. That done, the next task was to spiral a rope round the boom and sail to ensure it was all securely snuffed and under no circumstance able to whip loose and cause more damage. This was to be the most dangerous aspect of getting the boat back under control. To wrap the sail with a line meant that I had to abandon the safety of being in the prone position on all fours on the heaving deck to stand up and reach high over the boom, so lifting my centre of gravity higher than the guardrails that ran around the boat. As a precaution I had tightened the mainsheet rope down hard so that the boom was held strong and solid in the middle of the boat. It offered a good firm hold.

As I laboured on the sails, I kept an eye to windward and in particular towards the big seas that were rolling in and under *Pegasus*. A monster wave was approaching and the top broke just before it reached us, slamming with enormous force and a bang against the presented broadside of *Pegasus*. I dropped on to my belly on the cabin roof and held on as *Pegasus* rose on the wave. The angles started to increase and from my completely prone position on the deck all I could see was sky and cloud. Now it was the turn of the contents of the cabin below to sound their protest to conditions. Even above the shrieking wind I could hear crashing as God knows what ricocheted about the saloon. The wave pulsed on and we rolled back to the horizontal. We were still there, almost in one piece, and still afloat. I knew I had to get her safe and back on a course and away from this broadside attitude to the approaching seas. As *Pegasus* continued to roll, I set about the task of making good the mainsail. Between clinging to security on all fours and standing under the boom, I eventually managed to get a rope spiralled round and round the sail and boom until all was well and truly tied down tight. The mainsail was going nowhere!

I made my way back to the wheel, took control and engaged some throttle to give me some more steerage. Then I scoured the rigging to see if anything was amiss and to my huge relief it looked as if the rig, mast and deck fittings seemed to be sound and in one piece. It was on one of these inspections that I caught sight of the odd angle the radar dish had adopted. The big flying saucer-shaped dish fixed about three quarters of the way up the front of the mast was pointing not out to sea but hanging at a drunken angle to the mast. I knocked off the engine revs and inched forward again to the foot of the mast. Peering up I could see that the bracket supporting the radar had snapped at two of its three fixing struts. The radar was attached to *Pegasus* by some screws, cable and one bent aluminium strut! So now we had no radar in addition to no steering and no wind instruments. I let off a blast of oaths and resigned myself to sailing blind to Stromness. It was early morning so at least the passage would be in daylight, a real positive! I just could not believe that the force of coming off the top of that wave had burst the bracket. Just as well we were heading downwind and downsea or else hard hats would have been needed on deck as, at some point, it would be raining radar dishes.

I was back in control of *Pegasus* after a full hour of hard labour. I checked our course and heading: 150 degrees and still 75 miles to Stromness. Speed was lurching between 6 knots and a top of 8 knots coming off the top of waves. That is 10 hours at the wheel. 'Well, this is going to be a fun day', I thought. It was now an hour and a half past my check-in time of 06.00 hours and it struck me that I must make contact.

With the sat-phone gone, I had to open up the back-up sat-phone. It was down below in my survival grab bag, along with the hand-held VHF. With the engine back in neutral, *Pegasus* lay to the sea and I went below to find the valuable second phone. Below was not as bad as I had feared after the alarming crashing noises. The kettle must have come out of the sink where it had been stored, cleared the central console and landed on the settee on the other side of the cabin. Charts, books, binoculars, gloves, plates and cups were scattered about on the floor but, apart from that, all was well below and, most importantly, it was dry. One rice pudding pot had made a bid for freedom and was now smeared across the saloon floor, along with the teabags and contents of a cold pot of tea.

The grab bag was easily to hand by the companionway where it had been secured and, on the second dip into its contents, I pulled out the back-up sat-phone, powered it up and had soon picked up a satellite fix. I then made the call that I had never ever wanted to make. My priority was to let the coastguard know I was OK and under control. I also wanted to make sure that family were not worrying about me so I called Erik, who was a mightily relieved man when I spoke to him, and gave him the bad news. He set about relaying the information to family and the coastguard. The CG had been in touch with Erik asking about my whereabouts and my status after my six o'clock check-in was missed. After talking to Erik, I called the Shetland CG and spoke with them briefly to apprise them of my situation, assuring them that all was well. I told them that I had no structural damage, an engine capable of making way and enough fuel to get me to Stromness. We agreed to speak again in six hours.

The following six hours were the first half of a hellish 12-hour stint at the wheel. The sea was still rolling in from the west with creaming, cresting breakers all around us. Away to the west horizon it was bright but, above that, dark menacing clouds shrouded the light. Some of the white water broke beside *Pegasus*, some behind and some in front. Not once during the 12-hour passage to Stromness did I feel frightened or alarmed. *Pegasus* was entirely up to the challenge; this was the part of the trip when she had to look after me; this was her portion of the elephant to bite off and I was in her hands.

It was a long cold morning standing at the wheel trying to send *Pegasus* down the waves on a line of least resistance. We slewed and surfed onwards to Stromness. On several occasions water broke into the cockpit, not from breaking waves crashing down and onto us, but from waves that would break and slap hard on the hull sending water vertical and up and over into the cockpit. The only way to protect myself from the dump of salt water from above was to crouch down, turn my back and hang on to the wheel.

The day passed slowly and hour by hour we made good progress towards Stromness. My mind now shifted to entering the infamous Hoy Sound and its almost biblical warnings in sailing directions of the dangers of big seas and the conflict of wind over tide. If I arrived when the tide was racing out of the Sound and streaming straight into the rolling seas, all hell would be breaking loose as tide conflicted with wind and sea. The scenario of meeting more tidal standing waves, as we had done before off Islay, was getting to me, especially with the tail of a F8 gale, and as the hours passed it was starting

Day 4

Sunday 16th. 12.00 hrs – Sule Skerry 30 miles north-west of Stromness.

Pegasus under engine

463 nm run – 535 nm to Blyth

6 hr run – 38 nm – average speed 6.3 knots

24 hr run – 165 nm – average speed 6.9 knots

Sleep in last 24 hrs: 3 hr 0 min

to spook me. I feared it would have a terminal effect on my limp radar dome and that could cause damage to the decks if it were to fall. On my next scheduled connection with the coastguard I heard the words that most sailors dread. '*Pegasus*, I am calling the Stromness lifeboat to stand by as you approach Stromness.' I did not argue but I did reconfirm to him I had 100 horsepower, 50 feet and 14 tons of boat under me. He acknowledged all of this and calmly reconfirmed the lifeboat would stand by at the Hoy Sound.

The afternoon wore on and now the coastline or, more to the point, the western cliff line of Orkney had come into view. The long dark band now took on a personality as hills and cliff faces became discernible. The sea was green in the afternoon sun and the white breakers broke and rolled behind and in front of us. Ahead white water streaked in lines on the surface and spray was plucked up off the edge of waves as the wind sped it all forward. The hours dragged but I was busy, with a focus of getting to Stromness fixed clearly in my mind. Thankfully it was dry, sunny and bright. In foul wet weather the day would have taken on a completely different feel.

In amongst the white water ahead I could make out the pinprick of an orange spot, the lifeboat bashing its way out to sea towards me. In no time at all the spot became a shape and then the shape became the flying bridge of the Stromness lifeboat. She came up on my port side, circled round behind me and stood off by about 100 metres to my aft port quarter. Taking up station, she settled there for a couple of minutes and then called me on Channel 16. After a short exchange she pulled ahead; I was to follow her course into the Hoy Sound. The sea was beginning to take on a new rhythm and the rolling breaking waves were now more frequent and steeper as we entered more shallow water. *Pegasus* was surfing on the breakers and belting in at a tremendous speed. I pushed on some more revs and soon we were creaming up behind the lifeboat. Two of the crew appeared on the aft deck and flashes followed; they were taking snaps of the surfing and galloping horse. Over to my right the Old Man of Hoy stood tall and upright and watched without comment as another boat and skipper with a tale to tell passed by.

Soon we entered the mouth of the Sound and the water was not as bad as I had feared. The seas calmed and I knocked back the revs and resumed following my leader. We rounded the Skerry of Ness Light and I could see Stromness opening up behind Ness Point. We set off through the gap between the red and green buoys leading into the port of Stromness, heading for the North Pier that was tucked in behind the ro-ro ferry terminal. My next challenge was to get tied up alongside and face the locals and

Day 4

Sunday 16th, 18.00 hrs – approaches to Hoy Sound

Pegasus under engine

503 nm run – 495 nm to Blyth

6 hr run – 40 nm – average speed 6.7 knots

24 hr run – 167 nm – average speed 7.0 knots

Sleep in last 24 hrs: 1 hr 45 min

justify my being here, sailing alone in these waters in April. Would I be chastised? How was I to be received?

With my pilot book to hand I could see that yachts lie to the pontoons in the north harbour. The lifeboat slowed and one of the crew gestured for me to carry on round the pier and on into the marina. I waved and set about getting fenders and lines ready. The fenders are stowed in a large aft locker under the cockpit seat behind the port wheel. I opened the locker lid and got on my knees to pull out the fenders. Yanking them out and pitching them over my shoulder into the main cockpit, I had four of the six done when an air horn went off. Rather startled I looked up. *Pegasus* was now slipping along towards the shallows to the north-east of the pier. A quick glance at the depth sounder showed 0.00 metres! 'Holy shit, I was going to run aground'. The lads on the lifeboat were waving at me to head back in their direction. I gingerly engaged the throttle and turned *Pegasus* around 180 degrees and followed my track into the shallow waters. If I had not hit anything on the way in I would not hit anything on the way back. Safely back in deeper waters, I snapped the throttle astern to stop us dead and set about making fast the fenders and mooring lines. That all done, I gingerly nudged past the end of the big dark stone pier and, to my absolute joy and relief, there were three men standing on the hammerhead end of the pontoons ready and willing to take my mooring lines.

I set *Pegasus* up for a run at the pontoon and, taking it too timidly, totally screwed up, lost steerage and was blown off course and away from the pontoons. I waved a pathetic apology to the men and set off on a circle to try again. This time I put on some 'wellie' and banged the engine into astern as I arrived alongside. *Pegasus* shuddered to a halt as her big propeller below my feet dug into the water. The stern line was launched far and high into the air and soared over the head of one of the shoremen. I must have looked like a man keen to get alongside! I nipped along the side deck and the bow line set off like a missile and twanged into the rigging of the yacht sitting the other side of the pontoon. That was gathered by the chap up ahead, I tossed a breast line to the third man and, with his mates, they pulled the wounded *Pegasus* the couple of feet or so into the pontoon till the fenders kissed the rubber edging strip. We were secure and the men stood back, hands on their hips and I nodded to them and murmured an embarrassed thank you. I went aft and killed the engine, hitched up my sagging oilskin trousers, took a swig of water and stepped up onto the side deck to take my medicine from the locals. What do you say in such a circumstance to people of the sea? 'Bloody hell that was rough going,' or 'Thank you, thank you' – an abject grovelling apology for having their folk called out to this idiot trying to sail round Scotland in a big fancy yacht. 'You all right?' broke the silence and I, grateful for the approach, replied, 'Yes, but would not want to do that again.' The response was measured. A knowing inhaled 'Aye' was sucked through his teeth.

At this moment a large figure clad in the yellow of RNLI oilskins appeared at the end of the walkway leading to the pontoon and strode towards me. I went back to the side deck. He stopped and looked me in the eye. 'Everything OK?' to which I replied that all was OK and I thanked him for coming out to me. I hoped he knew that was from the bottom of my heart. My eyes were red raw with the sun, salt water and fatigue. What must he have thought as we passed polite conversation about *Pegasus*? Pleasantries done and a mug of tea declined, I switched into recovery mode and asked where or who I could contact to start repairs to the steering, radar and rigging. I was given a telephone number, the four men bade their farewells and disappeared back up the pontoon.

I was alone again, not at sea but tied up in Stromness marina with a broken boat and not sure what my next move was to be. I radioed the coastguard to confirm all was well and to thank him for his time and attention. He was aware that I was in, no doubt relayed from the lifeboat and he bade me good night. I was in mobile phone signal now so I called Shona and she was relieved to hear from me. I followed that up with a call to Erik and recounted the last 12 hours and a quick summary of damage to my warhorse. We agreed to speak again in the morning. Sleep was needed, lots of, and needed fast. I went down below and boiled a kettle and made up an instant noodle meal. That along with two mugs of tea and a slab of cake went down rapidly. I then climbed out of my oillies and lay on the bunk. I could not even get myself into my sleeping bag. I just curled up under the bag, pulling it up around my neck. My hands were swollen and ballooned with the effort of grappling with the steering wheel for 12 hours. They were hacked with deep splits that jagged with pain if I tried to clench my fist. One finger tip was split deep under the nail and it throbbed like hell; the rest of my fingers, claw-like, stiff and sore from hours at the wheel were hacked and painful. It had been fine earlier on and I had not even noticed the discomfort when wrestling with the wheel, gripping ropes, metalwork and hard nylon sails, but now to grip a soft sleeping bag was agony. My pain was amplified, in body and mind. I felt miserable, not only because of the situation I was in, but because I was utterly lost. I really did not know what I was going to do next. It was all too much for me and I started to bubble. I cried with frustration and anger that the show was really over. All the planning and time invested by so many people had ended up with a wrecked boat and a wrecked skipper stuck in Orkney. I turned to face the cabin wall and refocussed myself. 'It could be worse', I told myself. 'I am here in Stromness, screwed, but not totally screwed'. I smiled as I mused that I had the distinct taste of elephant arse in my mouth. I suppose it had to be dealt with somewhere along the trip and with these thoughts floating around my head I passed out into a deep sleep. I woke again sometime later, chilled, pushed my way into the bag and slipped off again.

Day 4

Sunday 16th, 18.52 hrs – Stromness marina

Pegasus secure to pontoons

508 nm run – 490 nm to Blyth

6 hr run – 5 nm – average speed 4.9 knots

24 hr run – 126 nm – average speed 5.3 knots

Sleep in last 24 hrs: 0 hr 45 min

5

STROMNESS

I woke with a start as a knock on the hull resounded throughout the boat. It was still daylight and it was couple of seconds before I realised that it was the next morning. I got up and poked my head out of the hatch. What a sight I must have looked. The figure standing on the pontoon piped up, 'I hear you may need some help.' I waved him aboard and put the kettle on. Over a brew we chatted about the damage and before I knew much more, Stewart and I were talking about how soon I could get going again and what jobs needed to be done. Steering, rigging, sails, running rigging and the radar all needed sorting. The next 48 hours were full-on as we set about making *Pegasus* seaworthy again. The full list of damages to sort was:

- Torn headsail and knotted sheets to replace
- Broken radar bracket to fix and make safe
- Broken mainsail cars to replace and repair
- Major bend to the boom (beyond repair) to jury rig
- Smashed deck mainsheet pulley block to replace
- Smashed runner pulley block to replace
- Torn sprayhood to patch
- Inoperative autohelm steering, to diagnose and fix
- Smashed heads mirror to tidy and make safe.

Before everything kicked off I made for the ferry terminal where Stewart had advised me there were some public showers. I entered the cubicle and soaked myself under the

A bruised and battered Pegasus *alongside Stromness marina*

steaming hot water. The salt in my hair and on my face ran off and tasted sour as it ran over my lips. My cracked hands, softened by the water, nipped and stung. In general my body was not in tip top condition. Having washed and refreshed myself, I had a stunning cup of machine coffee and then set off for the shops to get some bits and pieces. I found a hardware store and rummaged around in the chandlery section, coming away with an assortment of bolts, screws, nuts, washers and split pins. All good stuff for my toolbox, I thought. Perhaps it was just an attempt by a shaken skipper to make the boat that little bit more self-sufficient in the repairs department. I was keen to get on with the jobs in hand so back to the boat was the order of the day. The autopilot was dismantled and we could not find what was wrong so we called on a local firm, Hamnavoe Engineering, who sent two men down straight away to look into matters. Soon after they stepped aboard the culprit was found, a small matchstick-sized shear pin. The pin when loaded had simply given way as it should do but it had not sheared. Instead it had crumbled due to cumulative fatigue. The mechanic showed me the rusty residue that he rubbed between thumb and forefinger as proof of the problem. The whole challenge had failed because of a replaceable part that is part of a standard overhaul service procedure. Was it me or was it Beneteau and the yard at fault? Should I have been better prepared with knowledge of all the working parts? Yes! Should the guys who were part of the team who prepared *Pegasus* have checked this? Yes! Blame, blame, blame. That was the mode I was in when the true simplicity of the root cause of the project collapse was fully understood. I had to walk away from the engineers as I was spitting nails at this point and apoplectic with rage. A bag of shear pins was produced from a tool box and within five minutes we had the steering system fixed and the big hydraulic steering ram again responding to button commands. The plastic and metal cars that had come off the mast were reassembled and glued with two part epoxy glue. I swopped the most damaged ones with others from further up the sail where there is less of a strain and lateral pull away from the mast.

The radar was another story. I was hauled up the mast to survey the damage. No doubt when *Pegasus* had come off the top of a wave, the shock had been too much for the bracket to withstand. It had to come off and be welded, not a temporary repair job that I could effect. After much awkward work hanging out of a bosun's chair 15 metres off the deck, I had the whole kit disassembled and the offending bracket sent down on a halyard. The radar dish was made safe in a sail bag and strapped to the mast. The bracket was delivered over to Hamnavoe and they promised it back for first thing the next morning. With that work now in progress, I set about the entire minor task list of fixing or replacing the burst blocks and sail fastenings. The whole day sped by as job after job was completed. By late afternoon Stewart had departed for home

Author stripping the broken radar bracket from the mast and radar dish bagged for safe keeping

and left me to my own devices. I was exhausted and went below to eat and recover from the day's exertions and mental worry. After a good solid meal I rested for a few minutes and was soon back on deck to clear sails and general kit that was on the decks. The No.1 Genoa was a monster of a sail to manhandle on my own. I needed to get the sail off the foredeck, back along the side deck and then down below into the forward cabin. I thought for a moment that I should leave it until the next morning when Stewart could give me a hand but, no, I wanted to get decks clear for the morning. The effort was immense in moving the lump of dead weight over deck fittings that snagged and frustrated progress. I was at my wit's end with the wrestling match when, thankfully, the chap who was working on his boat two slots down the pontoon from *Pegasus* took pity and helped me complete the job. The sail was stuffed into the forward cabin and I said my thanks to the knight in shining armour. I collapsed, crashed out and slept deeply in a motionless state in my bunk.

The following morning Stewart arrived on site at 09.30 hours and the rest of the forenoon whizzed by with jobs getting ticked off one by one. The bracket reappeared in one piece and ready to go back onto the mast as promised, along with an invoice that was settled immediately. I was again hauled up the mast on the main halyard and set about the job. Working at a really awkward angle, it was difficult to get comfortable and a number of screws and bolts flipped out of my grip and spun down to bounce on the deck, with most of them taking a second bounce over the side and into the drink. The job was proving too much and there was seemingly no way that I was going to get the bracket screwed tight and the radar dome relocated onto the fixing pins. Each one required complete alignment for the whole fixture to come together. I returned to the deck three times to gather myself, grab a tea, collect whatever bits I could from the deck and return for more frustration on the end of a rope halfway up the mast.

After an hour or so we realised that enough was enough; this was not going to work and, with that point reached, Stewart decided to call in the cavalry. He went over to the Harbour Office and returned with a smile on his face. The harbour was going through some extension work and there was a crane operating on the site. We had two hours to get *Pegasus* round to the main ferry terminal and get the radar fixed before the ferry came in for the evening. I slipped lines, motored round to the terminal and secured *Pegasus* to the pier right under the tower of the large red crane. Stewart and I scrambled into the working cage and were slowly hoisted up to the offending radar bracket. The job was done in no more than 15 minutes thanks to the stable working platform and the fact that we could both get our hands on the offending fiddly nuts from our advantageous position. Back down on the pier I shook hands with the crane driver and offered him a few quid which, despite my protestations, he refused to take. I took *Pegasus* back to her berth in the marina. It was time to say good-bye to Stewart and, having paid him for his time, we shook hands and he headed off, having helped immeasurably to get the two of us back on the road again.

I surveyed the boom in an attempt to give a cold unbiased assessment as to its sea-worthiness. To set off for Muckle Flugga and then on down the entire east coast of Scotland with a boom that was going to give way would be madness. It needed to be up for the job and I needed to stand back from all emotional pressure and assess its condition. It was creased and bent but not beyond getting me back to Blyth. On a port tack there would be no problem; the boom would be braced on its good side and no harm would

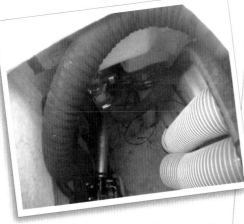

Below: Our saviour, the red crane, and means of getting the radar bracket fitted

Bottom of page: Long way down to the decks from the working basket hoisted up the mast

The autopilot drive, the source of all the problems

The new carbon headsail is bagged to be stowed away below decks

come. It would be a different matter on a starboard tack with the pressure of the mainsail pressing the long aluminium strut through the crease and so inviting the boom to fold and collapse under the strain. I decided that if I was to rig a line diagonally across the cockpit from the starboard winch to the aft end of the boom, I could control the weight on the boom by loading the support line on the winch. I checked the angles and the line of pull back to the winch seemed to be good. Other than the inconvenience of having to limbo under the obstacle as it reached across the cockpit, all would be fine. I talked this over with Erik during a long telephone conversation and his conclusion was that if I

Above: Damage sustained to the boom during crash gybe off Rona

Left: Pegasus *back in one piece and shipshape is ready to leave Stromness*

thought it looked OK, I should just go for it – brilliant positive support at every turn with that man. During all the work on *Pegasus* I kept a hot line to Fiona to understand what the weather was up to. I had completely lost the weather front that had swept me up the west coast and I did not have a clue what was coming next. Fiona advised that it was OK to go but there were some really nasty gales on their way and these we had to manage. The solution we came to was to get round Muckle Flugga and down to Lerwick. Safe in Lerwick I could sit out the impending gales. Bashing south into a southerly gale with a crippled boom was most certainly not the smart thing to do.

I had been in Stromness for nearly 48 hours and had not ventured away from the pontoons or harbour side other than that blissful shower and the rummage in the hardware shop. I took myself off to the lifeboat shed to see if any of the crew was there. I had been here over long not to have said my thanks to them in person. There was no-one there so I slipped a donation into the box and wandered around the quiet streets of Stromness and back to *Pegasus*, clear in my mind it was now time to go. I called both Erik and Gordon to tell them that all repairs were done and that *Pegasus* and I were ready and willing to go. Both were OK to go back on watch and we set up the schedule for the ensuing six-hourly check-ins. I called Lerwick Harbourmaster to request a berth for *Pegasus*. With a 50-foot boat it is best to call ahead as she is not the type of boat you can just pitch up and expect to slip into a little corner. He advised that they could take her and we agreed that I would make contact on my approach. Shona told me to be careful and, with all calls done, I settled down to get some sleep planning to set off at 06.00 hours the next morning.

6

Stromness to Lerwick

The plan was that I would set off from Stromness and get myself round the top of Shetland and down to Lerwick. In anticipation of some big winds coming in from the south, I really did not have an option to attempt a straight run to Blyth. There was absolutely no way I was going to set off into the North Sea expecting gales with the boom in its present condition. Fiona told me I had three days to get to Lerwick before the 'blow' was forecast to come in, and come in hard. I was not too perturbed that I was set for another stop-over in port as the non-stop ambitions had now been put to rest and I had come to terms with that disappointment. The thought of stopping was not the gut-wrenching feeling that I had endured when Stromness became the only option a couple of days before. I was not anguishing over what might have been, just more concerned now about getting the job done and heading for home.

It was now that an unexpected concern, or was it nerves, came over me. Yes, I was finding the thought of getting back on the horse after the fall very difficult indeed and was very unsettled and nervous about putting to sea again. The concern was across all departments: was I capable of completing this adventure? Would I make the wrong call in a situation off Muckle Flugga? Would the boat hold out and the damaged boom in particular? Worst of all, would I get into trouble and end up the cause of another lifeboat shout? The latter was my greatest fear. 'Capt Calamity blunders around Scotland' was the headline that played on my mind. The first three hours of this leg were to prove very uncomfortable as these thoughts overtook the fact that I was in a well-founded boat, the weather forecast was good and I was not a complete idiot. I have never felt so unsure of myself afloat or ashore as I did that morning. The feeling came without any real warning. I had taken a full breakfast and again run through the passage plan, as I had done twice the previous evening. The trip was about 180 miles out from Stromness to Muckle Flugga and then south to Lerwick. I had my boltholes planned and well-documented with approach bearings worked out and all easily to hand. I had several what-if scenarios noted and worked out. All the charts and pilot books were stored in sequence and marked up so, in passage planning terms, we were pretty well-set. The self-doubt hit me as I started to kit up and really kicked in when I set about preparing to slip the lines from the jetty. God, I was really nervous and not at all sure if I should even carry on. Would the sensible thing be to work my way back west and get the wounded *Pegasus* back to the familiarity of Oban, friendly faces and friendly waters? There was an internal struggle going on and I needed to grasp the situation. The fact that the self-doubt had hit right at the point of departure and not as I had been plotting and planning the passage to Lerwick the previous evening needed some thought. I tried to rationalise why it had got to me. It was irrational doubt and one that was not founded on anything more than nerves. If it had been more that that, it would have surfaced last night or as I had gone about the repairs and preparation to depart over the two previous days. So this was simply a reaction to the moment and was not based on logical thought. That was good enough for me. Another run through of systems and passage plan was undertaken and I decided that it was indeed time to get on with it. 06.00 hours was the planned time of departure from Stromness; it was now 06.15 hours, planning was complete so it was time to go.

Dawn and Pegasus *slips silently off the pontoons with a nervous skipper at the helm*

Morning reflections of the Stromness ferry

I slipped lines and carefully picked my way out of Stromness harbour. There was not another sound or motion stirring. The marina was completely silent and oblivious to my departure. The town lay, very quiet, over to the right and slept as *Pegasus* smoothed her way out from the inner harbour and on past the ferry and fishing boats. The sea was absolutely flat and reflected the sky blue hull of the ferry and the dark pier onto an upside down world. It was the time in the morning where the street lights provide enough luminescence to make a difference but if they were switched off you could get by without them. The sky had a turquoise hue and the sea was a reflected darker tone of the wondrous morning heavens above us. Behind the ferry pier, fishing boats sat absolutely motionless on the glass-flat sea. With the harbour left behind us, we moved away from the place that had breathed life back into *Pegasus* and her skipper. We continued to motor in quiet reverential manner along the shore line. Over to the right, stout stone gable ends faced the sea with the odd stone slipway connecting them to the water surface. Each building must have so many stories to tell, hard stories of life and some no doubt with heartbreak. As if to underline that thought, in between the shoreline buildings stood the old lifeboat shed, it too with a steep slipway reaching out to the water below. Lying still, a large yellow mooring buoy with a beard of seaweed lay redundant and suspended in the motionless water. The buoy and the weathered old red paint of the lifeboat hut were the only offerings of colour against the morning grey of old Stromness. The old fishing town sitting above the water was quiet and still in its rugged grey stone. Not much, I thought, will have changed for many a year from this vantage point. The town was a chaotic, higgledy-piggledy assortment of buildings to an uneducated or uninformed eye but had held the community together for hundreds of years.

A still and sleeping Stromness as Pegasus *sets off and the old Stromness lifeboat shed*

Day 7 —

Wednesday 19th, 06.15 hrs –
Stromness harbour

Pegasus under engine

508 nm run – 490 nm to Blyth

Sleep in last 24 hrs: 6 hr 00 min

*Centre of page: Stromness and the Hoy Sound
are left behind*

Above: The Old Man of Hoy looks on

I slipped on past the last house and made for the Skerry Ness Light that marks the turning point out to the Hoy Sound. The wind continued to be very light and *Pegasus* lolled around in the slight swell with sails slating and slopping from side to side, which added to the anxiety of the moment. I decided that I would start sailing at the mouth of the Sound of Hoy once beyond the island of Graemsay but I was not going to make my way out to the spot where it had all gone wrong. To motor for 12 hours out into the North Atlantic was an option for a purist approach, but the non-stop record was now gone and such detail was now secondary. I squared the rationale by taking the view that I was starting my sail northwards some 90 miles south-east of the point where I engaged the engine. The overall distance around Scotland was not shortened by this approach but in fact lengthened. Sure, it was not point to point but the extra distance of 10 miles made me feel comfortable that, should anyone pore over the detail picking faults, I had a good and reasoned case not to head away out to the Atlantic. As it was, I would not have chosen to do that in any case. I had three days to get to Lerwick before a southerly gale blew in and a detour back to a spot 80 miles north-east of Cape Wrath was simply just not going to happen.

The wind was very soft as I turned *Pegasus* north. I had to keep an eye over to my right to make sure I cleared Bragga Rock and Breck Ness Point. The Old Man of Hoy stood silent, just as he had done when he saw me two days ago. Perspectives of the shore line changed as we moved northwards; the Old Man saw me away and without as much as a nod or a word in my direction he stepped behind the headland to continue his look-out to sea for many more years. For how many more will he hold his position before the relentless seas take their man down? I was heading north with a gentle breeze sending us away from Stromness and away from any thought of turning back and heading to Oban and home. I set a course up the west shore of Orkney, passing cliffs and Skara Brae way over to my right. Sheer cliff faces dropped into the sea, each one topped with flat grasslands. Layer upon layer over the millennia sifted down through the deep waters only to be pushed upwards as continental plates met then tilted to create a cross section of time on earth. Progress on the water was slow and painful. We crawled our way north, more on the tide than thanks to sailing propulsion. This was of course all new sailing water to me and to *Pegasus*. The changing shoreline was captivating and slowly a more positive state of mind returned. Ness Point passed to starboard and we continued to sneak north. The day was warming up and I had shed my layers of jackets and fleeces and, at one point, only a thin thermal underlayer was enough to keep me comfortable. The morning passed away as we wafted our way northwards at what was a painfully slow pace. It had been an early breakfast so I sat down to enjoy an equally early large lunch, along with a can of Irn Bru and a read of the only lads' mag aboard. The movement about the boat after the time in Stromness had brought on some sharp jagging pains in my gammy knee so lunch was chased down by some painkillers.

The destruction of the wipeout meant that I was sailing on only 'three cylinders' so the joyous free sailing on the way to St Kilda was not on the cards. The new carbon headsail that was lying in a sorry mess down below decks had been replaced with a heavy Dacron high cut No.2 cruising headsail. It was solid stuff and fine in a blow but took no shape in a light wind. The main was also looking pretty sorry for itself. All my attempts to bind the plastic cars that connect sail to mast had failed so, unable to fly the whole sail, we were under one reef with a board-flat sail. All in all it was not a performance sail plan, but one that was taking me north so I should not complain. The hulk of the Orkney shoreline by Row Head, Kitchener's Memorial, MarWick and Brough Head did not give up easily as speeds struggled to get past 5 knots at best; at worst it was standstill. Progress was desperate, similar to the mood aboard.

Marwick Head and the Covenanter's memorial

The north shore of Brough Head slipped off to the east and Rousay Isle off Eynhallow Sound opened up to view. From here I had a stretch of open water over to the islands of Westray and Noup Head, the most northwesterly corner of Orkney. Tucked in behind was the island of Papa Westray. Oh, if this was not a self-imposed race I would be heading over there to explore these gorgeous islands, read about, dreamt about but not yet experienced. A neat black-hulled and white top-decked fishing boat came across my bow and I was given a hearty wave from the skipper who came to the wheelhouse window to salute *Pegasus*. I gave an equally enthusiastic wave back and watched *K76* as she rolled her way south-west.

Day 7

Wednesday 19th, 12.00 hrs - Ness Head

515 nm run - 483 nm to Blyth

6 hr run - 7 nm - average speed 1.2 knots

24 hr run - 0 nm - average speed 0.0 knots

Sleep in last 24 hrs: 6 hr 00 min

My mind flew way back to an experience that I doubt many kids of today would have the opportunity to relish. The family had adopted Carradale, a little fishing village on the Mull of Kintyre, as our summer holiday refuge and had become regular visitors each July. Over the years I had befriended a local lad, Robert MacDougal, and the two of us were invited to do an overnight trip on one of the local fishing boats. Game for this, I tentatively asked my parents if I could go and to my delight they agreed. Undeterred and at the age of 12 or 13, I made my way down to the harbour after tea on a perfect summer's evening to join up and go to sea – for one night. We were made welcome by the crew and soon were steaming out of harbour into the evening light in the Kilbrannan Sound. Robert and I were sent down below and were soon snug in the warm soporific atmosphere of the main saloon. I recall the distinct smell of the saloon being of stewed tea, cigarette smoke and of course fish. After what seemed an age it was action stations and we were called on deck as the nets were shot. Robert and I stood back in awe as, under the floodlights in the now pitch dark, what seemed like mile after mile of nets cascaded over the side. Following that show we were sent below again. After some cursory poking around our surroundings the two of us were soon mesmerized by the breasts of a page three model and, to confirm our position as hard as nails crew members, I had my first ever drag of a fag-butt, found smouldering in the ashtray. The night trip could not get any better! We were shouted back on deck as the nets were now grinding their way up and over the side and back aboard. Robert and I were both given brooms and told to stand fore and aft of the nets and whack any seagull that tried to swoop down to grab a fish. This task was clearly something just to keep us out of the way but as far as we were concerned the very catch depended upon us. Reaching out over the side of the boat over the dark waters of the Kilbrannan Sound, we swiped and waved our brooms at the gulls, never connecting with any single one of them. Once the nets were back aboard we had the job of nipping round the deck with a bucket to pick up any stragglers that had flipped their way in search of freedom from the net. The haul was made and we were sent back down below to make ourselves something to eat. Robert and I delighted in having the complete freedom from any maternal propriety so we made a stack of tomato ketchup sandwiches and wolfed them down. So good was the catch it was decided that our boat would head straight to Campbeltown to land the fish. We were going to Campbeltown but that did not suit the skipper so, after arranging a rendezvous with another Carradale boat, Robert and I completed our adventure by jumping ship in what seemed to us like the middle of the deep Atlantic Ocean. We steamed back to harbour and I wandered back to the guest house, a happy young lad. I clambered into bed and drifted off into a blissful sleep, smelling of fish. Could a kid do that today without Health and Safety Executive getting in the way or casting withering glances at my parents? I doubt it. What a stroke of luck being of that generation and having parents that really did let me experience literally all that was on offer.

Noup Head lighthouse, Westray

Fishing boat K76 heads off on a perfect day

It is strange but it was a turning point for the leg. I gave another much appreciated wave to fishing boat *K76* and smiled to myself. It was as if *K76* had been sent to break the stalemate as right at that moment a breeze started to fill in. *K76* also broke the stalemate that was lingering inside me; I had a boat to sail. The wind picked up and we were soon heading north with, at first light, rippling and dappling sounds, soon followed by a rushing sound and periodic surges of white water being splashed out from under the hull. *Pegasus* took the wind and heeled a fraction. She had what she wanted, wind to drive her forward at pace; she was in her comfort zone and we were now making distance north. With the pressure on the sails and with it jobs to do and tasks to attend to, my malaise and discomfort seemed to be tucked away.

We slipped along with little or no effort. Sail and breeze were propelling 14 tons of boat forwards and it all seemed to be totally free movement. We were slipping north leaving no trace, using no resource other than the free wind and not impacting on any other living thing. The propulsion of a yacht is a complex array of forces and reactions, yet they come together in effortless symmetry in light breezes on a flat sea. There is no resistance of wave pounding against the hull or beating of wind against taut and straining sails. A sailing yacht can be a relaxed and easy place, yet at other times ropes and sails are under tons of strain, with wire and metal braced against the elements. Today it was a loose and informal arrangement that *Pegasus* had with our surroundings.

So what makes a yacht sail, apparently with little or no effort? When two billiard balls collide they exert an equal force on each other. It is roughly the same story when the wind comes into contact with a sail. The sail exerts a force on the wind in order to deflect it and the wind exerts an equal force on the sail. The sail is the shape of a foil similar to that of the wing of an aeroplane. An aeroplane makes its own wind by the forward force of the jet or propeller-driven engine. At sea we rely on the wind blowing over our foil to create energy. Air accelerates along the windward surface, increasing in pressure, but behind the sail the wind is not compressed and is actually in lower pressure as the air has to move faster across the area, so creating a slight vacuum in comparison with the side facing into the boat and to the wind. All of this creates a low pressure on the back side of the sail relative to that on the windward side. The outcome of this is a force that is directed out and through the sail at right angles to the chord or belly of the sail. This is called the aerodynamic force. More force is generated towards the front edge of the sail, where there is more curve, like the leading edge of an aeroplane wing. So we now have a force that is driving directional aerodynamic force through the sail. The next question is, how does that almost-sideways force propel a yacht forwards? This is where the keel comes in. The keel acts just like the sail with the aerodynamic force generated by the sail above pushing the boat sideways and therefore the keel sideways. The keel comes up against the resistance of the water that simply does not like the idea of a broad keel being pushed sideways. If a boat does slip sideways we call it leeway. The same effect that is happening on the sails now takes part below the water and hydrodynamic forces come into play. A yacht's keel is shaped like a double-sided wing and, not willing to be pushed sideways, the water slips off and to the rear of the keel blade. Imagine squeezing a wedge-shaped bar of wet soap between your thumb (aerodynamic force) and forefinger (resistance). The bar shoots forwards, hey presto, hydrodynamic force has now just kicked in. Now the text book goes on a bit more into the complexities of variable wind strengths and angle of sailing towards or away from the wind but the simple principle is the same as above.

To the uneducated eye sails also have a myriad of ropes to adjust angle to the wind and depth of curve in the sail, each having a material effect on the angle of drive and efficiency of the sail. The mainsail on *Pegasus* has 10 control lines to affect the shape of the sail. These are namely: mainsheet, kicking strap, outhaul, flattener, halyard, Cunningham downhaul, leech line and three reefing lines. Each line pulls in different directions or on different parts of the sail, so allowing a sail trimmer to flatten and harden the sail twist off the top, or put a belly at the foot. Oh, and don't forget with a bit of effort the mast can be bent, so affecting the shape of the sail even more. Add a second sail fore and aft of each other and the speed of the wind over the leeward side is accelerated even more as it is squeezed through what we sailors call 'the slot'. So now we have an interrelationship between the two sails. The setting of each sail must be done in harmony. Tighten one in too much and at worst it stalls the other sail or at best it greatly enhances its efficiency.

Genoa and mainsail in perfect balance in light airs

Another service that is delivered by the keel is that its weight is low down and under the boat, so lowering the overall centre of gravity. This helps to keep the boat upright as pressure builds on the sails but, as the yacht heels over, the overall effectiveness of the keel and the hydrodynamic forces it generates are greatly reduced. So the ideal scenario is constant wind, balanced sails not creating too much heel, a flat and level boat, and then there is the sea state. A flat sea offers less wave slap and resistance so there is another variable to consider. In a dinghy, crew weight keeps you upright by shifting about the boat as mobile human ballast; in a yacht it is all down to the lump

of metal hanging below the hull. Have a longer and deeper keel, stick a bulb of metal at the end and you have a low centre of gravity which means you can carry more sail and so more speed follows. Some of the more modern hi-tech racing yachts have canting keels that, through a set of powerful hydraulic rams, tilt the keel to one side so as to maximise the righting moment or leverage. To add to the leverage of the keel, tanks loaded up with water ballast and stored on the windward side of the boat add a massive additional weight to the righting moment. With all of this 'ballast' and its positioning, modern ocean racing yachts can carry massive areas of sail, so producing speeds in excess of 30 knots. Such boats are light and powerful and skiff or, as it is known, 'plane' on the surface. Now with the boat lifted out of the water, there is less wetted surface and so friction and hull drag are reduced, all contributing to even more speed! By no stretch of the imagination does *Pegasus* fall into the racing class – she is more of a heavyweight cruiser type. However, she has a lot going for her; a big powerful rig, big sail area, a hefty 14 tons to hold her upright, plus a long waterline length. Now there is another factor at play as a boat that sails in the water is referred to as a displacement type and has a theoretical maximum speed that cannot be exceeded. This is all to do with wave drag and is too long a story to go into on these pages. The equation is 1.34 × √LWL (length of water line in feet). Taking this equation, a boat of 25 feet has a theoretical maximum speed of 6.7 knots and boat of 50 feet, being *Pegasus*, has a maximum speed of 9.5 knots. Any faster and the boat is out of the water and planing and in our case using a following momentum of a wave to accelerate you onwards. Put all of this little lot together and off you go! If you have all of these factors under control, sailing can be relaxing and, at times should you wish, exhilarating beyond belief!

It was time to check-in and the numbers were depressingly low with a disastrous average speed of a miserly 3.2 knots. In sailing it is very seldom that all points of a course or passage can be done at full whack. This was time to take my medicine in respect of light winds and slow progress.

The afternoon was warm with clear blue, almost cloudless skies that turned as the sun went down to a gorgeous vanilla blue and then filled with a pinkish red that comes with a beautiful uninterrupted sunset to the west. To see the sun set to the west, uninterrupted by islands or land is great at the best of times but to have the show put on at this latitude under clear skies is just stunning. The blue sky took on an aura where dark outer space and our world below that canopy seem to melt into one another. Tonight the array of colour was just magnificent, a bright orange ball surrounded by a halo of pearl and then up and up to a light blue, mixing into a heavy blue and then the neutral dark of outer space. There was still too much light to see the stars but the cloudless blue sky introduced a symphony of light to the canopy above us. The sun dropped below the sea and all bets were off regarding the range of colours that were to put on a show. Reds and oranges took over and the high altitude blue turned a slate grey and, with

Day 7

Wednesday 19th, 18.00 hrs – 12 miles north of Westray

535 nm run – 463 nm to Blyth

6 hr run – 20 nm – average speed 3.3 knots

24 hr run – 0 nm – average speed 0.0 knots

Sleep in last 24 hrs: 6 hr 15 min

Pegasus smoothes her way northwards after a difficult day

Sun sets on the open Atlantic west of Orkney

the waning light, dew settled on the deck as the night chill came calling on *Pegasus* and her crew. The first stars spangled above and there was new life in the heavens above us.

The day had passed and a large evening meal was taken, pasta chased down with custard and ginger cake and gallons of tea. *Pegasus* was set up for the night sail. The saloon was tidy and all items were stowed away easily to hand if called upon. I had a box of filled rolls; jam, ham and cheese, catering for whatever I took a notion to later that night. A flask of tea was also on standby should the sea pick up and easy instant hot sweet tea be needed. The housekeeping done, I turned my attention back to my passage plan and navigation needs. I was now north of Orkney and my next major island was Shetland. My immediate navigation concentration was centred on the island of Foula. In the dark the island would be difficult to spot and that lump of rock needed full attention and a wide berth. The light, bright blue day turned black very quickly and soon we were heading north in the pitch dark, sailing on plotter and dead reckoning. With the filling wind had come heavy cloud cover and the canopy of stars had been withdrawn from view for this evening. My focus was now all about when Foula Light should come into view. Boat speed was good and we were maintaining steady progress northwards. The sail to St Kilda had built my confidence in the navigation department so the course north and into the night was not really worrying me. Foula Light appeared on the scene as if to order, as predicted by the chart plotter and 'gut feel'. I have often wondered what it is that allows me to just have a feel for distance, heading and understanding of place at sea when on a hill I am almost incapable of reading a map, taking effective bearings or dead-reckoning of distance and place. Foula was identifiable by the three white flashes every 15 seconds of the light on its south shore. To ensure my plotter was working and we had no inaccuracy, I took out my hand-bearing compass and took a bearing to the light. Down below on the paper chart I drew the reciprocal bearing and bang on the line was my position confirmed on the electronic plotter. To do this properly I should take three hand-bearing fixes, plot each bearing on the chart and, if all is well, the point at which the three lines cross would coincide with my position on the electronic plotter. I was happy with one fix and initial confirmation from the electronic screen. It was absolutely spot-on with my position and I was content all was well.

Day 7

Wednesday 19th, 24.00 hrs –
Turbot Bank

34 miles north-west of Fair Isle

557 nm run – 441 nm to Blyth

6 hr run – 22 nm –average speed
3.7 knots

24 hr run – 0 nm – average
speed 0.0 knots

Sleep in last 24 hrs: 7 hr
30 min

We passed northwards and the light disappeared behind the island. My mind turned to the next target, Muckle Flugga (Old Norse *mikla flugey* – large steep-sided island). The following hours of darkness would see us past Papa Stour and the small but not to be ignored rocks that made up Ve Skerries that lay some six miles or so north-west of Papa Stour. Beyond that lay Esha Ness. The night sail passed without event and I managed to grab some good sleep, safe in the knowledge we were sailing parallel to the coastline and only a huge wind shift and alteration of course would take me the 12 miles or so over to the east and towards any dangers. To drop the 12 miles over to the right at current speed would take two hours and only if I turned a 90-degree change to my current heading. That was not going to happen so I was relaxed and enjoying this little sojourn up the west coast of Shetland. Sleeping was not a problem and I settled into a good period of 15-minute naps followed by a quick 360-degree look from the cockpit and a sniff of the air, a check of the sail-setting and then back down to my perch on the saloon settee. The night passed without incident and we made good time and ate up some good miles.

Morning announced itself with a stunning sunrise and the Shetland Islands presenting themselves in all their glory. My friend, the sun, had come back after it had shared its warmth around the globe. Sailing through the night made me very aware of our natural surroundings. With the sun making another appearance over to my right the world felt very round indeed. The coastline of Unst was, as expected, dramatic. To me it looked unspoilt and unchanged as it had stood there for thousands of years with no sign of man's hand. The stretch of coastline is clean of outlying rocks or islands with the sole exception of Muckle Ossa, a small and low-lying piece of stone that stopped me from sneaking close to the shore. The wind was out of the north-east so a close hauled sail-set was comfortable, made even more so by the flat sea in the lee of the mainland of Shetland. With the weather now settled I was also settled after the worries of the previous day. I had another successful well-planned, well-navigated and executed night sail under the keel.

Day 8

Thursday 20th 06.00 hrs - Ve
Skerries

593 nm run - 405 nm to Blyth

6 hr run - 36 nm - average
speed 6.0 knots

24 hr run - 85 nm - average
speed 3.5 knots

Sleep in last 24 hrs: 2 hr 40 min

All attention towards Muckle Flugga

I was now ready for Muckle Flugga and all she was likely to offer on what was a glorious sunny day with a wind of 15 knots from the north-east.

I cannot explain how much of an enjoyment that early morning sail was. I was still heading north, away from home but content. I was up for the task that lay ahead, the boat was up for it and the weather and tides of the moment were going to be as kind as I could have ever hoped for. The spit of rocks that makes up Muckle Flugga came into sight and very soon I was approaching the very top of Scotland and the guiding presence of yet another Stevenson lighthouse. The outcrop quickly became recognisable from the pictures that I had pored over during the previous months. The need for a light on this 'corner' of Scotland had been known for many years but in 1854 the light was finally completed to help the troop and supply ships onwards to the 1853–56 Crimean War. I came in peace and was wanting only a safe passage around this awesome last headland of our country that is savaged by North Atlantic gales. As with the island of Erraid, this place is also said to have influenced the writing of Robert Louis Stevenson. It is thought that the area and the island of Unst had a part to play in his thoughts when dreaming up his classic *Treasure Island*. I would soon be at that 'treasure island'; it was not far off from the ever-advancing *Pegasus* and then yet another big chunk of elephant would be a 'goner'. The headlands of Orknagable and Grunka Hellier were some five miles or so below me and we were on a perfect heading for the top of Scotland.

I hardened *Pegasus* onto a close haul north of the outcrop and gazed back down the west side of Unst. The sea state was 'slight' and I held the course for two hours, feeling confident I would clear Muckle Flugga on my next tack. I then set about readying *Pegasus* for an angle that would keep us clear of danger and any tidal eddies or holes in the wind that might lurk under the cliffs. Happy that I had enough in my pocket, I turned

Pegasus east and we were soon heading on a very comfortable close reach across the top of Scotland. One last look over to my right and I could see away down the west side, a view and perspective of Scotland that was soon to be in the past. Now this was a bite of the elephant that I had been dreaming about and here I was. It was as symbolic as St Kilda had been all that time ago. The sea was blue and the sun lit up the day. This was no grey day on the extremity of Scotland but a day to savour and enjoy. I simply could not keep my eyes off Muckle Flugga. Here I was sailing round Muckle Flugga, all was well; I was making good time and I would soon be homing in on Lerwick unless the forecast was to change. Now this scenario is a bit further on, I thought, from my first tentative meanderings in the Mirror dinghy across the Kilbrannan Sound and that gorgeous but defining trip around Mull in *Cloud Nine*. Thanks entirely to the opportunities given to me in life and my pal David, who put *Pegasus* in the water, here I was, Alan Rankin, sailing single-handed around the top of Scotland. Right now I was the most northerly Scot in Scotland and that was neat. I went down below and took a picture and filmed the plotter screen that showed a clearly discernible little blinking boat icon sitting at 60 degrees north. The furthest point north had been reached. Muckle Flugga and the outlier Out Stack was below me, as was the rest of my country.

For the next half hour I busied myself taking snaps and video to record the moment but it was soon time to leave this place that had on this occasion been so kind to me. I eased my course to the south and *Pegasus* liked the new free and open heading towards the eastern side of Unst. Soon Muckle Flugga was in profile and then, in no time, it had disappeared behind the headland and I was on a course of 175 degrees, that is south in anyone's book. The tide was good and

Muckle Flugga lighthouse, with Out Stack beyond, continues to keep watch (courtesy VisitShetland)

Above: Sixty degrees north – Pegasus rounds the very top of Scotland

Left: Muckle Flugga astern at last!

Below: Muckle Flugga is left behind as Pegasus heads south

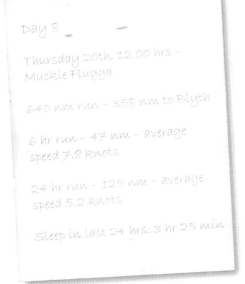

Day 8

Thursday 20th, 12.00 hrs - Muckle Flugga

640 nm run - 358 nm to Blyth

6 hr run - 47 nm - average speed 7.8 knots

24 hr run - 125 nm - average speed 5.2 knots

Sleep in last 24 hrs: 3 hr 25 min

ebbing south, the wind was 20 knots plus from the east and I was heading south, a lovely combination. The whole demeanour aboard *Pegasus* had changed from the day before. We had been holding some good speeds and I was keen to press on and get the most out of conditions and to maximise my own satisfaction of sailing in such special waters. I felt very lucky to be here.

We continued to hurtle south and recorded the third biggest six-hour run of 47 miles. As if on cue to help celebrate the moment, a school of dolphins suddenly appeared from nowhere and I had company. I tried to count them but was no match for them. Maybe five or six dolphins had decided to accompany *Pegasus* south. Their markings were the likes that I had never seen before. On many an occasion over on the west coast I had enjoyed the sights of bottlenose dolphins surging at the bow of a yacht but these chaps had more distinctive markings. My conclusion is that they were either common dolphins or white beaked dolphins. Each gorgeous creature would surge up from behind, slice through the water with their dorsal fin just breaking the surface, ride on the pressure of the bow wave and then dart back under the bow. A corkscrew movement followed to show their white bellies then, with a powerful flick of the tail, they disappeared down into the deep, only to reappear astern in a minute or two. Two of them added a show of airborne agility on a few passes when clear of the bow and, rather than digging back into the deep, launched themselves completely clear of the water, twisted in mid-air and landed on their flanks in a massive belly flop that sent water everywhere. To see this show and not be absolutely clear in your mind that this was fun and high jinks on their part would be impossible. Their motion through the water is spell-binding. Here was *Pegasus* surging south with all the power and technology required to propel her onwards. Tons of finely designed and hydrodynamically refined hull and superstructure, 16 metres of mast and hoisted sail, electronic plotters and autopilots and a skipper all hard at work to produce the momentum. Down below these beautiful creatures of the sea seemed to be generating forward pace with no real discernible movement. No frantic flailing of the tail or flexing of the body, yet they still managed to rush forward apparently toying with *Pegasus*. Nature at its sublime best was here for company. My dolphin pals were putting on a show to cheer me up and, like so many encounters with dolphins, they leave just as suddenly as they arrive. I had enjoyed their company for fully 10–15 minutes and had filled half a memory card and metres of movie tape with their antics. Then they were gone. 'Good luck and happy days to them', I thought, as the sea returned to a place of work rather than a fun-packed aquatics gymnasium.

Speed kept creeping over the 9-knot mark and held there for long periods. *Pegasus* then surged on the wave, tide and sea and held at around 10 knots for what was only 15 minutes or so, but boy was it enjoyable. I had a good wind and a following sea and the tide. What could be better? *Pegasus* started to lift her skirts and at one point we touched 13.2 knots. We were sprinting south now and the shoreline and its detail was slipping back and behind at speed. The little island of Balta was abeam. In no time I could see back in behind the lump of rock that protects the anchorage of Baltasound that, if things were not going to plan, was one of my boltholes. If I had been swept past Muckle Flugga in building gales, Baltasound was the first deep cut into Unst that would offer refuge. There was no need to dive for cover today; it was 'pedal to the metal' to get south to Lerwick.

Shetland was slipping past us and I was making a good heading to clear the island of Fetlar and a navigation headland of Head of Hosta. A slight alteration of course had

Out Skerries lighthouse
(courtesy VisitShetland)

us clear Fetlar but it soon became obvious that I was not going to wear Out Sherries some 12 miles or so south without a tack. The Out Skerries are the most eastern obstacles to spoil a very comfortable heading south down the North Sea coast of Shetland. They sit at the same latitude as their pals the Ve Skerries that had occupied me so much as I sailed north 36 hours before. The wind was gusting at what felt like blasts over 25 knots and it was very much more from the south-east. We tacked and spent a very unpleasant hour heading north-east to gain enough height to clear the Skerries.

With enough sea-room, I turned south again and, to my astonishment, a medium-sized fishing boat came in between me and the jagged white wave-spumed rocks. Clearly with absolute faith in his navigation but even more so in his engine, the skipper took a course so close to the point it defied belief. The Norse saw fit to view the place as a 'cast' or distinguished land and it is perfectly placed to catch the unaware or negligent of their navigation. The islands are home to yet another Stevenson light, this one courtesy of David and Thomas, first lit in 1854. It has survived the ravages of weather but also an attempt to blow it to kingdom come during the Second World War. In 1941 it was machine-gunned with no great or permanent damage, but in 1942 there was an altogether more serious event. The tower survived two runs of a German bomber who only managed to demolish the boatman's house but the unfortunate mother of the boatman sustained fatal injuries. There was much damage done to outhouses and living quarters but the tower itself escaped with only slight damage. Out Skerries light has left its colourful history behind and is now, like all the other lights, an automated sentinel of our shores. I called up the Lerwick Harbourmaster to advise him that I was about two hours off and asked for confirmation of my berth. He was a little vague, no doubt with more on his plate to occupy him than a yachtie looking for a berth. We agreed to speak again as I entered the North Sound into Lerwick.

Day 8

Thursday 20th, 18.00 hrs – 5 miles east of Whalsay

674 nm run – 324 nm to Blyth

6 hr run – 34 nm – average speed 5.7 knots

2 hr run – 139 nm – average speed 5.8 knots

Sleep in last 24 hrs: 3 hr 40 min

I turned my attention away from the cause of my detour and concentrated on the next job in hand, Lerwick and shelter from what was a lifting breeze. I cracked off my course a few degrees over to the south-west and reached off on a course direct to Lerwick. Concentration would be needed to make this new landfall and an entry via the tricky North Channel. Thoughts of carrying on south to Blyth hung with me for a few minutes but, having taken a real body blow off North Rona, I was not going to take on a southerly gale in a boat that was not bulletproof, with gear in which I did not have total confidence. I had 15 miles to run to Lerwick with only Whalsay and the little outcrop of Grif Skerry to worry about. It was daylight and, as I was quite happy with the course, my orientation to the land over to the west and my general state of well-being, we pressed on squeezing speed out of the sails. The names of the islands and outcrops in these parts are a delight, testament to the fact that Shetland is more than a few miles but a lifetime from mainland UK, never mind our capital city of Edinburgh. Moul of Eswick, Hoo Stack, Hawks Ness, Kebister Ness and Easter Rova Head all lay to the south-west, each place without doubt having a story to tell, but that perhaps is for another day and another sail.

At five miles out from the entrance to Lerwick the plotter screen in the cockpit went an ominous black and simply gave up the will to live. 'Brilliant!' I exclaimed to the gods. 'Just when it's needed, the bloody thing goes AWOL.' Raymarine had struck again; I would now have to enter the sound on paper charts and an electronic plotter at the navigation table in the saloon. I nipped down below and pulled out the appropriate paper chart from the OYTS portfolio that had been undisturbed in the aft cabin since Kirkcudbright. I had a detailed chart for Lerwick laid out and to hand.

The approach to Lerwick from the north is not overly complex but, on the back of two days at sea, some residual stress levels, a new landing, building winds and reducing daylight, it all made for a heightening of self-imposed pressures. Adding to my worries was that the berth for *Pegasus* might be up against a stone harbour wall. With gales forecast I could have my hands full. It was the accumulation of the unknowns that was getting to me and I was stressed as we entered the sound. To make matters worse a local fishing

Heading into Lerwick by the North Sound

boat was creaming up behind me and clearly would pass and, by the looks of things, at a narrow section of the channel. I moved slightly over from mid-channel and he steamed past. I immediately slipped in behind his course and knocked the revs up a notch to press on due to the gathering gloom. So this was Lerwick, busy with boats, ships and all sorts of shore activities. Large pelagic fishing boats lay tied up and sheds and buildings lined the shore. My target was the Small Boats Harbour or, as the pilot book called it, the Small Dock and I called up the Harbourmaster again to check arrangements. He advised me to lie in front of the small French yacht that was tied up immediately in front of the lifeboat, port side to. That said, I set the fenders and warps for a port side landing and hoped that there were plenty of hands to take my mooring lines. Sure enough as I inched my way forward past the wall of Victoria Pier I could see a man in an orange work jacket standing on the far harbour wall top just in front of a white yacht.

I slowly brought *Pegasus* in through the narrow harbour mouth and there on the far wall was the port authority welcoming party. Well, it was a welcoming party to me; one lad in a bright orange boiler suit standing over a bare stone harbour wall in front of a yacht flying the tricolour who was, in turn, in front of the lifeboat. 'Port side to' the man said and I was not turning back now. As *Pegasus* made for the harbour wall I swung her bow round and stabbed her astern, bringing her to a halt close to the wall. This was no time to repeat the half-hearted approach taken at Stromness. I darted forward to amidships and tossed up the breast line to the outstretched arm of the lad up top. He caught it and I nipped back along the side deck and jumped back into the cockpit to retake the wheel. With the breast now secured to a large bollard, I gently nudged ahead with helm full to starboard, so steering *Pegasus* away from the wall. The breast line slowly tightened and then gently drew us in to the wall. With complete control *Pegasus* gently touched her fenders to the harbour wall. With drive still held on, I nipped forward and tossed up to my new best friend on the harbour wall my bow line. In a couple of minutes the engine was off and *Pegasus* was snug to the Lerwick Small Boats Harbour wall. 'What a bulletproof corner', I thought, as I surveyed my new surroundings, not knowing that this was to be home for the coming seven days.

Now the Small Boats Harbour in Lerwick is a place to savour for a tired yachtsman. It is a small harbour with a narrow entrance and on three sides a

Day 8

Thursday 20th, 20.10 hrs – Lerwick Small Boats Harbour

688 nm run – 310 nm to Blyth

2 hr run – 14 nm – average speed 7.0 knots

20 hr run – 131 nm – average speed 6.6 knots

Sleep in last 24 hrs: 2 hr 25 min

steep and solid stone harbour wall that looks as if it will be there for ever and a day. No doubt in its heyday it would have been full with fishing boats. I just adore the old photographs of such harbours at the peak of the fishing industry when they were packed with so many boats that it looked as if you could walk from one side of the harbour to another from deck to deck, a feat that would not be possible in this modern age. Today the harbour was completely empty apart from the Lerwick lifeboat, the French yacht and *Pegasus*. At the top or inner end of the harbour and along the north wall, new wooden pontoons had been established for visiting yachts. Beached and pulled up on to the hard beyond the top pontoon lay a handful of small dinghies. Beyond this little maritime sanctuary lay the busy town of Lerwick, with its magnificent old stone buildings, and the islands of Shetland that I was to taste and enjoy in the days to come.

After phone calls home and to Erik and Gordon, I was fit for nothing so I had a big bowl of pasta and turned in. I slept solidly for 12 hours that night, a quiet, motionless, contented, deep sleep, with no timer clipped to my lapel, no radar pinging the surroundings and no motion. The next morning I woke with a fuggy head and had cereal and tea before venturing out to explore my new surroundings. Most important of all I had to pay my dues at the Harbour Office and get a key to the Lerwick Boating Club where visiting yacht crews had use of the showers and laundry facilities. I clambered up the vertical iron ladder that was fixed with rusty bolts to the old stone and, on reaching the harbour top, had a good look down on *Pegasus* to survey her condition, tidiness and general demeanour. All was well.

Wandering in the general direction of the town, I asked a taxi driver where I could find the Harbour Office. It was the red shed building beyond the next harbour quay. Once through the front door, I noticed the working smell and the walls festooned with prints of tall ships, tankers and fishing boats. Reception was on the first floor, behind a sliding glass service hatch. The glass slid back and with beaming smile the lady spoke in what was only my first real encounter of the local brogue. 'Wow', I thought, 'what a lovely accent'. That took me by surprise. It was just like going away on holiday asking for a coffee in the arrival terminal to be greeted by a foreign or heavily accented tongue. I snapped to and gave her my story and she in turn provided me with the necessary paperwork to fill in. That done and paid for I was now a temporary resident of Lerwick and had some exploring to do but my priority was to use the key to the Lerwick Boat Club. At that moment a wave of disappointment came over me as it hit home that I was to be ensconced in Lerwick for a few days. But to banish the negative thought, I asked myself when else would I get a chance to come here and explore at my leisure a place I had never been to before. I made my way back to *Pegasus* and collected clothes and my wash kit and, oh boy, was I looking forward to a shower. Armed with directions from the lovely helpful receptionist, I found the club just beyond the Small Boats Harbour down one of Lerwick's narrow sea front streets in the Lodberries area. Once inside I cautiously made my way down to the shower room and saw right next door to the showers the laundry. Delighted that no one else was in the building, I stripped off in front of the washing machine and threw every stitch I was wearing and all the contents of my bag into the drum, closed the door, put my money in the slot and said good-bye to the 'whiff' that had been company for the last few days. Living in sailing gear does build up a certain odour that catches you unaware at times. The design of sailing trousers is prone to knocking you for six when you bend down and the air around you and inside the trousers is suddenly exhausted up your front and out and over your face. It can be a real wow at times! Happy that the machine had not been repulsed by my clothing, I made my way through to the shower room and stepped into the cubicle. No sooner had my £1 clicked into the coin box than the water came and I stood in a state of delirium under the hot steaming shower. What bliss! It was the second time this trip that I had tasted the sea running off my face, out of my hair and over my lips. Having soaked myself for the 5-minute running time I fed another £1 in for good measure and soaked for another few moments of delight. That done and a shave to scrape off the last four days of growth, I ventured out, intent on seeing what Lerwick had to offer.

Old Lerwick, the Lodberries from the Small Boats Harbour

7

LERWICK

Having checked the mooring lines and happy that *Pegasus* was secure to the wall, I stood back from the harbour edge and surveyed what lay before me. We were moored up against the south wall of the Small Boats Harbour and I could not have asked for a better spot. Snug in this corner any southerly gale would blow her off the hard unforgiving stone, concrete and metalled wall. Clear of the previous night's deep sleep-induced fug in my head, I could now fully take in my surroundings. The harbour is right in the middle of Lerwick and as such is an integral part of the town. The whole waterfront had a buzz and a busy feel both on shore and afloat. Turning my back on the water and boats I made my way into the town to explore what lay beyond. Traditional old stone buildings lined the road at the top end of the harbour. 'Yes, I like this', I thought. There was no sign of a town that had been disconnected from its waterfront through planning folly. There seemed to be no modern developments that had separated Lerwick from the sea or through necessity required a false slab of reclaimed land to support the capacity of the waterfront. This looked and felt like a community which lived and worked on and around the sea. Some of the harbour area had been given over to car parking and a line of taxis stood waiting for custom, their drivers hanging around, chatting with each other. Beyond that lay sheds, an open wharf, ships and the general to-ing and fro-ing of craft along the waterfront.

Walking up the incline of a narrow lane, I came out onto the pedestrianised main street. Commercial Street was narrow and also bustling with people going about their business. I set off along the street, window shopping and trying to take in my new surroundings. After about half an hour of aimless wandering, I was tired and needed another kip just to top up the batteries. When I got back down to the harbour I could see two people standing over *Pegasus*, the first of what would be a very welcome series of visitors over the coming week. I said my hellos to the admirers and exchanged pleasantries and had 10 minutes of chat about my trip and the general set-up of *Pegasus*. That done, went below and slept for a couple of hours before setting off once again to explore the town.

First stop was a coffee shop. This little oasis served the most delicious cappuccinos, bacon rolls and warm pastries. Along with some salad and mayonnaise in a fresh soft roll, the crispy and very well-fired bacon was just fabulous. I had a paper to read and a seat by the window to watch Lerwick walk by. *Pegasus* was safe and secure; I was happy and relaxed and felt a warm contentment come over me. Wandering around this delightful little town, taking in the sights and sounds, I did some further window shopping then meandered back along to the Boat Club to collect my washing. Some washroom fairy had folded my gear and it was sitting bone-dry and neatly stacked on a shelf by the washing machine. I dawdled back along the Lodberries and back to *Pegasus* where I slipped off into another sound sleep for a couple of hours. It was tea-time when I woke, groggy and spaced out, so I made myself a brew and a concoction of all sorts of things out of the fridge. The gruel was shifted very quickly and chased down with a couple of tins of beer. Buoyed by the beer and grub I decided to venture out again.

Having checked the mooring warps, I set off again along the lane to the Boat Club to see if there was any crack to be had. On opening the front door of the club I heard the noise of chat and people coming from the bar on the first floor. It all sounded very cheery if not slightly raucous. Making for the bar upstairs, I asked if it was in order for me to have a pint and if I needed to be signed in. The barman nodded and asked what I wanted to drink and the chap standing next to me said he would sign me in. It was fast-forward from that point on, well, what I can remember anyway! I was given a hale and hearty welcome into the club and asked to join a group at a nearby table. From that point on it was fast and furious pints and nips. Well, it seemed that way to me. To be in such relaxed and accommodating company was just great and all my worries were history. The chat was great fun and it was really interesting to hear all about the sailing activities in the area. My hosts were also very interested to hear my tales of the trip so far. There was a classic moment of dialogue that gave me my first insight to the fierce pride that is common to the residents of Shetland. I threw into conversation my observation that the Norwegian vessels were all flying as their courtesy flag a blue and white crossed flag that I assumed to be the Shetland flag and that I must get one. There was a pause in conversation and one chap offered, 'Aye, we noticed.' The point had been made and next day I was flying a Shetland courtesy flag. It had never even occurred to me that when sailing around Scotland I would be sailing in waters that required a courtesy flag. After all, that is only done when you are sailing in foreign waters. I was wrong, so very wrong.

The pints slipped down and before long I was under the influence of not just the beer but the infectious hospitality and conversation. I had a few too many by the time I said my thanks for the company and made my exit to set off for my bed in that stupor induced by drink, where walking requires a high level of studious concentration just to get the basics right. Not quite staggering but not far off it, I made my way back along the quayside to *Pegasus* to what was likely to be a more dangerous manoeuvre than securing the sail in the storm-lashed seas off North Rona, the task of getting myself safely down the iron ladder to the deck of *Pegasus*. It was low tide and *Pegasus* was some 10 feet below street level. About half way down the ladder I lost my grip and fell off, landing with a drunken thump on the side deck. Possibly anaesthetised by the drink, I felt no pain and was probably so inebriated that I landed in a relaxed state. It sobered me up a tad as, if I had landed the other side of the guardrail in the harbour, it would have been a different story. Undeterred by my little mishap I poured myself down the companionway, made a cup of tea and then crashed out in my bunk. The next morning I had a head that felt as if an axe had split me open above the right eyebrow. The day was taken very slowly. I dozed and slept off the hangover well into the afternoon before sticking my head out into the fresh air and then took another wander around the docks and main seafront. I had the presence of mind to buy my Shetland courtesy flag. Back on *Pegasus* the afternoon was spent dozing and reading *It's not about the Bike* by Lance Armstrong. What a guy! I turned in at eight o'clock and slept all the way through to eight the next morning.

The next day dawned and I promised myself that I would make more of it and stay off the drink. Breakfast was large and scoffed down as I was starving. I felt really good and thought that today I should have a good look round the area by bike. I also wanted to visit the Coastguard Station to express my thanks for all their attention over the past few days. I set about cutting the ties on the bike that held it tight to the bare frame of the bunks in the forward cabin. Careful not to scratch any of the woodwork in the main saloon, I eased the bike frame followed by its front wheel out to the cockpit. There the machine was assembled and left propped up against the side of the cockpit. It looked so incongruous. Here was a performance, part carbon fibre bike with snazzy racing wheels sitting in the cockpit of a yacht, not exactly peaches and cream but more like apples and pears, two different worlds sitting side by side. It struck me at that point how divorced the two looked but to me they were perfect bed partners and they were the two bits of kit that I needed to pull off this challenge.

It was high tide so it was not a problem to lift the bike up from the side deck to the pier. Propped against the guardrail, I tied a rope to the cross frame and tossed the loose end up to the pier. I stepped gingerly away from the bike and climbed the two rungs up to the pier. The bike was light and I was feeling strong so, with a straight arm, I pulled the bike up and away from the guardrail and pier wall and fielded it as it came up to waist level. The bike shone in the bright Shetland light and it seemed to be saying to me, 'Is it my time yet?' Kitted up in helmet, glasses, gloves and Lycra shorts, and with my silver Nike cycling shoes on, I stood by the bike feeling a little alien to my surroundings. I had been at one with oillies, boots and thermal layers, but now I stood in skin-tight shorts and DayGlo yellow top. I mounted and gently pedalled off to explore.

I had decided that I was going to cycle to Scalloway over on the west shore of the island. All I knew was that there was a bloody big hill between Lerwick and Scalloway. I am not sure how many cyclists enjoy their sport on Shetland but there are two natural features of the place that immediately struck me – hills and wind, the perfect turn off for me as a cyclist. There is no way out of Lerwick that I could find that did not involve a lung-busting climb up a steep hill. In addition, when out of the lee and shelter of the town of Lerwick, the wind is either your enemy or your ally. It either blasts you in the face and slows the most strenuous of pedalling to a crawl or allows you a free ride as it whistles you onwards. I set off on what I saw as the low road that passed North Taing and carried on through the south-west built-up area of Lerwick and out past Sandy Loch Reservoir. The first part of the ride was agony as I climbed Run Hill in the teeth of a very strong wind. My legs had been used to standing, sitting and sleeping, certainly not pumping the pedals up hills. My lungs heaved and my back ached. Up and up the road dragged and all into the wind for good measure as it was by now blowing hard. The undersides of the verge-side grass shone as the wind streaked across the surface, making it look almost fluid in appearance. After about 20 minutes of hard graft I started down the long decline to the appropriately-named Wind Hamars and on to the west coast of Shetland. Scalloway lay before me and I stopped to take a quick snap of the town and its partnership with the sea. Below I could see the conflict of heritage and hard industry. An old castle was the dominant landmark but its place in the town was outgunned by the sprawling sheds and buildings of the docks, each shed, box-like and light in construction and so much in contrast to the weathered old stone of the castle. Nestled right below me was a marina with three pontoon fingers, each berth busy with small craft tied up alongside. Beyond the old town lay Port Arthur and beyond that the scattering of islets and rocks that protect the stretch of water between Scalloway, the island of Trondra and the open waters beyond. I carried on down the hill, back to sea level again. Now exposed to the western and open side of the island, I could see very well why Fiona had recommended a stop-over at Lerwick. It was blowing like old boots up the inlet of the East Voe of Scalloway. I would have been mincemeat out there in a wounded boat.

I passed a couple of houses and the school where two kids were playing. Both stopped and stared at me as I cycled passed. 'Stranger in town', I mused as I grunted and pressed my way to the crown of the hill. Below lay the harbour of Scalloway and it was a much appreciated freewheel down to the bottom of the hill. Down to the left I could see a large yacht alongside the pier, a fishing boat and various other working craft in and around the harbour.

Ahead lay the gates to the working harbour. Ignoring all the signs that indicated authorised personnel only, I carried on into the port and made for the main area where the larger boats were tied up. There were two large deep ocean fishing boats and what looked like a government patrol boat. I needed to get out of the driving wind so pulled up in the lee of a skip parked on the quayside and dismounted. The wind howled and ripped across the pier and sent scudding squalls across the flat harbour water. Even the puddles at my feet and on the harbour top darkened as ripples of wind shot across the surfaces. Not wanting to hang around for too long, I got back on the bike and made for the exit. I could see an interesting arrangement of channels coming into the harbour. On a good day they would have been studied with great interest but today white-topped waves were chasing across the open area of water. The wind chill effect on a warm, well-exercised body had just sent the first shiver through me.

Feeling cold and hungry I was hoping to find a café or tea room, somewhere to get a cup of coffee. I did a loop round the western side of the harbour and pedalled across a large concreted flat area. As if by order a café sign appeared pointing up the slight rise. I carried on and, yes, there it was, a white traditional stone terraced building and inside, tea and warm scones awaited. Outside the front door was a welcoming wooden bench which was a great bike prop and seat to kick off my shoes. So strong was the wind that when the bike was buffeted by a particularly strong blast, it slipped down the front edge of the seat to the stone floor with a horrible sort of tangly metal crash. I left the bike flat on the ground which seemed the best tactic for anything moveable in this wind and kept just my cycle shoes on. Across the narrow road stood Scalloway Castle, or what was left of it. My little guide book back on *Pegasus* had said that it was built in 1600 by the Earl of Orkney and had been the administrative centre of the old capital town of Shetland. The book also commented that the Earl was renowned for his cruelty. 'Try bloody cycling in this wind, mate, if you want cruelty', I thought to myself.

I gathered myself and teetered the few steps from the bench to the front door with juices now flowing in anticipation of some good nosh. I opened the door to my little oasis and what greeted me did surprise me and, yes, initially disappointed. Facing me was a shiny metal and glass fish and chip counter with two smiling Chinese faces looking welcomingly at me. 'A chippie', I thought, 'not what I was expecting'. I crossed the lino floor in my cycling shoes and held the counter for balance. 'Do you do teas or coffee?' Again a big smile was forthcoming and 'Yes' was the answer. With a wave to my left my hosts pointed to the door tucked behind the sweetie counter and the upright cold drinks dispenser. I made for the door and then realised I was on a skating rink. Either my shoes and the lino were incompatible or there was a layer of grease on the floor. Holding on to walls, counters and anything I

Scalloway Castle – the old capital of the Shetland Isles
(courtesy VisitShetland)

could, I slowly made my way through to the back room where four tables awaited. I sat down and heaved a sigh of relief that I had not fallen my length and that I was soon to get some grub. A cheeseburger and coffee were soon in front of me and they were despatched, followed by a coffee and a Tunnocks Caramel Wafer. As I sat there reading the *Daily Record* two men dressed in orange boiler suits came into the little café. Their working boots made light work of the skating rink for sure. They were soon presented with a plate of macaroni cheese and chips the size of which I have never seen before and never likely to see again. I decided it was time to get going again and, nodding to my fellow diners, I carefully made my way to the safety of the loo, a room shared with the stock of cleaning materials. Safely back out to the front shop, I paid my dues, bade my farewells to my hosts and congratulated them on a great burger. Never mind the surroundings, the burger and coffee had hit the mark and I was restored and ready to take on the wind and the hills.

Back on the bike I juddered down a cobbled lane and returned to the main tarmac road, through the town centre and on the road leading to the Port Arthur fisheries college. The road was open and exposed to the sea on my left; a hill to my right only helped to funnel the wind in my direction. It was blowing with a vengeance so that forward motion was hard going. Well down my gears, at one point I had to stand in the pedals just to maintain forward momentum on a perfectly flat road. Enough was enough so I pulled over and took two minutes to look at the small boats marina. It was hard to stand still and I was keen to experience the wind behind me so I remounted and took off back to Scalloway. Sitting up straight in the saddle and coasting my way back into town – this was sailing again, on wheels and not on water!

Evening light sets in and one last look at Scalloway before cycling back to Lerwick

I retraced my tracks to the main street in Scalloway and decided to head straight back to *Pegasus* in Lerwick. The return trip to the capital was a completely different proposition to the energy-sapping outbound slog to Scalloway. I flew through the town and was soon at the foot of the steep hill that led back over the moor to Lerwick. With a good deal of grunt I took the hill in bottom gear but made it in one go, pleased with the way I responded as my heart rate climbed and came under real aerobic demand again. It was a good exorcism of the excesses of the Boat Club and the deep sleeping over the past couple of days. The long downhill stretch back to the main junction was done at speed, reckless speed if the truth be known. I carried on up the hill, not turning off to the right and back via North Taing but onwards and downwards to the Bridge of Fitch junction. I was screaming down the hill in top gear with a good powerful rotation of the pedals. Speed was creeping up and with one final effort I touched 40 miles per hour. At that point I thought it would be bloody stupid to end up on the deck, injured and not able to sail down to Blyth so I backed off and coasted on down the decreasing incline, sitting up in the saddle to offer a wind brake and so keep some heat out of my brake pads. I pulled into the lay-by just before the junction and whooped with the exhilaration of the descent. I ground up the next hill but did experience what I consider to be the 'Holy Grail' of cycling, being blown up the hill with nothing more than an easy rotation of the pedals. Over to the left lay the golf course and I marvelled at how anyone could keep a ball on the fairway in such a howling wind. With the climb conquered I screamed down the next decline, having happily forgotten the telling off I had given myself at the foot of the last descent; not quite 40 but a credible 38 miles per hour and very much in control. The last piece of road down into Lerwick I took very canny as there was more traffic about and the hill was very steep and one that could create a problem if I chose to gun it. The road swept me back into the north end of Lerwick at Gremista and at the foot of the hill I swung left to look round the boatyard and marina. I spent 15 minutes dawdling round the yard looking at a quite amazing array of boats. A small classic wooden day yacht was laid up between two giant pelagic fishing craft, the old and the new side by side and a lifetime of stories apart. Happy that I had exercised enough my legs, heart and lungs, I cruised through the town and back to *Pegasus*.

As I approached *Peggy* I could see four people standing over her taking in the detail of her decks and rigging. 'Well, there is no mistaking you then,' uttered one of the men as I dismounted beside them. 'You are in the right place here alright,' he added, no doubt referring to the gale that was blowing from the south and my snug position in the Small Boats Harbour. 'You bet I am, although cycling is bit of a challenge in this wind,' I retorted. That drew a smile from the chap. 'Care for a look aboard?' My offer was taken up with an even bigger smile. He and his pals nodded. What was even better, I now had four pairs of hands to help me get the bike down onto the deck. With the bike stowed in the aft cockpit by the port wheel I gave the lads, who were all in their early sixties by my reckoning, a tour of the deck. As they prowled up and down the side decks taking in all the detail, I slipped below and did a quick tidy up of the saloon. They chatted

Top: *The Norwegian queen of the seas the* Statsraad Lehmkuhl *berthed at Lerwick*

Centre: *A study of the complex rigging of a tall ship*

Above: *The* Statsraad Lehmkuhl *moves off into the Bressay Sound and another adventure*

with me for about 10 minutes and, content they had a first-hand understanding of this gleaming white plastic boat and its skipper, thanked me, wished me luck and departed. They wandered off, curiosities satisfied and able to report facts and not supposition to their mates about the big visiting yacht. When on deck I could see a crowd gathering on the Victoria Pier and thought it must be another Norwegian cruise boat about to arrive. From the south channel three masts appeared. It was a tall ship, flying a Norwegian flag and a Shetland courtesy flag. At least the skipper knew the ropes around these parts! As she came into view the penny dropped; she was the *Statsraad Lehmkuhl,* one of the most glorious examples of the world's great tall ships. She gracefully moved towards Lerwick and came alongside the main pier. I had the delight of visiting the great ship in her home port of Bergen in 1999 with my friend Greg Bertram. We had actually made the trip over with the objective of chartering her to re-enact the great voyage of the Royal Research Ship *Discovery* to Antarctica, as part of the 2001 centenary celebration of the launch of the *Discovery* in Dundee back in 1901. At that time I was director of Discovery Point Museum Dundee, where RRS *Discovery* sits afloat in her dock. To celebrate her centenary some great plans were dreamed up; some came off, some did not. Unfortunately the sailing of a tall ship from the UK via Cape Town and New Zealand, then down to McMurdo Sound in Antarctica did not attract a sponsor. We could not secure sufficient sponsorship despite the very best of efforts of Greg and myself, supported by Scottish Enterprise and some of the folks of Dundee. The big trip was to be a voyage of a lifetime, sailing around the world on a tall ship re-enacting history. Although that brainwave did not come off we did some great projects in 2001, supporting the centenary celebrations of the old ship.

We encouraged NASA to take a piece of the deck of RRS *Discovery* aboard the shuttle *Discovery* and, after its 'wee' trip in space, it was brought back to Dundee and is now on display at the museum. As the shuttle was orbiting, we hooked up a satellite link that had local Dundee kids speak from the bridge of the RRS *Discovery* with the astronauts and cosmonaut on the bridge of the USS *Discovery*. That was a really neat day; we secured national coverage on the main BBC channels and had widespread press coverage the following day. I still have a chuckle to myself as, during the day, the BBC asked if they could do a live feed to the lunchtime news bulletin. This would entail a slight change to plan and a small technical challenge. In response to the producer's request, I uttered the unforgettable words, 'I will need to clear that with NASA.' NASA were fine about it and we went out live. What a day!

Frustrated that the big voyage south to Antarctica had not come off, I managed to persuade 12 tall ships to stop over at Dundee on their way back to the UK from Esbjerg in Denmark. They had completed the annual Tall Ships Race so, to head back to the south coast of England where the next event was to take place, seemed an easy decision to stop off at the Tay. Dundee City Council and Scottish Enterprise came up trumps and underwrote the event so, with that vital and much-needed support in place, I set about organising a weekend of sail and celebration for the old lady. We engaged DF Concerts, who manage the now massive T in the Park Music Festival. They did a brilliant job in coordinating the whole weekend and all the crowd safety management issues. We entertained 50,000 people at the docks over a wet weekend in June 2001. The star attraction was the 90.5 metre (270 feet) 1,800 tons *Cuauhtémoc* of the Mexican navy. She is a gleaming, immaculately-presented tall ship, a joy to watch and a joy to board. Dundee did not know what had hit it when the starch-sharp uniformed cadets of the *Cuauhtémoc* took to the streets. We had a very hospitable Tequila reception aboard the ship one evening. Officers and crew were perfect gentlemen in every sense. At the other end of the spectrum one master of an Eastern Bloc-based tall ship, which I refuse to name, invited me to tea and proceeded to demand £500 cash as a thank you for deigning to come to Dundee. It was a particularly uncomfortable couple of hours where voices where raised and I do believe I was threatened. We shook hands and I got back on the quayside. Not wanting to have her slip her lines before the grand finale on the Sunday, I returned with £300 in a brown envelope. They were not very nice people at all and ones that I would not like to meet again.

The Tall Ships weekend was a great success with live music, a fairground, fireworks and all sorts of activities in and around the harbour of Dundee. Another event to savour that year was the black-tie centenary dinner with the theme 'Discovery; Past Present and Future'. Our speakers that evening included Sir Ranulph Fiennes, speaking on the golden era of polar exploration of Scott, Amundsen and Shackleton. Professor Sir David Laing spoke on the groundbreaking medical work taking place in Dundee, the City of Discovery, especially in his field of discovering the cancer genome. To top it all, we had the American astronaut Dr. Bonnie Dunbar who spoke of future discoveries in outer space and where that may lead. As a very nervous MC to an audience of over 200, I had the job of supporting these three great speakers. The real icing on the cake for me that night was to host the late, great and much-lamented Sir Wally Herbert, the first man to have crossed the Arctic on foot. I had the good fortune to meet Wally on a handful of occasions but, what a man, and what a gentleman; marvellous days and ones that I remember with a great deal of satisfaction and fondness.

It was time to get washed-up for the evening so I grabbed a few items of clothing and made my way to the Boat Club for a shower and shave. On returning to the *Pegasus* there was an elderly chap standing over her dressed in a blue boiler suit and a smart skipper's cap. He greeted me and made some very complimentary remarks about *Pegasus* and the way in which she was set up; he obviously approved. I offered hospitality, which he refused, adding that he was just over for a quick look. As he turned to go he pulled out his wallet from his back pocket and took one of the two notes in it and handed me a tenner. 'That's for your trip, good luck and don't be in a hurry to leave.' I was taken aback by the man's generosity and his genuine interest in *Pegasus*, the charitable causes and my well-being. 'I will, and thank you.' I uttered and warmly shook his hand. Off he went and I was genuinely rocked by the kindness of this stranger. That moment with the blue boiler-suited gent is one of my defining memories of the trip and one that really did make it all feel worthwhile.

Pegasus, the centre of attention in the Small Boats Harbour, Lerwick

The stopover at Lerwick was to last one whole week and it was a long one. I would have much preferred to have shared it with Shona and my daughters Jennifer and Katrina but having a few days to kick my heels was luxury. Fiona made it clear that the foul weather would continue, with strong southerly gales pushing north for at least four more days, so I resigned myself to doing some rooting around Lerwick.

When I had contacted the harbourmaster seeking confirmation of a berth, he advised me to tie up in front of a French yacht, which I duly did. It was time to meet my neighbours. I could see movement aboard so I gave them a shout and a head popped up from the hatch. I waved and it was reciprocated so I shouted over to see if they would like a cup of tea and cake. The chap clambered up on deck and came to the bow of his boat and we exchanged pleasantries. He said he would come over in an hour as he and his wife were working on their electrics and did not want to stop before any more light was lost. In an hour they arrived and came aboard. He was a canny-looking chap who, it transpired, ran a sailing school in France. His wife was a typical French woman, slightly built, sallow-skinned with great hair. A shock of wiry curly locks tied back behind her head set off this French beauty. They inspected the decks, massive winches, fittings and running rigging. Wearing big grins they came down into the main saloon and let out a whoop of joy and surprise at the massive space. A quick tour of down below was followed by tea, cake and Tunnocks Mallow Snowballs. An hour passed and we chatted about my trip. In turn, I was fascinated by their great adventure. From Lerwick they were bound for Norway and then on past the Arctic Circle to Svalbard. What an adventure! I felt a little jealous that they had the time and energy to head off across the seas following their dreams and fancies. We said our goodnights and they wandered back to their floating life. I had a dram and settled down to a really peaceful sleep.

The following day was all about tidying up and making *Pegasus* absolutely spick and span. I wanted her to be in showroom condition should anyone else come aboard for a visit. Good company arrived on the pier in the shape of Leslie Irvine, who came down to check out *Pegasus*. Leslie owns and operates a local builders' merchants and I took to him very early on in our chat over a brew. He was a sailor and planning to take part in the 2006 Round Britain Race. Over the following days Leslie shared his house and hospitality, along with time to visit the local swimming baths and, of course, a trip to have a close look over his yacht. She was built to go north and Leslie had plans to sail to Svalbard and explore the icy north. He was great company and a really sound guy who was good to share time with.

I was cross with myself as I had not yet visited the Shetland Coastguard Station to thank them in person for their vigilance and attention to my plight off Stromness. Having phoned them immediately on my arrival that I was secure and safe in the harbour, it was time to go and see these folks. It was lashing with rain so I just headed straight for their station on Nabb Road on the South Ness. Soaked and cold, I arrived at the front door and rang the bell. A voice answered and I was buzzed in. Once up the stairs, I entered the nerve centre of the operation that looks after shipping and leisure craft safety and movements in the Orkney and Shetland waters. I must have looked a sight. I was supposed to be a hardened sailor but here before them stood a dripping cold chap dressed in skin-tight leggings, tight cycling top and stupid 'clacky' cycling shoes. I was offered a cup of tea that was readily accepted and we had a good chat for half an hour, during which time I was given a tour of their control room. I really do hope that I managed to get across to the guys on duty how grateful I was for their patience and listening out for me, not just during the steering gear debacle but also throughout my time on their patch. I said my thanks again, mounted my bike and sped off back to *Pegasus* to get dried out. I was just back in dry clothes when I took a call from Sue to say that BBC Radio Shetland wanted to do an interview. No sooner had I hung up than there was a shout from the harbour top; it was the reporter holding his recorder close to his side. Never one to say no to getting the challenge into the public domain, I invited him aboard and, after a cup of coffee, did a recorded piece that went out that evening. By the end of the challenge, between Sue and Andrea, we had racked up over 40 media trackings in the press, TV and radio, leaving aside the masses of Internet links. The press exposure the challenge created for both OYTS and PDS was great and it was all down to the unstinting efforts of my PR gurus Sue McKichan of Marketing Matters and Andrea Tofta, Senior Media Officer at PDS.

Another open door was offered to me was by the staff of the local VisitShetland office. The Visitor Information Centre in Lerwick has an imposing position and is one of those VICs that just looks as if it means business. Having recently been refurbished, it was very well laid out and presented the Shetland tourism product well. I took up residence on one of the PCs that is available to the public and from there I had open access to e-mails and weather forecasts. I was back in communication with one and all. Cups of coffee were freely on offer and I had a really good chat with their staff. Unfortunately Andy Stevens, the director of the Shetland office, was on leave that week and I did not get a chance to catch up with him and retune from sailor to tourism commentator and lobbyist. I would have particularly liked to chat with Andy as Shetland was increasingly moving towards self-determination in respect of tourism which was a 'live' political and major issue for debate around tourism structures in Scotland – and there is the rub. The Shetland Islanders, as I had discovered in the Boat Club on the first evening, are fiercely proud and see themselves more as members of the northern isles. They are more Nordic in the truest sense rather than Scottish with the islands frequently seen as an insert on a map of Scotland, never mind of the UK. I was a 'sooth-moother' who hailed from the mainland. The haven of the VisitShetland office was much appreciated both in providing a communications link with the team but also for the chat and company. Another thing I liked about the VIC was that it had the feel of an information centre and not of a cheap tourist nick-nack shop, as some have ended up. The Lerwick VIC did have retail goods on sale but not to the detriment of its core purpose. This is a matter that has been long discussed in the tourism industry and the debate still runs and runs.

I wandered back to *Pegasus* at a bit of a loose end, wondering what I would do for the rest of the day. I took out all my charts and pilot books and set about doing some passage planning for the trip down the North Sea. 'Ahoy down there,' came a voice from up on the quayside. Another visitor, I thought, and an excuse to put a brew on and a chat. I popped my head out of the hatch to see a chap in his fifties standing with what could only be described as a rather expectant look on his face. On being invited to come aboard, he was down the ladder and standing in the cockpit shaking my hand. 'Stuart Hill is the name and I thought I would come and give you a visit; heard all about your trip on the radio,' he rattled off without taking breath. I did the usual tour of the decks and then offered a cup of tea that was readily accepted. The chat flowed and before too long and to my amazement I realised that I had the real 'Captain Calamity' aboard *Pegasus*. Stuart has the ignominy of being the most-rescued sailor in the record books. Being at a particularly rocky stage in his life, he upped sticks from his family and set off to sail around Britain. It's been done before, but in an old steel rowing boat with a windsurfer sail and mast as the rig? – unlikely. Reports vary on how many times he was rescued by lifeboat or helicopter but they go well into double figures. On one single day he was rescued twice by the same lifeboat and yet still had the brass neck to continue on his way. His final wrecking off Shetland meant that he landed on the island penniless, boatless and, some might say, clueless. His wife, it was reported, had sold their house and done a runner with the kids to France, along with the proceeds of the house, and there was no invite extended to her wayward husband. He decided to settle in Shetland and was, as I was about to learn, planning his next harebrained scheme. Before I had finished my first mug of tea I had been sounded out to invest in his revolutionary sail mould, which would turn conventional sail-making on its head. How lucky could I get? A chance to come in at the start of a design revolution, and all for £10,000. I choked on the dregs of tea in my mug and declined his offer of riches. The chat carried on but he was undaunted by my knock-back. He would not let it drop. Without being rude, I brought our chat to a close under the pretence that I had to head to the shops for supplies. Before much more was said, I was on my feet with rucksack in hand ushering him up the companionway and off *Pegasus*.

Over the previous couple of days I had been giving my mainsail a great deal of thought; well, the lack of mainsail more to the point. The bottom car was completely broken and no amount of Araldite would bond it back together. I also tried a bolt through the plastic sheathing but there was not enough robust plastic to get a hold of. I even looked into getting a replacement shipped up to Shetland but decided that sod's law would have it turn up the day after I had left, so that idea was abandoned. How could I jury-rig the mainsail so that I could hoist the full sail and get so much more power from a well-shaped foil? The hard flat board that a reefed sail presents to the elements is fine in a blow but, with anything less, it drastically reduces sail efficiency and therefore speeds. The idea struck me while looking at the rigging on the *Statsraad Lehmkuhl* with her complex lines and halyards and yardarms. Rope! Why not rig a loop of rope round the mast and through the reefing cringle eyelet in the sail. If the rope was looped round the mast, I might manage to tension it just the right amount to allow it to slip up the mast with the sail. When hoisted, lateral tension would build, pulling the sail away from the mast, and the rope would hold firm. I set about the port locker where all the bits of rope and warps were kept. A short piece of rope that could easily have been binned as being useless came to hand. 'Never throw away bits of rope' is a great motto when one has a boat! I scrambled up onto the boom and led the line around the mast and running rigging lines and tied it off in a reef knot. There was not a puff of wind in the harbour that evening so I hoisted the main and, just as I had hoped, the sail slid up, pulling the rope loop with it. I could still reach it from my position standing on the boom and, with a little adjustment to the tensioning, I had a perfect rope mainsail car. Very happy with my work, I now had a full sail to get south and, with lighter winds forecast for later on in the week, it would mean that I could maintain that all-important boat speed.

On the fifth day I decided I was going to explore the island of Bressay that lies just a short mile from Lerwick across the unsurprisingly-named Bressay Sound. The island protects the port of Lerwick from the prevailing northeasterlies and, to put it simply, without Bressay there would be no port of Lerwick as it is the only thing between Lerwick and Norway. The island is low-lying and, because of that topographic feature, seemed to me to be a good place to go on a bike. A ferry serves as the communication link and plies its trade on a fairly regular basis to and from each shoreline from Lerwick to the little village of Maryfield. Clad in my biking gear, I bought my ticket and felt thrilled being back at sea as we crossed the flat water. Once on the island I meandered my way up from the ferry pier and enjoyed just sniffing around the first few houses and on up to the little shop and a T-junction. I turned south and set off along the beautiful single-track road passing farms, fields, cottages and sheds. On and on, past Glebe and the scattering of houses at Grindiscot until the road started to rise towards the south end of the island. My goal was Kirkabister Ness Lighthouse that stands sentry to the south entrance to the Bressay Sound. The sky was a stunning blue and, with the effort, I was sweating and really enjoying my outing. I reached the lighthouse after a bit of a puff up the hill and left the bike against a solid iron gate that broke the well-maintained white line of the lighthouse perimeter wall. The wall was a brilliant white against the lush grassy surround and above was the clear blue sky, a photographer's dream composition of bright and vibrant colours. I clicked my way down the short tarmac path and then wandered on right round the tower and its outbuildings. This lighthouse, like all the others, had the most amazing views away off to the south along the Ord cliffs, to the north-west up the sound into the heart of Lerwick and over to the south-west along cliffs down to Dedda Skerry and on out to the North Sea. In a pitch dark approach to Lerwick from the south a ship could, without too much of an error, end up being pushed on a southwesterly gale straight onto the cliffs below. With all that bounty being delivered onto the shoreline, it would make for rich pickings. Way over to my left was Bard Head, the outermost south-east extremity of Bressay and my mind drifted to when I might be saying good-bye to that cliff face from the cockpit of *Pegasus*. Looking out to sea it was perfectly clear why I was here sightseeing and not out at sea. The wind had settled in for the last few days and the large rolling waves being sent north crashed against the immovable Ord cliffs. Fluid force against immovable object sent the waves upwards in an explosion of brilliant white water and foam. The sea was shiny slate grey and further out it looked immense yet sublime. The waves rolled serenely northwards but where they were goaded by the

Above: Wild seas beat against the Ord cliffs

Right: Kirkabister Ness lighthouse, Bressay

unyielding cliffs they turned ferocious as they burst in anger against Bressay. I had picked up a flavour of the sea over at Scalloway but this uninterrupted view down into the inhospitable-looking North Sea was a sobering sight. Fiona was right again; this was the right place to be.

I lay on the grass lawn under the column of the light and gazed up at the whitewashed stone and azure blue sky. So strong was the glare off the tower that I slipped my shades down off my head, closed my eyes and lay there cooking in the reflected heat. Tucked in behind the white-painted stone dyke and in direct line of sight to the sun, was a great suntrap and it was hot, not just warm. I lay there and nodded off for a few moments, letting the heat soak into me. After a lovely 15 minutes of dozing, I decided it was time to look around the rest of the island. The trip back north was faster with the wind whistling me onwards. I was back at the T-junction very quickly and kicked hard on the pedals for a few more miles. I pulled to a halt and was looking at an option of picking a side lane that seemed to head down to the shore on the left with more fields and smallholdings. I chose right as it had an intriguing signpost pointing towards Globa. The track sliced off across more flat grazed fields until it came to a dead end at the buildings that constituted Globa. That ticked off, I pedalled back up the single-track lane and turned right which led me on to Gunnista and Beosetter. Content that I had seen both ends of Bressay, I turned and puffed my way back to the T-junction. I could see the ferry steaming over to the island from Lerwick so I freewheeled on down to the jetty, still with enough time to have a quick look at the little harbour. Within the comfort of the stone walls, a couple of small fishing boats hung on limp mooring warps suspended in the crystal clear waters. The island of Bressay had been worth every second.

The ferry was bang on time and, with no cars making the trip, the half dozen or so foot passengers were ushered on. I made for the covered passenger area that runs along the side of the top deck and took up a seat in the cabin with the three or four other folks making the short trip. Behind me a young lad of about 25 nodded and asked if I was OK. I nodded and said thanks. 'Are you the guy who is sailing around Scotland? Heard you on the radio yesterday.' We entered into a very easy chat about *Pegasus*, the gear failure, why I was in Lerwick and how much I had enjoyed the Boat Club hospitality. He told me he was out of work and looking to get back onto a fishing boat but if that did not happen, he was off to Glasgow. Just as we were pulling in to the pier he pulled out a handful of change, picked out two £1 coins and gave them to me, saying that I should put that towards my fund-raising. For the second time, I was really taken aback by the genuine generosity of the folk of Lerwick. I warmly shook his hand and gave him my heartfelt thanks. What a kind gesture the lad had made! It fair made my day. Back ashore I made my way back to *Pegasus*, gathered my toilet bag, showered at the Boat Club and then made for my favourite café for a late afternoon coffee and bacon roll. That evening I went into the town and enjoyed a couple of pints and some company with a visiting lorry driver and a lad who was waiting for the engine of his fishing boat to be repaired. The chat that evening was really easy and relaxed and, having said my goodbyes, I wandered back to *Pegasus,* content that I had just had a really good day.

Reflections of the esplanade in perfect still water

129

The following morning I decided that a trip further afield was needed. Scouring my OS map, I struck on Hamnavoe on the island of West Burra as somewhere that looked interesting to explore. I set off on my trusty set of wheels and followed the same road out of Lerwick as on the windswept trip to Scalloway, but this day was altogether much better for pedalling. I reached the top of the Hill of Dale road in much easier fashion and then whistled down the hill to East Voe. Then, rather than turning right for Scalloway, I headed off left and was soon over the low causeway bridge and on the island of Trondra. This was a different world, with some of the most mouth-watering views out to the west and the profusion of small islands. Cracking on, for this was a day when the miles came easy, I was soon off Trondra and crossing the piers to West Burra at Ux Ness. From there, an easy spin took me down into Hamnavoe. The weather was really a treat and I was positive in spirit and energy. Stopping off at the bottom of the steep hill down to the harbour, I bought a Cornetto and sat on the stones by the pier baking in the sun, sheltered from the omnipresent wind with my face glowing. Having despatched my Cornetto before it melted, I lay back and dozed for what might have been 10 minutes. Stirred by the squawk of the gulls, I mounted up again and dawdled out of this little piece of heaven. Over my shoulder lay such tantalising islands as Papa, Oxna and Hildasay that would just have to be visited some other day.

This indeed was a different place to the Scotland I knew. The names, the flags, the people and the lie of the land shouted out, 'We are our own islands'. I had sympathy and a full realisation of the cause Shetland has with our centralised marketing agency of VisitScotland. Here in Hamnavoe with the islands and lands laid out before me, I could see no relationship between the City Breaks campaigns, Cool Metro-Scotland, the Highlands and Western Islands and the ubiquitous tartan, castles, mountains, glens and shortbread images promoted around the world. I pedalled on, still throwing around in my mind the challenge that exists between Shetland and our national tourism agency. To me this land was growing in identity and in its own sense, and I was now getting in tune with the frequency of this northern place. Before I am excommunicated by VisitScotland (some may say again!) I have to say that I have every admiration for the well-researched and thoroughly professional marketing set up in their HQ at Ocean Point in Leith. Their trophy cabinet is groaning with awards from their marketing peers. Their customer segmentation and product portfolio approach have many fans, including me. However, not much of what I have seen as the core call to action at the tail end of every advert promoting Scotland connected with this place and it was a place I was coming to like more and more. Yes, this was Scotland, but not quite – it had more affinity with its Norse neighbours Iceland, the Faroes and Norway. The view back up Lang Sound from Grunnasound and Meml was just breathtaking. The sun was lowering in the blue, almost cloud-free sky, the sea was the most vibrant and bright aquatic turquoise blue that I had ever witnessed. This, I concluded, was a different land.

Standing on the rise near the Standing Stones just above Loch of Sandwick I looked back north to a stunning vista back up the Lang Sound. To complete the moment a pair

Below: Wester Quarff from Burra

Above: Clift Sound

Below: Looking south to East Burra causeway

Bridge End Outdoor Centre and marina – Burra

*Some of the locals look on with Bridge
End in the background*

Looking south towards Fitful Head from Burra

of Shetland ponies stood with their rumps to me and the wind. One casually cocked his head round his flank as if to say, 'not a bad view?' I snapped the moment with my camera and the photo sits at home as a touchstone of that moment in life. I cycled on a bit more southwards and came to the little settlement of Papil. Again, another stunning sight of colour and shape, it was just sheer Shetland. My cup was full and it was time to head back to Lerwick. A quick check of the map confirmed that I was about 20 kilometres away from Lerwick. It was mid-afternoon and with the wind behind me, I followed my route the way I had come and enjoyed every minute of it. I felt guilty; here was I enjoying myself again but I was on my own. I could see Shona in particular enjoying all of this, especially coasting back on the luxury of a following wind to a holiday home or a bed and breakfast. These thoughts troubled me and the pedal back over to Lerwick was quiet and a touch subdued as I mulled over a few things in my mind.

Heading back to Scalloway after a stunning day on the bike

Determined not to be too morose about life, I decided I needed company that evening. On getting back to *Pegasus* the bike was stowed away and I made a beeline to the Boat Club for a shower. I was determined to get in and out without getting caught up in a session at the bar as I had a gut feeling that the weather had changed and, if today was anything to go by, I would soon be off. No belly full of booze for me tonight! I scoffed tea aboard and headed out and found a pub with company and a TV. Perching at the end of the bar, I enjoyed watching a football game, a few pints and some chat with folks that were coming in and out. Before long I heard, 'Are you the guy sailing around Scotland?' and '... you must be mad'. It was a really good evening and one that cheered me up again after the surprising low at the end of my cycle run.

My time in Lerwick was coming to an end. Fiona confirmed by e-mail that the weather was to break in two days and I would have north-westerlies that would take me south. The following day was all about getting ready to move out. I decided that I should top up to a full tank of diesel. If I was to lose the boom and found it necessary to motor to shore, I wanted to have 'belt and braces' levels of fuel in the tank. After making enquiries at the Harbour Office, I set about taking *Pegasus* round to the fuel berth in the Albert Dock. It was an excursion I was not looking forward to. I walked round to the dock to check out the lie of the land and where I should aim *Pegasus*. The last thing I wanted to do was make a fool of myself in the heart of the port of Lerwick. I slipped lines, enjoyed the short motor along the sea wall of Victoria Pier and then swung into Albert Dock. The lad who was to fuel me was nowhere to be seen so I was going solo again! I nipped *Pegasus* up to the harbour wall and stomped on astern to stop her dead in the water. I took a breast line with me up the metal rung ladder that was perfectly positioned at her beam. Three steps and I was up on the quayside and making the line fast; *Peggy* was now secure and going nowhere. I went back down onto her deck and slung a bow and stern line up onto the pier and was delighted to see my absent fuelling friend now on station. He took the lines and made her fast. We fuelled right up to the top of the inflow pipe which meant I had enough fuel to allow me to motor for about 240 miles, depending on the weather. That done, I went into the office and paid my bill, which was not inconsiderable, then slipped lines and made for my berth back in the Small Boats Harbour. A repeat single-handed performance was played out with the breast line doing the business and we were snug again.

I had some shopping to do – a present for Shona and groceries so I helped the local economy with the purchase of a lovely item of Shetland knitwear and three bags of food and grub from the supermarket. We were ready for departure the next morning. I made one last trip to the VisitShetland office before they closed for the evening and checked my e-mails. The most important one was from Fiona and it was 'Go!' The weather was now stable and the gale had moved through; a steady but moderate northwesterly would fill in within the next 24 hours. Such a wind would send me down the North Sea on a reach and would be just ideal, not too strong but good enough for some good boat speed. I headed back to *Pegasus* to

Pegasus sitting snug in the Small Boats Harbour

set about getting ready and to let my French neighbours know that it was time for me to head off. They too were going to leave the next day so, to celebrate our collective release from Lerwick, they invited me over for some lunch and I readily accepted. Armed with a fruitcake I climbed up to the pier and then down onto their yacht. She was about a 33-footer and in immaculate condition, everything ordered, in perfect place, the decks and cockpit business-like. She was armed and ready to head north and who knows what sort of adventures lay ahead for the two of them. We shook hands and I was ushered below to have my senses ambushed. The smell of fresh coffee hit me and the hostess was looking flawless. What is it about French women, oh and their coffee? Their saloon was small and perfectly ordered with charts, books and general kit all perfectly stowed. There was not an inch of space wasted. Laid out on the saloon table was a French lunch extraordinaire of wine, cheeses, bread, salami and a bowl of olives. I held my fruitcake behind me cringing within as to the 'Scottishness' of my shrink-wrapped, processed token. The coffee pot was perking away on the stove and I could not help but be impressed with the whole set-up. Here they were living in cramped conditions with really not much room and we had such a simple but civilised spread laid out to enjoy. It was a great lunch and I fell in love with the food and the company. After two hours of swapping stories of life and sailing plans, I said my farewells, we embraced, wished each other well and fair winds and I dragged my feet back to *Pegasus*.

My cavernous and cathedral-like saloon was neat and gleaming, with bare shelves and surfaces; bare floors, no doors and stripped-out all for the satisfaction and indulgence of one passenger. Laid out on one settee were my battle fatigues: waterproofs, harness, lifeline thermal gloves, balaclava and sat-phone. I felt very lonely after the intimate company of the last couple of hours. Oh how much I wished I was here on a cruise with Shona and my girls, enjoying the sights, sounds and experiences of these northern parts. My self-accusatorial thoughts ran out of control, released by the moment. 'You take three weeks off work, the first time you have ever taken three weeks off work, ever!' For most of the last 20 years, only one week had been grabbed each year with family and loved ones. Yet here I was on a boat, having the trip of a life-time and not sharing it with anyone. The mood darkened and I swilled around in my head all sorts of instances when I had been doing things for me, and how much time this challenge had taken out of the lives of my family. How many weekends had the preparation taken up and so denied time with my two daughters who were growing up in another dimension to the one I was so consumed by? Was this a driven competitiveness I had lodged deep inside me, one, no matter how hard I tried, I was just not able to shake? Was it a focussed determination towards this project that my internal make-up would not allow me to walk away from or was it cheap fame that drove me? All I knew was that I lacked some element within that could take a balanced position when such decisions were needed. I was damn proud to have got this far after the Irish false start and the massive diversions of work, getting the inaugural of Scottish Tourism Week successfully delivered, and then the wipeout. Yes, the wipeout that rendered the whole project almost but not quite obsolete. I was still chasing something and deep inside I was not content with my lot. I still needed to push and prove something to myself, or was it to everybody else? I needed to reach that bit further than what life was offering me and, along the way, it meant that not everyone could come along, and that was just plain fact.

I thought about my brother and how he had moved on from a highly successful and competitive level of rugby to be a brilliant professional coach. He had held senior professional coaching jobs at club, regional and national levels yet he managed, from my perspective, to keep family, farm and friends in equilibrium, unlike me. He was a team player through and through and there was no doubting that. Meanwhile I had touched on team games but my sports ended up as athletics, hill running, golf and single-handed sailing, each a one-man effort at the point of competition. Perhaps I was not a team player, although I thought I was. I could never have 'retired' from competitive sport and taken on the role of coach as I would simply not have had the patience or the gift of the time needed to nurture talent. Is that selfishness or just who I am? Whatever it is, the end result is that with most things in life I feel a frustration that what I have done is not the very best in the world or the very best I could achieve. Typifying the whole mix, here I was sitting it out in Lerwick, having to make second best of my triple crown of being 'the first', setting a world record and raising cash for charity. To compound all of these thoughts, the challenge and its partial failure was twisting the knot of frustration inside me. Yet, like my athletics and working careers, here I was 'grinding out' a result.

The malaise that came over me on my bike ride, which had taken me by surprise had returned with a vengeance. Here I was sitting in a 'wonder boat' that many could only dream of, tied up in a place many could only hope of sailing to and I was hogging the whole show, sharing it with no-one. I was angry and annoyed and that feeling remained with me for a good couple of hours. Time was up on this trip and I needed to get on my way and home. Slowly the mist lifted and thoughts turned to how to get the trip over and done with. I had really had enough of Lerwick and felt very homesick. I am not sure if was nerves coming to the surface or some suppressed subconscious guilt that I had been carrying for some time, now released as a result of the cumulative fatigue and stress. Whatever it was it made my last afternoon on Lerwick miserable. As evening came I set about double-checking charts, pilot books, bolthole locations and bearings and running a full systems check-up on *Pegasus*.

I had been here long enough and on this occasion I was very happy to get back on the horse, and in a completely different state of mind to when I was leaving Stromness. Rather than being nervous I was desperate to get away and back to sea. I ate well and topped up all the water tanks and generally made *Pegasus* ready for departure. Leslie popped down to say his farewells and said that he would nip down to Scattland Point to wave me on my way. We chatted for a few minutes and he had a dram to wish me luck. We shook hands and he headed off home. I made one last call to Shona and also to Erik and Gordon to say that all was well and that we were ready to sail. Texts were sent to Jenny and Katrina and, with that done, I crashed out.

Above: The port of Lerwick from the air
(courtesy VisitShetland)

Below: The author sets sail from Lerwick on a wet day

Day 15 –

Thursday 27th, 13.20 hrs – Lerwick

688 nm run – 310 nm to Blyth

Sleep in last 24 hrs: 7 hr 00 min

The next morning was a wet and grey start as I slipped my lines and said farewell to my big stone wall that had, over the course of the last seven days, considerably aged my fenders. As I edged *Peggy* out of the Small Boats Harbour; there was no sign of my French friends. They would be warm and snug below decks, so I threw them a wave for good luck. In the Bressay Sound outside the harbour the mainsail was rattled up the mast and I motor-sailed north with Lerwick to my left and port side. If I had turned south out of the harbour and away to the open sea I would have passed inside Bressay and Noss, yes inside, and would have been looking at 'solo round Scotland except Bressay and Noss', never mind 'except Rockall', an easy mistake and one I was not going to make. Sure as he had promised, Leslie was on the pier at Laurenson Quay waving as we rumbled past under engine. I waved back, happy that I had made his acquaintance and then turned to get on with the job. I was soon out of the protective waters around Lerwick and as we neared Easter Rova Head I killed the engine and bore away to the east along the north shore of Bressay. I had to ensure we had enough sea room to sail past a little brick of a rock called Holm of Beosetter that lay directly in line to Score Head, the most northerly tip of Bressay. Boat speed was great; *Pegasus* dug her starboard gunwale down into the water and off we streaked with Blyth and the north-east coast of England in mind.

8

THE NORTH SEA

We fetched along the north shore of Bressay and cleared Score Head with a good quarter mile to spare. With that done, I pulled the wheel down to the right and to starboard and gybed through the wind. *Pegasus* responded with a further surge of speed as we eased further off the wind and were heading south again. After all the time in Lerwick it was good to see some southerly numbers showing again on the compass. The Island of Noss lies directly east of Bressay so, once abeam of the Noss Head cliffs, I had a straight line to Blyth. This was it, my North Sea leg was about to unfold.

Over to our right the cliffs of Noss and Bressay were sheer, dark and stunning. Away to my left lay the open North Sea. Ahead to the south lay Orkney, Fair Isle and the Scottish mainland with the entire length of its coastline to the North Sea. It was going to be a long sail south and I needed favourable winds to get the 300 miles or so down to Blyth. At this point a great wind was pushing us south at speed and right now all was just perfect. Bard Head at the southernmost tip of Bressay slipped by and I was in the open water south of Lerwick, in the water that had only a few days ago been a seething torment of wave, spray and spume crashing against cliffs. Now it was benign running waves, each one helping me south and home.

As we thundered along holding 8 knots under full mainsail and full Genoa, it seemed it was not just me that wanted to get home, *Pegasus* was at a gallop. My rope jury mainsail car was snug and working a treat. The main was full and pulling and that was nice to see again. Life aboard very quickly settled down to the routine of cups of tea, tweaking sails and steering the waves for boat speed. I glanced back to catch a last look at the Shetland Isles and, happy that they were being left behind, I turned and braced myself for the long

Sailing south looking over to the cliffs of Noss

sail south to Blyth. The boat was well-set and I was ready and willing for the sail and keen to keep the foot down and push on for boat speed. Gone were the unease and concerns I had felt when setting off from Stromness; this time I was keen, rested and restored and just desperate to get the job done and get down south. All the negativity around my thoughts of being selfish and not sharing *Pegasus* were blown away by the fresh breeze. I knew I had been away for too long now and I just wanted to get home and get the job done, but done well. My little huff of last evening had left me but had served to sharpen the intent to get home safe and sound. The afternoon passed without any incident, I was relaxed and in control, energy reserves were high as was morale and, what's more, we were honking south at a rate of knots. Some herbal tea along with a pork pie and cake were enjoyed along with a couple of painkillers as my knee was aching again and I needed to free it up for the nocturnal activities ahead.

The euphoria of speed was fairly short-lived as the wind started to ease and the gushing, deflected water that whooshed out from under *Pegasus* was soon reduced to an odd slap and then to a gentle dappling sound. The wind started to die late afternoon and speed dropped to a painful crawl but I was not really too worried about that. I was happy to be heading south. As far as I was concerned these were all 'free' miles. I was so laid back and relaxed and not really having to working too hard to keep *Peggy* moving.

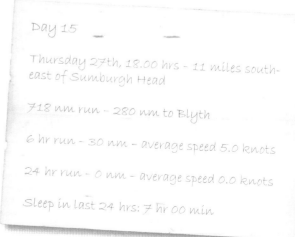

Day 15

Thursday 27th, 18.00 hrs – 11 miles south-east of Sumburgh Head

718 nm run – 280 nm to Blyth

6 hr run – 30 nm – average speed 5.0 knots

24 hr run – 0 nm – average speed 0.0 knots

Sleep in last 24 hrs: 7 hr 00 min

The evening settled in and it was looking like it would be a cold clear night, but a night with wind that was forecast to pick up again. Having learnt from the St Kilda leg, I was determined to get some good sleep and not to get carried away with boat speed and progress. I needed to arrive in Blyth capable and in a frame of mind that would let me get fired into the cycle leg and all the challenges that might come my way. I ate well and slept on and off through dusk as a starry night sky settled in above me. The canopy of twinkling stars on show that night was just amazing and deserved closer inspection. I adopted the *Pegasus* stargazing position, one that has been used sitting at anchor on many clear nights during weekend trips on the west coast. Lying flat out on my back in the cockpit with a cushion behind my head and binoculars fixed on the light show above is the best possible way I know to stargaze. The sights out there that night almost defied description. The naked eye reveals only a fraction of what is going on in the heavens. The thought never fails me, each time I look out to space through binoculars, that we just cannot be alone and there is a heck of a story to be unravelled by those who can delve deeper into outer space and beyond. Galaxies and swirls of stars take your eye further and further away from this world, each one being seen as it was perhaps millions of years ago. Who knows, one may have exploded tens of thousands of years ago and, by doing so, signed the death warrant of planet earth. But when is the warrant to be served, another 50,000 years from now? Anyway I was sure, absolutely sure, that out on another planet there was a guy lying on a boat looking back at me thinking much the same. The other theory I aired to myself that evening is we are but a part of an atom in someone else's universe and, in turn, each atom on this earth contains countless universes, each dependent on each other. Where are we in this chain, I wonder? Looking out into the great beyond, the larger stars almost create light pollution in themselves. Their brightness spoils seeing even greater marvels in the clusters and layers of minute white lights twitching and fading in and out of vision.

Watching the stars from a boat sailing south, balanced by sail and rudder, only heightened my appetite for the night that lay ahead. So much of this trip was mind games, preparation, risk assessment, percentage play, holding the risk position and downright hard graft. Here was a phase of complete relaxation and deep contemplation of greater matters than merely sailing a boat around Scotland. It is moments like this that bring me back to boats and probably will do so for the rest of my life. The night was also going to offer the satisfaction of navigation by the heavenly stars. To steer at night following a star rather than a digital readout of a compass is an absolute delight. A digital readout or swivelling compass on a binnacle (pedestal at the wheel) both have the ability to make you go cross-eyed after a few hours. To sail by a star is so much more satisfying. Any night sail like this takes me back to a favourite passage in one of my library of sailing and adventure books. The accumulation of such books fills the shelves at home, much to the consternation of Shona, but she invariably makes no comment as I sneak another one into the house. The passage of text I refer to comes from a book that has brought me so much enjoyment each time it has been taken down to be read. Whilst sailing in the open Pacific on his epic circumnavigation of 1895–98, Joshua Slocum writes:

I sailed with a free wind day after day, marking the position of my ship on the chart with considerable precision; but it was done by intuition, I think, more than by lavish calculations. For one whole month my vessel held her course true; I had not, the while, so much a light in the binnacle. The Southern Cross I saw every night abeam. The sun every morning came up astern; every evening it went down ahead. I wished for no other compass to guide me, for these were true. If I doubted my reckoning after a long time at sea I verified it by reading the clock aloft made by the Great Architect, and it was right.

—*Sailing Alone Around The World – The first solo voyage around the world*
Joshua Slocum

I had seen the sun rise and set around me as I headed north to Muckle Flugga and now I had the stars, just like my friend Joshua. My little trip paled into insignificance compared with his. But I had tasted, even if it was only once, the experience of watching the sun go down on our port side and for the ball of fire to rise on our starboard. Now I was steering by the stars, I was happy.

Day 15

Thursday 27th, 24.00 hrs – Dutch
Bank 46 miles east of Orkney

751 nm run – 247 nm to Blyth

6 hr run – 33 nm – average speed
5.5 knots

24 hr run – 0 nm – average speed
0.0 knots

Sleep in last 24 hrs: 2 hr 00 min

I was rudely brought back to earth, in fact brought back to reality that on earth my position was east of the Pentland Firth, one of the earth's busier pieces of water. A dim white glow lit the horizon; I was back into the shipping areas that fed ships into and out from the Pentland Firth. The binoculars were now needed to observe lights of a different nature, not heavenly light but harsh commercial merchant shipping that owned this water and did not expect to be sharing it with an insignificant white plastic sailing yacht. The cushion that had comforted my head was tossed below to the saloon and a watch of a different intensity and resolve started. I checked the radar and nothing was showing. Which I thought was strange as the white glow had turned from a glow to a discernible white light – the two of us were getting closer. I trained the binoculars on the light and soon a red bow light was also visible. This monster was heading south and over this way so I had to keep an eye on her. There was still no trace of the ship on the radar and I was starting to feel concerned that repairs in Stromness were not as successful as I had hoped. The readings gathered in the harbour in Stromness seemed to confirm all was well but out at sea it was a different matter. Another glow appeared north and behind my first visitor so now I had two ships to monitor and assess respective courses and levels of danger. Ship 1 carried on and passed well ahead and away to the south of us. The red bow light was hidden from view by the ship's superstructure and the bright white stern light confirmed she was steaming away from us, but more importantly, out of our lives forever.

As part of my pre-voyage preparation or risk assessment I needed to know what I might be facing in respect of shipping traffic. If I knew roughly how many ships transit through the Pentland Firth I could establish the likelihood I would have of encountering traffic. I was horrified to find that an estimated 6,500 ships transit the Firth each year. Running a calculator over that gives an average of 18 ships a day! Allowing for some seasonal adjustment for the foul months of winter, I estimated that 20 ships a day would come funnelling in and out of the Firth, an average of one ship every 1 hour 10 minutes. If one was to make an assumption that ships enter or leave the Firth through a gate some 40 miles wide and I was sailing at, say, 6 knots, I would be in the danger zone or zone of intensity for about 6.5 hours. That would mean I was likely to see six ships as I sailed the length of my imaginary gate. So like it or not there was going to be very little sleep in the coming hours as I still had some 15 miles to my 'gate' and here arriving on stage was my first big mama. Forewarned is forearmed in my book so with that data tucked away I knew I was in for a night of stress and 'heavy metal'.

Ship 2 appeared and seemed to be holding the same course as Ship 1. On that basis I had an understanding of the shipping lane, likely routes and was pretty happy that it was in 'gate' territory. As I proceeded south I would at some point cross this imaginary motorway so I just had to cross at a time when no leviathan was coursing east or west. Ship 2 slipped silently on ahead and was soon just a glow on the eastern horizon. Now what is the first rule of the sea? 'Power gives way to sail'. I was not going to move from the theory that I have always held when it comes to that specific rule and that is 'Might has right!'

An hour passed and then it all kicked off. Ship 3 appeared from the expected area over to the west, followed not long after by Ship 4 looming from the east. Within the next 30 minutes Ships 5, 6, 7 and 8 all made their appearance on the stage. I had six different ships on the move, each thundering along at possibly 15–20 knots. I had each set of lights covered and in my mind's eye a basic understanding of what each ship was doing and where it was heading. Then it all went pear-shaped and in a big way. A set of lights I had assessed to be passing behind me from east to west changed from green to all horrors, a red and green – meaning that it was heading straight for me. After 10 minutes or so the light changed to green and passed *Pegasus* a

Night shift on the North Sea

good way off ahead following a north-west course. Just as that scenario had unravelled I made a further assessment of two other sets of lights as both had changed their aspect; a reappraisal of their course did not in any way resemble my initial assessment. During all of this I darted up and down to the navigation station to see what it all looked like on the radar screen. Well actually, it looked like a walk in the park as there was nothing to be seen. 'Strike four, not three for Raymarine', I thought. First it had been the wind speed, second and with calamitous effect the autopilot and now the radar and, oh yes, also the cockpit plotter. 'Welcome to the blind, hand-steering, don't-know-how-much-wind-there-is Raymarine Panto!'

This was the first night out from Lerwick and it was hard work. Gone was the easy-go-lucky relaxed demeanour of the early evening. I had just enjoyed six days of sleeping and recovery after the tension and trials of the first part of the trip and I was now starting to stress with my current situation. What would I have been like if this had been at the end of four or five days at sea, short on sleep and with nerves frayed? If I had sailed on round Muckle Flugga with no autopilot, then on down the east coast of Shetland, out beyond Fair Isle and into this 'merchant shipping soup', could I have coped with all it was throwing at me? Maybe, maybe not. I knew the situation before me with all these navigation lights needed clear, rational thought and interpretation. If I had sailed on with no autopilot and been forced to hand steer, hove to for sleep and then hand steer again for hours on end I would have done myself some damage. This was the only point during the trip when I knew for certain that the decision to quit the non-stop attempt had been absolutely right.

On returning to the deck I took a quick headcount of my night-time company. It was 03.00 hours in the morning and pitch black; I was sailing single-handed in the North Sea and had five sets of lights circling me, not the average day in the life of a desk-bound commuter. I took another belt of strong coffee and a large lump of fruitcake and continued to monitor the situation. Two lights passed into what I saw as a safety zone, i.e. I could see their white stern lights so they were steaming away. One set of red lights over to starboard and to the west was maintaining a constant bearing that held for over 20 minutes. I rechecked again and again with my hand-bearing compass. The bearing was not changing, which meant that we were on a collision course. 'OK son, what is the decision here?' I asked myself. I went through the options and closed in on two courses of action. The first was to heave to and stop the boat in her tracks. I could slam *Pegasus* into a tack and hold her Genoa aback; free off the mainsail to the point of balance and she would hold a position with slight drift off to the east, or I could put in a tack and head over to the north-west and ensure I was in control of my position with the approaching hulk. I had to make my intentions clear to the ship, that is, if they had even spotted me yet. I decided to stick in a tack. I was heading south on a southwesterly, I was not the stand-on vessel so the rules of the road meant that I should give way. Anyway 'might has right'. It is nonsense to believe that power will give way to sail in these conditions so I was going to tack, show my port side to him and we would pass port to port, my red light to his red light – text book stuff.

The lights on the approaching ship were now crystal clear. The red port light was distinct and bright, as were the two small white lights above the red indicating she was a ship under motor and over 50 metres in length. The clutter of lights of the ship's bridge was now clear to the naked eye and she was a big one! I took my search torch lantern and lit up the white sails which dazzled me with the bright reflection. I was hoping I had woken up the watch on the bridge of the brute that was creaming its way in my direction. Sweeping the light across the foredeck to ensure all ropes and sheets were clear to tack, I doused the light and threw the wheel over and slipped the Genoa sheet. On the port tack I was now heading north-west. More importantly the green light that I had been showing to the ship was now the red of my port side and we would now pass red to red, port to port. I held the course and watched the black visitor pulse on by. When she had passed me I swung *Pegasus* back onto the starboard tack and returned to a southerly course. The white stern light of the tanker was lost in the haze of bright domestic lights around the huge deckhouse and bridge; we were about 3 miles apart and that was way too close. I congratulated myself over the decision-making process and execution of the whole event. I was back on course, not panicked by the encounter and in control. Would it have been so if I was at the end of my fifth day at sea; how would I have managed the situation? To avoid the mental conflict I decided that if I had not been holed up in Lerwick for six days I would not have been here right now, so I would not have met her. The sails were retrimmed for the resumed course and I sat down at the wheel for a session of steering and concentration on what was coming our way, not what might have been. It was the here and now that needed all hands.

No sooner had I settled to the wheel than a thumper of a sore head kicked in. Was it too much coffee, or tension as a result of the last hours or was it lack of sleep starting to lodge a protest with management? I did not have time to worry too much about the headache as directly ahead was a cluster of very bright lights. These were not navigation lights and it was not long before I could make out that it was a fishing boat with working deck lights. The fishing boat proceeded to put on a performance of boat ballet as she swerved and turned to chase whatever shoal of fish she had fixed on with her electronic fish-finder. The lights turned again and headed away from *Pegasus*; I was relieved and very glad to see the back of her. I went below to get myself another cappuccino 'coffee hit' along with an obligatory wedge of cake. On returning to the wheel, I was horrified to see that although the bright stern working lights were gone, for the second time on the trip I was confronted with red and green navigation lights staring straight at me. They remained constant for about 10 minutes and then just as I was getting nervy the fishing boat suddenly changed course, veered away and took up a course out of harm's way. The boat accelerated and was soon behind me and showing her back end of bright working lights. She continued this course and before long she too was out of my life for good.

The rest of the night passed without any excitement. Now it was just all about getting some miles under the keel and being further south. The morning light came in from across the open North Sea; the sky was clear and it was going to be a good day which was offering a southwesterly wind over what was still a fairly flat sea. It all looked good for a day where we could hit 180 miles or more and bring Blyth even closer.

Breakfast was full on, big, fried and not really all that healthy. Sausage, eggs, tomatoes and bacon, all cooked in and served from one pot. The North Sea fry went down and was followed by two marmalade rolls and three mugs of tea. What a wonderful life it can be – a sunny 06.00 a.m. breakfast, trucking south with 360-degree sea all around me; nothing but sea, sky, wind and a straight line course to 'destination Blyth'. Wow, what a start to the day! Last night was done and dusted. We had made it and I had a big bright blue day ahead of me. Two shipping areas remained ahead of us, Aberdeen and the Firth of Forth.

Day 16

Thursday 28th. 06.00 hrs - 62 miles east of John o' Groats

784 nm run - 214 nm to Blyth

6 hr run - 33 nm - average speed 5.5 knots

24 hr run - 0 nm - average speed 0.0 knots

Sleep in last 24 hrs: 2 hr 15 min

A new approach to one-pot cooking!

Away over to the east the shape of an oil rig appeared. It was far enough over to the left not to need a course alteration. The shape grew in size, along with the now discernible shape of a support vessel hovering near the massive superstructure. I passed a good 6 or 7 miles to the west of the obstruction but no sooner had it reduced in size behind me than another shape formed on the horizon bang on my heading. The second oil rig was making no attempt to hide itself and was sporting a bright orange flare shooting out from one side. I hardened up my course to windward and changed course a good 20 degrees to swing round to the west of the obstacle. It was not moving unlike my pals of last night and at current boat speed it was over an hour off. I set my alarm for 30 minutes and lay down in the cockpit for a nap. I fell asleep very easily and the alarm came about in what seemed to be no time at all. I was either tiring or getting comfortable with my ability to nap aboard. The oil rig was now safely over to the left and I was happy with circumstances and our respective positions. The day was hotting up. I took a few snaps of the rig and carried on with a morning of napping, cups of tea and tweaking the sails. Away over to the right and out of sight was mainland Scotland and the north-east coast.

The wind was constant, behind the spreaders and at right angles to us, so the option of flying the spinnaker was definitely there. I monitored the wind for a further 15 minutes and then decided to hoist. The spinnaker was stored in the forecabin and easily hauled up onto deck through the hatch. The big sail was prepared and ready for action. It had been carefully packed in its sail bag before the start of the voyage for such an occasion and it was now needed to do its stuff. I laid it out on the deck to make sure there were no knots or crossovers that would cause mischief during the hoist. All running rigging was in place and it took no time at all to get ready. I pulled on the halyard and soon had the long sausage-shaped bag of nylon that holds the sail hoisted the full 16-metre height of the mast. To open the sail out from the sausage snuffer, a position is taken at the foot of

the mast. A continuous cord that leads up the outside of the snuffer to the head and back down inside the bag to the deck acts almost like a rip cord for the sail. Heaving the up-haul line, the protective sock is dragged higher and higher and the sail fans out, now unrestricted by the snuffer sock. I pulled on the rope and, with a satisfying rustle of fresh dry nylon, the sail opened out and filled. *Pegasus* responded immediately by lifting her skirts and set off a good knot and half faster. After securing the cord to the chrome bars at the mast, I went aft and attended to the control ropes and soon had the spinnaker set just off that optimum position where the luff edge curls. I had no grumpy Hugh Scott aboard to throw the sheet lines to, so it was all down to me.

For the following two hours the big sky-blue and green-coloured spinnaker pulled and pulled *Pegasus* south. I maintained a watch over the stern and over to the north-west just to make sure no wind squall was going to catch me unawares. It was not relaxing sailing. 'Don't stuff up now', a voice kept reminding me. A big foul-up and the spinnaker wrapped round the mast would not be a good thing to do right now.

Confident that the sail was pulling well and all was settled, I called in my numbers on the sat-phone. The check-in was a light-hearted affair and we dallied a tad too long on the very expensive gold-bar-a-minute sat-phone. Fiona's forecast relayed by Gordon indicated that

Asymmetric spinnaker pulls Pegasus *south in a splash of colour*

the wind was to increase in the afternoon and overnight. We sailed on for another hour with 'percentage sailing' very much at the front of my mind, especially now that I was on the home leg and making good time to Blyth. Away behind me I could see clouds filling in and there were darker streaks of water indicating that wind and change were on the way. The decision was easy – the spinnaker had to come down and come down now. I went forward and prepared to drop the big sail. Standing on the foredeck, I realised that I had kept the sail up too long and it was now pulling hard. The rustles shooting over the surface of the

Day 16

Thursday 28th, 12.00 hrs – 38 miles north-east of Kinnaird Head

819 nm run – 179 nm to Blyth

6 hr run – 35 nm – average speed 5.8 knots

24 hr run – 131 nm – average speed 5.5 knots

Sleep in last 24 hrs: 3 hr 00 min

sail-cloth intensified as the wind piped up. It was clear that there was mounting pressure on the sail. Boat speed was just great but we were now in a danger zone. It was a state of affairs I did not like as the massive spinnaker is a handful when fully crewed. On my own I knew I was in for a bit of a wrestle. I nipped back to the cockpit and set a new course more downwind with the wind directly behind. The spinnaker was immediately depowered behind the mainsail so I set about the drop, having rehearsed in my mind specific moves and a sequence of events. The drop was completed without any real panic or struggle thanks to the snuffer and all the moves going to plan. I soon had the whole sail lowered and safely on the deck. The arrangement for the asymmetric spinnaker on *Pegasus* was another Owen Sails solution, nothing earth shatteringly innovative but, most important of all, the system worked like clockwork. With the sail now snuffed into its long sock, I elected to pack the sail away carefully into its sail bag. I knew then this was the first and last drop of this sail before the end of the trip and was surprised how I was thinking, for the first time, about the end of the trip, even though I still had over 24 hours to run to Blyth. The wind picked up quickly and soon *Pegasus* was surging south with a building wind from the north-west. The sail drop was exactly the right decision.

Now back under two white sails, the level of stress aboard immediately dropped and we settled down to a fresh evening breeze. I was feeling perky so pulled out the movie camera and wandered around the deck looking for an interesting angle. The sea was not exciting enough to film so I decided to get an aerial shot. With the camera in my pocket I scrambled up onto the boom and stood some 6 feet off the deck looking down on my domain. I cast a shadow over the deck and over the sprayhood. So I filmed the black man of *Pegasus* and made a childish running commentary that when replayed gave a clear indication of my state of mind. I was skittish and silly to the camera, hanging on with one hand to the mast, standing on one foot and waving the other one to capture the waving foot shadow on the deck. It was plain daft. A slip and I would be prostrate on the deck and feeling stupid if not rather sore. I clambered down and settled back in the cockpit, bored and looking for something to do. Over to the east a supply ship for the rigs moved northwards and was far enough away not to cause me any real worry. Almost in defiance of the North Sea I went down below and I pulled out the set of road route maps for the cycle from Blyth to Kirkcudbright. 'My, I am getting pretty cocky', I thought, 'looking out the road maps with an overnight sail still to do'. It was now clear to me that I just had to keep my nose clean tonight and it would be Blyth by midday tomorrow. I called Shona on the sat-phone and we spoke for a few minutes. She needed to know roughly what my arrival time would be in order to pack the car and get herself down from Blairgowrie to Blyth. She also needed to alert Nick at OYTS to call up the crew who were sailing *Pegasus* back to home waters and Dunstaffnage marina near Oban. I also called Linda Lane-Thornton, my contact at Blyth, to give her a rough idea of my ETA. The little session of logistics management was comforting on a number of fronts. I was nearly there, the trip was now looking eminently doable but, most of all, it was conversation with others.

I ate a big evening meal as I thought it was going to be a long cold night. A pot of chicken and pasta was followed by ginger cake and custard, all washed down with strong coffee. Clouds had filled in and it was to be a dark night. Tonight I would be crossing the open sea east of the Forth estuary and that meant more merchant shipping, and it would be pitch dark. I had not seen a trace of the Scottish coast since Fair Isle disappeared astern so long ago and I felt a bit cheated that I had not been able to track my progress against landmarks or lights. The evening wore on without any excitement or bother. We were on a fairly relaxed reach south and speed was good.

It was at 22.50 hours when I had my first encounter with the merchant shipping that plies its trade to Leith or perhaps the Hound Point oil terminal that sits not far from the Forth Rail Bridge. Steaming from the south-west, a silent dark shape moved swiftly across my bow, a good 5–6 miles away heading to the North Sea. I shrank inside as I knew I was in for another night of Russian roulette with our merchant shipping mates. I had not researched the shipping levels of this piece of water and, to be honest, the area was a bit of a black hole in my passage plan. I had neither thought nor worried too much about it and was annoyed that I had overlooked this element in my passage planning regime. I had my course and my bail-out option of the Forth to Granton or Port Edgar noted but one key aspect was shipping levels. To cheer myself up I thought that it could

Day 16

Thursday 28th, 18.00 hrs - 35 miles due east of Aberdeen

859 nm run. - 139 nm to Blyth

6 hr run - 40 nm - average speed 6.7 knots

24 hr run - 141 nm - average speed 5.9 knots

Sleep in last 24 hrs: 4 hr 15 min

The author waves to his 'crew' from atop the boom

not be worse than the 'Pentland experience'. I had not banked on a night of ship watching but it was exactly that. During the night three ships caused me real concern. Each one was moving west to east but more of a concern was that, as I covered ground southwards, I seemed to be more and more on the same course as my nocturnal visitors. One monster passed behind me, too close for comfort but not at a distance that constituted danger or required evasive action. The Pentland Firth had offered up a spaghetti junction of shipping but down here these big monsters adopted a more consistent track.

One success of the North Sea leg was my jury-rig for the boom. Having tied a sound rope to the rear end of the boom, I had led the line across the cockpit and secured it to the main starboard winch. With this arrangement in place, I could put a few turns on the winch and the taut line took some of the load at the back end of the boom. The rig was sound as a pound in my view, and at no time did the boom cause me any real worry, but by no stretch of the imagination would I have liked to beat a long course into the teeth of a strong wind. The boom had a definite lean to the left!

Going below to record the statistics for the log and the midnight check-in did not give any relief from the cold as once down below and with gloves off the backs of my hands were numb and I found it difficult to write. My head felt as if it was going to explode as I rubbed, clawed and scratched at it. I had put on my balaclava to keep my head warm but the fleece material was driving me to despair. I was at the very bottom; even the long haul to Stromness was not as bad as this. I went back on deck for air.

Pegasus was slipping on at 7.0 knots, her white stern light shining brightly onto the white foam of the wake. I stood facing aft with arms hung up and round the twin back stays and watched in a hypnotic trance as water bubbled and turned as it rolled out from under *Pegasus* then disappeared off into the dark night behind us. I could not believe that someone could design a boat that would have its stern sit absolutely on the water surface, not just under or just above but just right on the surface. My mind drifted back to my first ever night sail on a yacht. Cousin Ian had asked if I wanted to help deliver a boat from

Day 16

Thursday 28th, 24.00 hrs - 40 miles due east of Dundee

894 nm run - 104 nm to Blyth

6 hr run - 35 nm - average speed 5.8 knots

24 hr run - 143 nm - average speed 6.0 knots

Sleep in last 24 hrs: 5 hr 30 min

Banff down to Dundee and I jumped at the chance. I was an inland loch sailor and the thought of a passage sail down the east coast was too good to resist. We assembled in Banff and aboard Ali Summers' Ruffian 26 (he of throwing the sheets at Hugh some years later). A crew of four settled into a great evening sail and then it got dark. I must admit to being less than comfortable at the prospect of sailing at night as I did not have an idea about navigation or the positioning of navigation lights. The highlight of the sail was thrashing headlong into the pitch dark with the spinnaker hoisted and white water rushing all around us. What an experience and one that stuck with me! The low point of that trip was just how long it took us to get past Aberdeen. I went to my bed for a kip with Aberdeen visible at a bearing of about 2 o'clock. I slept for an age and when given a knock to come back on deck for my watch, Aberdeen was no more than at 4 o'clock. It clearly did not put me off!

The night of 28th/29th April was bitterly raw. In fact it was miserable and had me chilled to the core and shaking with cold and fatigue. I lost my inner heat and resilience early on in the night and never managed to heat myself up again. Sleep that night was also miserable, fitful and draining. I was not at ease so the 15-minute naps down below were not topping me up in any way. If anything, they added to the stress and when down below I was worrying about another fast-approaching tanker bearing down on me from behind, both of us on much the same course. I elected to sit up in the cockpit and spent the agonising time between 03.00 hours and 06.00 hours slipping off into fitful shivery sleeps. To fight this hell I threw down more coffee and cake. My hat itched my scalp, the soft skin under my chin was wet and irritated by the jacket collar zip and my stubble was scratchy. I had drunk too much coffee and I had the buzzes that were adding to my jitters and shakes and, to prove the diuretic properties of coffee, I passed what felt like gallons over the side. The first few had been done over the stern of the boat but I recognised that I was toiling and for safety's sake all others were made down below at the heads.

The night wore away and light came in for my last day at sea. Morning light brought some warmth and the relief of being able to take off some of the layers and get some fresh cool air around my frazzled head.

9

THE FINAL REEF

Day 17

Saturday 29th, 06.00 hrs -
50 miles east of the Forth Estuary

928 nm run - 70 nm to Blyth

64 hr run - 144 nm - average
speed 6.0 knots

24 hr run - 144 nm - average
speed 6.0 knots

Sleep in last 24 hrs: 5 hr 45 min

Morning of the last day at sea

The morning of what would be our last day at sea filled in; it was bright and the wind was strengthening by the minute. Glancing astern I could see more and more white tops breaking in the dark squalls that were now scudding across the surface. Gusts were now pressing *Pegasus* hard and the helm was becoming more and more of a handful to keep on course. I had the full main and a full Genoa set and it was time to take in sail and return a sense of balance between boat and elements. The Genoa was reefed away to about 50% and I sat back to see what difference that would make. *Pegasus* settled to her new sail plan but I knew that it would not be long before the main and the now reduced Genoa would be out of balance and a heavy and awkward helm would return. The early morning sail became frantic, with me wrestling the wheel as the power of the sails threatened to have their way rather than obey the wheel and heavily-pressurised rudder. The water behind was getting darker and darker as clouds started to fill in and squalls chased after us. It was all getting quite hairy and tension was high. The first broach overpowered us and *Pegasus* started to screw up to wind and, with the cavitating rudder now having lost its bite, she rounded up further; with all equilibrium now surrendered to the wind, she lay over on her side. Water breached her side decks and she lay floundering. Both sails flogged violently and then, slowly and predictably, she came upright and the sails filled again and off we went careering down the waves. I cursed myself for not having had a reef in the main before this wind had struck. It was a basic that I had applied on all trips. Perhaps it was the fact that Blyth lay within reach that I had lost concentration and missed the opportunity to reduce sail. The notion of rounding the boat to the now 25 knot plus wind was daunting. I was tired and had started to think about Blyth too much and not the job in hand.

Wham, a second broach put *Pegasus* on her side and all hell broke loose again with the sails flogging and flailing as she sat there helpless to the imbalanced forces that had overtaken my wit and the power of the rudder. A broach in a yacht is when the force of the wind on available canvas simply overpowers the steering capacity of the boat. The pressure builds until the direction of the boat is dictated by the wind. Even with full lock on the wheel the power in the sails is too much for the rudder to cope with. Equilibrium between sail, hull and rudder is lost, the rudder loses its grip on the water, it cavitates and the power of the wind takes total control. With no bite or grip of the water, the rudder is useless and a yacht will turn to windward and, in the process, load the sails even more. At that point the boat is pressed over and laid flat on her side. With the sails laid flat to the wind, the pressure is reduced and a yacht will sit back upright. The sails now presented to the wind load up and off you go again, the cycle repeated until the wind drops or sail area is reduced.

Again, the sail filled with an alarming crack and off we roasted down wind and wave. We touched speeds of over 10 knots for spells and rounded up again and again, each time losing speed down to less than 5 knots. It was a wrestling match between boat, sail, rudder and helmsman and one that a submission from us and not the elements was the more likely. I took a look back astern and could see that the water was getting angrier and that a reef in the main was the only real option, either that or I would break something. We broached again and *Pegasus* complained to me as she lay prone in the water, sails flogging and flailing with attached ropes cracking and banging on the decks. She had had enough of this and was now demanding some respect. She deserved better than this.

I set about preparing for a reef and made good all the lines. The halyard was laid out on the cockpit floor to run easily when asked to let the mainsail down the mast. The reefing lines were hand-pulled as far as possible and the mainsheet and vang were let go to loosen the mainsail. At that moment we broached yet again and, like before, *Pegasus* surrendered to the forces of nature. She lay on her side and the sails flogged as before but with one major difference. The rope rigged to hold the sail to the mast shook free in the commotion and the sail pulled away from the mast. *Pegasus* came upright again and the loading built on the mainsail. Bang!, went the second car and the sail took on a horrible crease line from the back of the boom to a quarter of the way up the mast. I had to get the sail down before the strain on the remaining cars was too much and I lost the mainsail. I rounded *Pegasus* to the wind and popped on the autopilot to hold her off the wind. With the boom run out on a free sheet the sail now flapped in line with the wind. The pressure was off the sail, thank God. The Genoa remained powered up, offering enough drive to keep her on course. The main halyard was released and the main crumpled on the mast. I had a horrible replay evolving right in front of me, just as it had been away off Rona; I had now to snuff a flogging and broken sail to a bent and surrendered boom. There was no time to hang around and think about the meaning of life as every flog of the sail threatened to break the remaining cars and render the sail totally useless. I was quickly to the mast, not clipped on and not really caring. My absolute priority was to snuff the sail down and minimise the damage. In an absolute rage I set about making the sail safe and soon had a rope spiralled around the boom and sail. The noise of flogging cloth subsided and I had *Pegasus* back under control. With that job done I returned to the wheel and set *Pegasus* back to her course on Blyth. I cursed myself for not having put a reef in the mainsail in time to save the damage; we were limping home now.

Down to the last sail after the mainsail is dropped

The injured soldier that she was did well and immediately settled into a sort of rolling run with the sea and to my delight held a speed of just over 6.5 knots. The fact that I was now down to my last sail and that the last few hours had sapped me meant that I was at my lowest point of the whole trip. Panic flashed through me that if there was a sudden drop in the wind or, God forbid, it was to come out of the south I would not be able to reach Blyth under headsail alone. The conspiracy theories ran wild and I sat slumped in the cockpit, physically and mentally shattered. I went down below and had a can of cold Coke and guzzled half a pack of Jaffa cakes, both of which helped morale. A few minutes of self-pity passed and I gathered my thoughts. It was unlikely that the wind would shift 180 degrees and that it would drop to nothing, so I would get to Blyth. It would just not be as soon as I would have hoped, and not in the style that I would have wished for. I was still in one piece, even if the boat was not. The boat was not needed for the next leg; I was needed and I was needed in good order to pedal with conviction the 160 miles back to Kirkcudbright. I was on my way to Blyth and nothing was going to stop me getting there. I nipped back down below and selected *Queen's Greatest Hits* and *We Are the Champions* was let rip at full volume from the speakers; two fingers to such defeatist thoughts – they had absolutely no place on *Pegasus*. I roared an off-key accompaniment to that great classic track that was set at such a volume that the speakers vibrated and buzzed in protest.

Anticipation builds as the coast of England appears

That was it, this was likely to be my last check-in from sea. The numbers were read and noted and I joked with Gordon that he could stuff the weather forecast where the sun does not shine. We chatted for a few minutes and I told him I could see Blyth in the distance. We had some more idle banter and Gordon wished me luck and apologised again that he could not be at Blyth to help me in. We sailed on under Genoa and all was well; it was warm, I was happy and all was good with life. Blyth was now in clear view, the towers, chimneys and cooling towers in stark contrast to the last shoreline I had seen, the beautiful cliffs of Noss and Bressay. What a difference, a complete geographical and cultural schism if ever there was one! 'My goodness', I thought, 'I have just sailed around Scotland and, besides my time in Stromness and Lerwick, I had hardly seen anything of Scotland'. My course had taken me away from shore and, of the 1000-mile passage, this last slice of shoreline was part of the mere 80 miles or so that had been visible during the whole trip. Blyth dragged closer and closer and soon it would be time to stable the horse. The last couple of hours went really slowly as we lolled and slapped around in the waves and the now-reducing afternoon breeze. The CD player had been put into play and there was a veritable celebration of classic tracks booming out from *Peggy*.

Making it all worthwhile

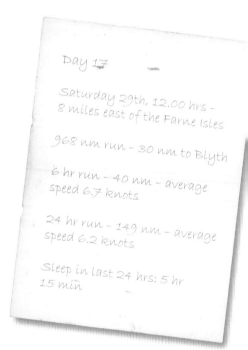

Day 17

Saturday 29th, 12.00 hrs –
8 miles east of the Farne Isles

968 nm run – 30 nm to Blyth

6 hr run – 40 nm – average
speed 6.7 knots

24 hr run – 149 nm – average
speed 6.2 knots

Sleep in last 24 hrs: 5 hr
15 min

10

BLYTH AND BUST

Day 17

Thursday 29th, 16.42 hrs – Blyth fairway
buoy

998 nm run – 0 nm to Blyth

4 hr 45 min run – 30 nm – average speed
6.3 knots

22 hr 45 min run – 139 nm – average
speed 6.1 knots

Sleep in last 24 hrs: 4 hr 00 min

Having taken a very conservative course keeping well off the low-lying Seaton Sea Rocks that jut out from Blyth, I rounded the fairway buoy marking the channel into the port of Blyth. That was it, 'trip over', as they say. The Genoa folded as we turned into the wind and, with all propulsion removed, we wallowed in the swell. I took one more glance over the fairway buoy and over to the shore and I was sure I was now north of the buoy and therefore, job done. My watch said 16.42 hours. I started the engine, engaged the throttle and rolled away the headsail. 'Wow that was it, really it', I thought. We motored up the main channel into the port of Blyth. Over to my right was the long harbour breakwater wall of the East Pier. It was lined with big wind turbines, each one arcing round and round in the late afternoon breeze. On the left was the Outer West Pier, the long finger of stone I had surveyed when down checking the place out all those weeks ago. I knew exactly where I was heading, sharp left at the end of Inner West Pier, double back on myself and into the South Harbour and on into the marina. The marina berths were tucked in the far corner and I was looking forward to getting tied up and getting some rest and sleep, but I had to get *Pegasus* alongside before I could relax.

The original plan had been to arrive at Blyth and have Erik and Gordon come out in a Royal Northumberland Yacht Club dinghy and help take *Pegasus* to the pontoons. I was about eight days late and neither guys could be there because of work commitments. RNYC had proved to be a little difficult to liaise with prior to the challenge due to a distinct lack of communication and, had it not been for their secretary Linda Lane-Thornton, it would have been a pretty miserable, lonely landing. With Erik and Gordon off the scene, Linda was my only point of contact on the shore. I hoped she was wearing a pink carnation. I

Almost there, Blyth marina our final goal

rounded the main harbour head and scoured the pontoons ahead of me for any sign of movement and assistance. There she was with her husband waving me in from the end of the pontoons. The berth I was expecting had been taken so she was pointing me round and into the heart of the marina. Over to my right a large merchant ship was slipping lines and getting ready to set off. Massive whirlpools of water shot out from her as her bow thrusters started to turn her in her own length. These huge monsters were still chasing me right up to the very end!

Waved on past the outer pontoon, I turned sharp right along the back end of fingers and sterns of berthed boats. 'Away in there, you must be joking', I thought to myself. Linda was pointing me to a berth that had a short finger, was tucked in at the end of the horseshoe of pontoons and, yes, had an off-berth breeze thrown in for good measure. I was not about to replay the mismanaged attempt to bring *Pegasus* alongside that I had served up at Stromness; this time there would be no mistake. My mouth was dry as I went for it and 'slotted' *Pegasus* in the berth and, more importantly, did not biff her bow at the top end of the pontoon. I did have a wee smile to myself as I sped towards the berth, an approach at speed that was being observed with saucer-shaped eyes by Linda, clearly alarmed at my technique. With astern slammed on, *Pegasus* came to an abrupt stop, I stepped forward from the wheel, tossed my lines to the eager hands on the pontoons and we were made fast. After a few minutes of adjusting the warps, *Pegasus* was still; she had reached the end of her voyage around Scotland. I switched off the engine and all was quiet.

A little ripple of applause broke out from the very relieved onlookers of which there were about half a dozen who had sprung up from nowhere. Before jumping down onto the pontoon to thank my little welcoming party, I went down below under the pretence of something I needed to attend to in the cabin. Once down below I took a few seconds to myself, clenched my fists and had a big inward shout to myself – 'Yes, done it! I have just got *Pegasus* and myself safely around Scotland and here I am in Blyth'. I was elated. All the chart work, passage planning course checks, navigation checks and tidal checks had worked and seen me safely to my destination. Hours and hours over charts on the dining room table through the winter had delivered *Pegasus* and me to Blyth. I did a little jig, had a look around the cabin, wiped the huge grin from my face and went back up into the bright evening sunlight to share what was an intensely personal moment with the strangers on the pontoon.

I jumped down from the side deck and shook the hands of the people that had gathered. I was, however,

Skipper pauses before stepping ashore

missing known faces. I was missing family and friends, the people with whom I wanted to share the moment. The helpful and kind 'unknowns' soon wandered off and after there had been a quick tour of *Pegasus* for the remaining inquisitive ones I was on my own again. I wondered what to do next. I called home to let Shona know all was well and then called my Mum to report in. Both were relieved to hear I was in Blyth, safe and sound. After 20 minutes or so Linda returned and asked if I wanted to come for a drink or check e-mails or whatever. I opted for a cup of tea back at her house and a quick bash on the computer to e-mail the news to all that I was back on dry land. After that task was done I was given a lift back to the boat – good people the Lane-Thorntons. I knew that RNYC was not in a position to let me off with the berthing fees for an extended handover period, but I must admit to being more than a little disappointed that even my one overnight stay was not going to attract any charity from the club. On hearing that a bill was to be presented to me, Linda was not having that for one moment and made a commitment to cover the cost herself. As I say, good people the Lane-Thorntons.

Back on board I gathered my thoughts and drank a can of beer but most of all I needed a shower to wash away the North Sea. I gathered my shower kit and wandered up to the club to have a good soak. Now, Royal Blyth's clubhouse is not your average clubhouse. It is, in fact, a clubship, the HY *Tyne* which stands the club in very good stead, but not being a square building, it has some features that I was about to become intimately aware of. I found my way to the shower room, stripped off and stood under the shower and, for the third time, tasted the salt on my lips, not quite as strong as it had been in Stromness and Lerwick, it was North Sea salt this time, but it was a good feeling. After a long soak, long enough to have prune-like fingers, I dried, and went to have a shave and in the process nearly did myself in. In a sort of semi-daze, being very tired and with the slight wooziness induced from the can of beer injected into the blood system, I misjudged the height of a low roof beam and, wallop, collided with solid oak. I hit the floor and felt a splitting pain across my forehead. I got up from the floor and sat down on a plastic chair by the door. I thought this must be a visitor recovery chair and wondered how many strangers had sat here holding their head. I made my way back to *Pegasus* and after a few phone calls set about refuelling, knowing that I had to stoke the boiler with carbohydrates for the next day. Oh yes, the next day; I had the little matter of cycling across the country, so I kept eating. Pasta and rice puddings disappeared down the hatch, along with cake and coffee, a further can of beer and biscuits and crisps. Undaunted by the onsetting alcoholic fug, I made for the club as social company was now needed.

On entering the bar, it was like the clichéd scene from a spaghetti western. Stranger walks through the door, locals stop, turn, and all goes quiet. I nodded uncomfortably to the room, made for the haven of the first bar stool and ordered a pint. Once through the first gulp, a chap next to me broke the silence, congratulated me on my trip and the next couple of hours were an absolute hoot and a laugh. The group standing at the bar was the crew of a visiting yacht. Here was I with 50 feet to myself and they had seven or eight of them in a 35-footer. They were game all right and good company. After the third pint and a bellyful of laughs, I knew the needle was at 'full' so I made my excuses and slipped away back to *Pegasus*. In a hazy mist I passed out into a deep and peaceful sleep.

Job done, Blyth marina

The next morning was again lovely and a day to do some biking. The only problem was that my knee was again giving me gyp; a dull throb, almost like toothache and it worried me. To help ease me into the day I threw down a couple of Ibuprofen and had a brew. The forecast indicated that it was to be a good calm day and evening. Shona was due down early afternoon and the lads from OYTS were expected mid-morning to get ready to take *Pegasus* back to Oban. The biggest surprise of the day so far was that I did not have the slightest nip in the head after the excesses of the previous night. No axe injury this morning! After breakfast of porridge, eggy bread, bananas and cake I set about doing some tidying and getting ready. Then it was time to cut the bike free from its lashings in the forward cabin. The frame and wheels were carefully taken up on deck and then handed down onto the pontoon. There it was reassembled and made ready to go. The bike felt foreign to me and I worried about the day's pedalling that lay ahead as I was not feeling great. I was edgy, lethargic and just not at all comfortable so I lay down in the saloon and dozed for an hour. It was a very strange feeling that had come over me. I hauled myself out from under my sleeping bag and went to the heads to brush my teeth and splash my face with water. What a sight greeted me! My face was swollen and my lower eyelids and top lip were puffy. I looked a right sight. I wondered what on earth was going on here and decided to go and lie on the saloon couch for another 30 minutes. A knock on the side of the boat announced Andy, the first of the OYTS crew. I recall Andy taking a second look at me as I met him in the cockpit; I was not looking my best. It was only after the trip that it became apparent I had developed an allergy to Ibuprofen, which persists to this day. I had been stoking too many down the hatch during the build-up to the trip and en route. My knee told me it needed them but in the long run my intake of these painkillers had been too high. The other crew members arrived one by one over the next hour and helped to get things in order. A couple of hours swept by and just after midday Shona arrived at the marina and we met with a long, squeezing tight hug and a tear.

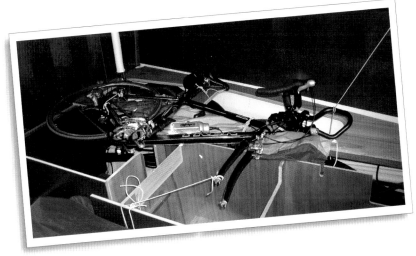

Next mode of transport lies ready for the road

The afternoon took care of itself with final handover issues with the now fully-assembled OYTS crew, whilst I ate and drank. I was embarrassed by the general state of repair of *Pegasus*. The guys were facing a trip in a crippled boat, not quite what the advert claimed when the offer to sail a spanking big 50-foot Beneteau back to Scotland was first circulated by Nick. We had managed to sort two of the mainsail cars, but there was nothing we could do about the boom; they would just have to take it easy. I was very grateful that all the hassle and issues surrounding getting the boat back to Oban, a not inconsiderable voyage, had been wiped off my plate. Their plan was to head back up the east coast, stopping at Montrose and from there on to Inverness and through the Caledonian Canal to Fort William. From there on to Dunstaffnage it would be familiar waters for *Pegasus*. When I returned to her a couple of weeks later, she was like a new pin, with decks and saloon gleaming, running rigging bundled and coiled like a showboat and not a single drop of beer or whisky left aboard! They deserved every single last drop.

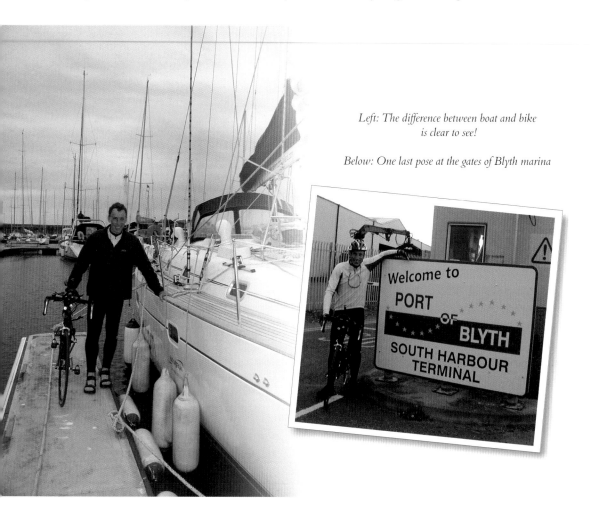

Left: The difference between boat and bike is clear to see!

Below: One last pose at the gates of Blyth marina

Come five o'clock and it was time to go. Mocking a sailing celebrity, I kissed the side deck on *Pegasus* and walked on down the pontoon with cycling shoes in one hand and pushing a bike with the other. I headed on up the walkway to the main pier and on to the car park. It was time to switch from boater to biker. By the time I reached the end of the walkway I was a cyclist and in a clichéd scene of the TV show *Stars in Their Eyes*. Standing there, Robin Knox-Johnston utters, 'Tonight Matthew, I am going to be Lance Armstrong,' and I step through the dry ice smoked doorway into the spotlight and start pedalling. It felt so bizarre that I was about to leave *Pegasus* and her charts, winds, tides and waves and enter the realm of tarmac, pedals and Ordnance Survey maps. My heart was beating fast and I had butterflies in my stomach. Shona had the boot of the car open and I sat on the back ledge and took off the deck shoes and squeezed into the cycling shoes. I still did not feel all that great and had a horrible tangy taste in my mouth, almost like I was chewing silver paper. Stripping off the extra layers of clothing, I swung my leg over the saddle and prepared to do the job that was next in line. I pushed off and clipped into the pedals and coasted on out of the marina area and headed for the main port gates. The gateman politely lifted the barrier and I nodded as I passed his booth. I wondered if he had the slightest notion of what was in my mind and what I was about to take on. Having posed for Shona to take a photo at the gates, I turned to the road end and crossed the main road at the entrance to the harbour. I was on my way. What pain would this bring? I wondered if I would have the staying power to cycle three times further than I had ever cycled before, after 1000 miles and 16 days on board *Pegasus*. I coasted through Blyth town centre and was soon on my way to Cramlington and looking out for signs to Morpeth. Shona was in the car and she passed me with a wave, the first of many times she would slip past keeping a watchful eye on progress. My eyes were still puffy; I could see the bags on my lower eyelids as I looked down to the road below my wheels. I told myself that I was feeling fine and it was time that I just got on with things.

After an hour I had settled into a good rhythm and felt very comfortable cycling along the suburban roads. I sped down the steep hill on the A192 into Morpeth and then took the rise on a sharp turn to the right. All the landmarks were as I had committed to memory and all was looking good. The road took me over the A1 and, once on the west side of the main north and south artery, I really felt as if I was on my way. The urban sprawl of Blyth, Bedlington and Morpeth were behind me and it was onwards to the west and open countryside. The evening wore on and we made good progress and, in what seemed a short time, I was through Whalton and navigating the lanes of the B6308 heading directly south until Stamfordham. I needed to make sure I hooked a right in this village or I would be off back east, in sailing terms a massive header off course. I was through the village, took a right and then on down the hill to the reservoir and turning right onto the long B6318 that would be my friend and enemy for the next few hours. The last 25 miles had been a case of cycling not the most direct route but, in my mind, the safest route, safest in terms of navigation. On studying the map of the area I knew there was a myriad of back lanes and sneaky roads that could have shaved off distance, potentially a huge bonus, but at what cost? I would have been continually turning and spotting little lanes, each with varying levels of signage and surface condition. Taking the selected route was slightly further but one that would not have me going round in circles and concentrating on navigation rather than body position, form and relaxed cycling. I slipped down the hill from Stamfordham through the zig-zagging course of the road. It was a peculiar stretch of road that had 200–300 metre straights broken by right-angled bends and then another short straight to another bend. I stopped and attached the camcorder to the bracket I had taped to my handlebars and recorded a sequence of rolling footage. The recording is a hazy fuzz due to vibration from the rough lanes up through the solidly-pumped tyres and rigid frame of my bike. I came to a stop at the gates to Milecastle Reservoir, not a remarkable piece of English landscape but to me it was another chunk of my elephant consigned to the 'just done it' file.

With Stanfordham done and dusted, I was now on my first soul-destroying long straight road. Cycling is great as long as you cannot see for more than half a mile in front of you – it's the same as running in my book. Being able to see away into the distance on a straight inclining road is just not good for you. I passed a lady cyclist who was startled by my presence as I appeared from behind, but no exchange took place between us. I was focussed on the task in hand and was for the first time on this leg of the challenge digging in and working hard. The road went on and on and kept rising ahead of me; it was a real case of converging parallels of the side ditches. Halton Shields was my reward at the end of the haul. The next hour was a mixture of slogging up steep inclines and whistling down descents. Cresting a hill at Brunton Bank, I relaxed as I freewheeled down the steep slope to the River North Tyne and one of my key section markers, the town of Chollerford. I decided it was time for the first real refuelling stop. I pulled over about a mile out of Chollerford at the gates to Chesters Roman camp and was alarmed to find how stiff I was when dismounting the bike. Oh boy, it was really starting to sink in that I was in for a battle. I was on page three of the nine laminated sides of OS maps that Willie had supplied, less than a third of the way, and I was already struggling.

Shona pulled up beside me lifted up the boot lid and opened up her glorious bag of goodies. I tucked into a feast of tattie salads, pasta, sandwiches, tea and all sorts of cake and snacks. I ate well, drank well and got myself back onto the bike. The first stretch after the food stop was an uphill rise that quickly brought pulse and body heat up and deep belches from a protesting stomach. It was there and then that I vowed never to stop for a rest or for food at the foot of a hill. The slog up the hill was a killer forcing me to strip off the waterproof jacket that I had donned to stop a chill setting in at the food stop. Once I was up the hill at the Roman camp at Carrawburgh, it was a little easier as the road rose and fell in a much more accommodating manner across the open moorland. I was now on the old Roman road and had my first sight of Hadrian's Wall close by on my right. 'Not much left of that', I thought to myself as I whistled past various amounts of assembled stone and loose masonry lying around on the grass. The Wall, or what was left of it, was not as obvious as I thought it might have been. Apart from the regular signs

Above: Another cross-roads to test the navigation!

*Right: Some vital fuel taken aboard at Collerford
for the road ahead*

reminding you of this great example of our national heritage, it could be easily missed. Perhaps that view was simply a reflection of my reason for being in the area; it was not for sightseeing so perhaps I did it an injustice.

It was over the next two hours that I managed to get into a groove that was quite exhilarating. Road speed kept building and leg rotational speed was not an issue. I kept the bike in a reasonably high gear and the speed just kept on coming. I was not aware of a following wind but I can only put down this magic patch to a following breeze. The miles literally sped by as I sent the bike bowling west. The undulating hills on the moor offered little problem. The hills had been in my mind as big chunks of the elephant but that night they were just little snacks and nibbles. Shona kept a regular distance ahead then pulled in to a lay-by until I caught up and we exchanged thumbs up or some snatched smart aleck comment as I whooshed past her open window. Very soon I had the evening sussed. Each passing of Shona in the car represented a segment of the overall distance, each one manageable and all with the reward of a quip or big smile; simple things but enough to fix my mind on without losing concentration on keeping form, leg speed and rhythm. It is amazing how much you have to think when you are running or, on this occasion, cycling. Long distance is a mind game and it takes a lot of concentration to keep a good shape on the bike, keeping the elbows tucked in, and grab any chance to get down onto the aero bars. With the instant reward of the crouched position allowing me to ease up yet still maintain the same speed and, most importantly of all, save energy.

We passed through the quaintly-named Once Brewed and Twice Brewed, another couple of target landmarks. Twice Brewed has a pub and it looked a really nice English pub when I had driven past on the recce. I must admit to having a thought of jagging on the brakes and getting off to take a half pint of the local brew and raise some cash for the challenge from the punters. However, the thought quickly passed and the rhythm of the evening was not broken. Time and distance continued but I started to slow as darkness came in over the next hour. I was struggling and needed to play some mind games to keep the momentum going. If my mind had run a bit awry at sea, fearing phantom knock-downs and stowaways, that was nothing to the mind games that night. I was sprinting as hard as I could to the finish line of a running race and I just could not beat the guy ahead of me. White singlets, bare feet on grass, whitewash track markings, screaming and shouting parents were all sharply in focus. It was my school sports day, June 1968, and I was coming in second in the primary 440 yards. I was in P6 and was beaten by a P7 boy and it was my first ever running medal. The memory was as sharp as a pin and was my first experience of the excitement of track and field and one that stayed with me for 18 years until my last medal as Scottish Decathlon Champion in 1986. That little trip into memory lane helped me through a few miles. I relived other key sporting moments in my life, visualised athletic events and dissected every movement of a successful pole vault. I re-enacted in my mind throwing a discus, a successful high jump, the technique of a javelin throw; anything associated with positive thoughts and sporting achievements. I relived the day in a British Athletics League meeting in London when I was third man in the Edinburgh Southern Harriers relay team. Running leg two that day was the soon-to-be-crowned Olympic gold medallist, Alan Wells. A smooth baton change in a 4 × 100 metres relay is when the inbound runner reaches forward to the outstretched hand of the outgoing runner. I knew I had to set off early to build speed ahead of the inbound missile. That day Alan, having slowed as he passed me, turned and thrust the baton in my hand before we exited the front end of the change-over zone. These were all positive thoughts with no room for failures or fluffed attempts. After I had exhausted track and field moments I sang songs and counted pedalling leg rotations up to 50, then up to 100, and then 50 again. I passed Shona but there was no chirpy wisecrack from either car or bike. The long straight moorland stretch was coming to an end and I was in for some more navigation. Now 10 o'clock, it was dark and there was the slight spit of rain in the air.

My next chunk of elephant was at Greenhead and it was here that the wheels almost came off the trip. There was a key junction and point of navigation which called for a steep descent to the old pub and a right turn, keeping on the B6318 towards Gilsland, West Hall and Hethersgill. After that, I had to pick up the A6071 at Smithfield and on to Longtown. I swung round the corner and 'road closed' signs greeted me. My sneaky back road was off limits and a quick look at the map confirmed my fears that the only plausible alternative route was to take the busy A69 trunk road for 10 miles or so to Brampton, before swinging off on to the small A6071 to Longtown. So it was with some trepidation that I set off on the A69. Shona sat in behind me with her hazard lights on as it was now pitch dark and raining quite heavily. I felt vulnerable as I was easy fodder for some large articulated lorry thundering along the main east–west artery across the north of

England. Trucks, vans and cars sped past and heavy spray soaked my every effort. It was 10 miles of misery. In an effort to get the stretch of road done, I pushed on hard and, in the process, completely emptied my 'fuel tanks'. I swung off the main road to the sanctuary of Brampton, soaked and tired.

It was now pitch dark and I was tiring fast and struggling to keep momentum. I needed a hot drink and some sugar. Ahead shone the bright lights of a filling station so in we went and, sure enough, there was a hot drinks machine in the shop. Shona had pulled up in the side car park. I plonked myself down in the luxury of the soft front passenger seat but was not able to fully enjoy the moment as cramp seized my left thigh and calf. I shot upright and out of the car, tottering around the forecourt grimacing and trying to stretch off the cramp. I was oblivious to the car parked at the pumps and a little girl staring from the back seat who, when I caught her eye, looked very bemused, and so she might. What must I have looked like? Here was a man in black leggings with cycling shoes that made him walk on his heels, topped off with a red Day-Glo jacket, a fleece over his shoulders and a hard hat with a red light flashing at the back of it. At that point Shona emerged with two steaming cups of coffee, mine with extra sugar, and a Mars bar. The coffee was slurped, the Mars bar wolfed down and Shona despatched for seconds. I was getting chilled and, like it or not, I had to get on my way again.

Kitted up with zips pulled up to my neck and muff rolled up and over my chin, I looked more like a highway robber than a cyclist. I set the bike rolling, this time with

Grinding out the miles

little relish; I was really not at all happy. The tank was getting empty despite the food stop and it would not be too long before I needed some real rest and some solid food. From the filling station we coasted down into Brampton and made the right turn in the town centre, following the A6071. Normal positions were resumed with Shona hanging back to protect my rear end and me pushing on in front. Another hour went by and we made good progress. I was back up to speed but it was hard. I had to push down on each stroke of the pedal to keep rotation and momentum going. I was tired and, as if to rub salt in my gaping psychological wound, the rain was now a heavy downpour. I set myself the target of getting to Longtown, my next portion of elephant, before giving in for the night. That was a sign I was weakening, because two hours earlier my target had been Gretna, only 5 miles or so on from Longtown. I was now happy to cut that target and settle for Longtown, it was 01.00 hours, tipping down with rain and just horrible; my resolve was weakening by the minute. We came next into the lit streets of Smithfield and I coasted down a slight slope into the heart of the village where I stopped to grab a drink of juice and adjust my neck gear as water was now running down my neck. I clipped back into the pedal and pushed on to build up bike speed but there was no real response from my legs; they were done in. I was in trouble and the truth of the matter was I was broken. All I wanted to do was stop and sleep. It was an amazing feeling, worse than hitting the wall in a marathon and was as if a switch had been thrown. I had to get off the bike and pulled to a halt at a junction that opened into a tidy little street of houses. Shona came to a stop right beside me. I was hanging my head and the rain was running off my helmet and dripping down onto the handlebars. She asked if I was OK and I muttered that I had to stop for a rest. She did not offer a motivational reply of 'Just try a little bit further dear'. She must have seen the message that I needed a rest. We decided to carry on and find the first lay-by and pull in for the night. I pedalled out of town and found, in a very dark and wet tree-lined road, a lay-by opposite a large farmhouse. I pulled up and Shona tucked the car close to the verge while I propped the bike against the wet hedge and was in the car as quickly as I could.

I sat motionless and absolutely done in. Shona urged me to get out of the wet layers which I partially managed and just sat there in my leggings and put on a dry fleece top. Taking my shoes off was agony as the wet socks held the shoes tight and really needed huge efforts just to pull them off my feet. My strength had completely gone. After the battle to take my shoes off, I just lay back and sat motionless feeling very sorry for myself, my whole body aching from top to toe. My feet were wet and felt crushed by the hard-soled cycle shoes, my knees, legs and back throbbed with fatigue and my neck was stiff and sore. To add to the misery, I had rubbed both eyes very hard and the contact lenses were now narking and my eyes felt sore. Shona meanwhile had a fruitcake and juice ready for me. The rain was belting down hard and, as we were parked under trees, the rain was accentuated by large drops coming off the leaves and 'donking' on the roof of the car. I wound the seat-back down as far as it would go and closed my eyes. It was 01.35 hours on day 18, with 1,000 miles under the keel, 97 miles under the wheels and some 60 or so still to go. All I needed was a few hours of sleep and some food just to get me going again. The rain continued to pelt down and I drifted off, conscious of wet socks, a wet backside, stiff legs and throbbing knees. My knee was aching like hell and, being cramped in the car, I could not fully straighten it. I slept fitfully, each time I woke making an adjustment to my aching and protesting legs and stiff back. In the middle of the night Shona woke shivering so I managed to do something for her by hauling a sleeping bag from the back of the car and helped her into it. She slept better after that. I caught a glimpse of my Ibuprofen-induced puffy face in the rear view mirror, shivered and fidgeted a bit more. I slipped off to sleep.

11

TEARS ON THE HILL

At 04.30 hours it was still raining hard outside and large drops of water continued to 'ding' on the roof as they dropped from the sodden leaves above. The night had been one to remember and the day was going to be even more of an event. I was not looking forward at all to stepping out into the heavy rain and getting soaked to the skin. What a nightmare of a day it would be if the rain continued! I was stiff, had a sore backside and my eyes were red with lack of sleep, fatigue and a reaction to my contact lenses being rubbed. I lay there hunched, uncomfortable and not at all happy. I knew that I had more than 60 miles still to go and it was not hard to work out that if I wanted to arrive back at Kirkcudbright at midday, it meant I needed to get going and soon. I slipped off into another phase of fitful napping and at 05.43 hours I knew there was nothing else for it but to get out and back on the bike.

Shona was also stirring and, God bless her in her sleepy haze, she immediately set about sorting a breakfast of sorts for me. As per the night before, everything seemed to be within easy reach from the front seats. I stuffed down a couple of pots of rice pudding, a banana and a cereal bar, along with juice, an apple and some jelly babies, the latter in the hope that sugar might kick-start the day. After food I squeezed my damp feet into the wet cycle shoes and zipped on my neoprene over-socks. This was it, time to go. I opened the car door and swung my stiff, cramped and damp legs out into the rain and, with a grunt and a puff like an old man getting out of an armchair, I levered myself out of the door and creaked upright. Quickly donning my waterproof jacket, I kitted up with helmet, gloves and neck scarf, all the time being dripped on by the soggy leaves above. The bike was dripping and propped up against a very wet hedge, where I had dumped it just a few hours before. I was not a happy chap right at that moment, feeling cold and shivering with a mix of nervousness, chill ache and fatigue. It was without doubt the low point of the trip in respect of well-being, beating the other lows by a distance. I got onto the saddle, snapped in my right foot to the pedal clip and creaked a few yards before trying to secure my left foot shoe clip. It took a few more yards of teetering and then the balance came in and I was cycling again, heading in the right direction. The first mile was agony; it was cold, my hands felt frozen, I had deep shivers and generally felt miserable to the core. My backside hurt and my gammy knee was stiff and almost seized.

After 3 miles I was still cold and getting wetter by the minute as the rain lashed down all around me. Shona passed by carefully pulling wide of me to avoid the surface water puddles and disappeared ahead in the grey morning light and spray. It was time just to get on with it. I was cheesed off that I had not made Gretna the night before so the next bite-sized chunk that I loaded in my mind was Gretna and the 10 miles or so between me and my next goal. I was back on track with my mind fixed on the positives. Soon the wet and cold began to subside as insurmountable problems and obstacles to my progress. Longtown came into view, dull and wet, and I passed through this markettown seeing and being seen by no-one. Many of the roads around these parts are long and straight, just as they had been earlier in the trip. The long straight views into the distance have a multiplying effect of what I felt was visual distance fatigue. I crossed the River Esk on the west side of Longtown where only 5 miles downstream it feeds into the Solway Firth. I was getting there! Over to my left was the site of Longtown Market, where the first animal with foot-and-mouth disease was sold in 2001. Because of the size and reach of the market, and the number of animals bought and sold, the infection spread across the country causing devastation, loss and hardship to so many. A few more rotations of the pedals and I was out of Longtown. With another key point passed, I now had my sights set on Gretna. I eased along the road, passing the old munitions factory that was at one time the largest bullet and bomb factory in Western Europe. Line upon line of neat, shed-like buildings covered acres of ground. It was from this quiet border area that the explosives, shells and munitions were produced during the First World War, and used to such devastation.

'Gretna', the sign said, and I whooped with relief. It is strange how passing a sign at the side of the road can have such a major impact. I was on the border and nearly back in Scotland. I swept down the slope under the A74 and whooshed by the 'Welcome to Scotland' sign. It was a pity Shona was not here to take a snap, but I had a new-found energy, a new leg speed and confident rhythm and I eagerly pushed on the pedals rather than letting them circle with the least resistance or effort. Being back in Scotland was a tonic and I was much happier.

I negotiated my way through Gretna without any real problem. At one point during the planning I had thought about Gretna as a stopping point and had sent a letter to Gretna FC hoping to tie up some mutual PR link. My idea had been to call on the services of their physiotherapist to rub life back into my aching limbs, suggesting they might get some press out of it. The letter went without a reply, so no joy there. Through the other side of Gretna, I called my brother, Ian, and sister, Helen, to see where they were and where we might meet up. Our plan was to cycle together the last miles to Kirkcudbright, the Rankins doing it for their sorely-missed Dad. Contact was established; they were about an hour away so it looked as if we would meet at Annan. Ian confirmed that he had worked out a solution with cousin Derek to getting his car back to Kirkcudbright, and that he and Helen were keen to do the 58 miles or so from Annan to Kirkcudbright. I despatched Eastriggs behind the back wheel, buoyed up from the conversation with my big brother. At last family were close to hand. The next few miles skimmed by with my new-found vigour and purpose. About 3 miles short of Annan, I was conscious of a car pulling up alongside me, I turned and there, smiling from inside the warm car, were Ian and Helen. Another surge of energy appeared from nowhere, having now seen friendly faces. We exchanged some idle chat and a couple of sarcastic comments and digs. With that family ritual duly done, off they zoomed, followed by Shona, to get themselves ready for the Annan rendezvous.

Town square in Annan saw a family gathering and hugs all round. No sooner had I pulled up when Derek and Mairi arrived, having come over from Kirkcudbright. It felt like the team was complete, that I was not on my own but amongst family and nothing would stop me reaching Kirkcudbright. This was so much better than the well-wishing strangers at Blyth; this was family and it all meant so much more now. Shona went to a bakery shop and returned with steaming hot cups of tea and freshly-baked warm cr-

oissants. They were wolfed down and af-ter a few minutes of idle nervous banter it was time to get going. The three of us set off abreast along Annan High Street. The Rankins were in town and going places together.

I was intrigued as to how we would settle into an agreeable pace. We had not cycled with each other before, perhaps not for 35 years, and that was probably getting a 'backie' from Ian. He had bought a new Trek road bike especially for the trip and Helen had done a fair bit of cycling over the last few years so she was on her trusty steed. Nevertheless we did look an odd trio: Ian, in his tracksuit, shades and helmet looking as if he was on his way to a rugby coaching session; Helen in a bright fluorescent rain top and handlebar panniers, cycling

Ian, Helen and the author are ready to roll.

with effortless rhythm; and myself in skin-tight leggings, go-faster oversocks and tight top, hunched down on my aero bars at the head of the group. Pace was not a problem. On we went, covering the miles with infrequent stops. It soon panned out that my pace was faster than Helen's who was doing cycling at set speed. Ian just seemed to vary his pace for what was required. A regular pattern emerged: I would bang on ahead at my settled pace followed by Ian and then Helen, or Ian beside Helen with the two of them chatting away. When both were out of sight behind me, I would stop and wait for the pair to appear and off we went again. Cummertrees came and went and we bore down to Stanhope, within spitting distance of the Solway. I was becoming frustrated by this stop–start progress and went into a couple of real huffs as I cycled on, only to have to stop and wait for these two. Later in the day, these stops and the company of Ian and Helen would turn out to be my saving grace as I started to run out of energy and will-power. At Bankhead we faced a frustrating looping turn south down to the Solway shore. An easy option would have been to take the most direct route to Dumfries but that would have meant missing out a corner of Scotland, a small corner but a corner all the same. The route took us away from where we wanted to head and was soul-destroying. Once down at Caerlaverock Nature Reserve, we swung round back to a westwards heading and set off on the picturesque shoreside road to Dumfries.

Another, not totally unexpected, phenomenon emerged. If Ian had set off first after a stop and was 100 yards ahead of me, I would really push hard and pull him in to re-establish the lead. Whilst this was not a race, I have a deep-rooted automatic response when Ian is around – compete to win. No doubt this was ingrained in me from our youth when, as the younger brother, regular sibling beatings were a part of life. He had, in my eyes, always been one step ahead of me and a better big brother I could not wish for. What would life be like without a deep-rooted competitive instinctive reaction to my big brother? It may subside some day, perhaps when we are doddery old buffers. We rolled into Dumfries and it was a bit of a navigational nightmare, none of us being familiar with the town. After a few meanderings we picked up the A710 out of town. New Abbey led on to Kirkbean and soon we were back down at the water's edge at Mersehead Sands. We were now entering a more hilly section of the route as we swung away from the water and headed inland towards Dalbeattie. The maps showed lots of contour lines and they matched what was lodged in my mind. I had fixed the hills and slopes as end-of-journey inconveniences when the route had been driven, but from my saddle they were taking on more than just an air of inconvenience!

Very soon I was really working hard not just to climb the inclines but also to keep a good pace into the now buffeting headwind. Each hill was picked off and each one drained me. I was now entering a zone where mind games would dictate getting to Kirkcudbright or not. I never for a moment thought that I would not get the job done but in what state would I be and how long would it take me? I had been in this position before in various hill running jaunts and, of course, on the mountain running legs of the Scottish Islands Peaks Race. In my default state of mind I repeat the mantra 'Do not stop, do not stop'. It is one that I have used time and time again and tunes the mind to one matter only. Having one thing to think about blocks off opportunities for weak thoughts to creep in, thoughts that can weaken the state of mind. If, however, that default line of mental defence had been broached by fatigue, mealy-mouthed thoughts or weakness, my second default is rewind the brain back to my decathlon days. At the end of the decathlon, the 10th and final event is the 1,500 metres, an event that a decathlete does not really train for, nor is equipped to run. The decathlon is all about speed and power, certainly not the attributes of a 1,500-metre runner. To add to the challenge of running a 1,500 metre race, nine disciplines have just been completed over two days, you are dog-tired and ready to drop. I would be physically sick before some 1,500s, safe in the knowledge that the next four and a bit minutes were going to be absolute agony. It was also nerves and being scared rigid that I might not win. The decathlon is an event where athletes gather an accumulation of points awarded for their performances in each of the 10 events (day 1: 100 metres, long jump, shot putt, high jump, 400 metres. Day 2: 110 metre hurdles, discus, pole vault, javelin) and the last event, the 1,500, offers a further opportunity to amass points from the scoring tables. Distances and times in each of the 10 events are set against a set of tables awarding higher points for the better result. This means that, by the last event, you know by how many seconds you have to beat someone, or not be further behind at the finish in order to have a higher overall cumulative score. The situation at the end of a decathlon has been one of the best-ever life lessons for me and I continue to apply it to this day. The 1,500 metres is three and three quarter laps of the track, a real sod for a decathlete. The mental toughness required to maintain pace is critical, no matter how much your lungs rasp or how heavy your legs and arms feel.

This torture presented itself every year in the Scottish Decathlon Championships and more times than not my arch rival, Ben Thomson, and I would be neck and neck on points going into the last event. Invariably Ben was slightly behind me on points come the dreaded 1,500 metres. Knowing by how many points I was ahead of him meant that, with a cross-check to the decathlon scoring tables, I knew exactly how many seconds I could be behind him at the finish in order to win the overall championship. I never lost such an encounter and won the title on seven occasions. He was by far the better 1,500-metre runner than I, so all I had to do was hang on to his coat tails and dig in. By the third lap, as lactic acid was building in my weary legs and pain levels were increasing, my mindset defaulted into an internal chant, 'Stay on pace, stay on pace'. If I slipped and lost contact with Ben, I would be done for. The chant worked and he never managed to break me. One year in a fairly blatant attempt to psych him out, I drew up to his shoulder at the end of lap 3 and stared at him. That sort of thing is not really the 'done thing' in athletics but I had a job to do. On that day I was close to blowing it and my last roll of the dice was to use what little energy I had left to show him I was right there and ready to mix it all the way to the finish line. I detected a slight droop in his shoulders, so I just hooked myself to his elbow, stayed on the pace and ran well enough in the last 400 metres to win the championship.

When I came to each of the hills later that day, the 'do not stop' mantra was brought into play and, when that line of defence was broached, I took myself back 20 years or so to when I was on the track on lap 3 and not going to be beaten. Even the indestructible and well-proven mantra of 'stay on pace' was broached that afternoon as I struggled into the wind and hills. Stage 3, and my last resolve to avoid the easy option of stopping, was to roar in pure anger at the thought of wimping out. Goodness knows what an innocent walker would have thought if they had heard my profane roars and mumbling chants to myself.

To keep myself going, my mind would also run off into all sorts of cul-de-sacs and open blue-sky thinking, anything but letting the torment of fatigue take a grip upstairs between the ears. I thought of Dad and experiences as a kid on boats, bikes and playing fields. I re-ran some rugby try scoring moments and all sorts of days at sea in *Cloud Nine*. I had a distinctly clear vision and memory of the family on holiday in Carradale when my brother and I challenged Dad to a sprint race. He had been a speedy winger in his day and, when in the army, had won several 100 yards races. We knew of his speed from the old yellowed newspaper cuttings of his rugby days in family scrapbooks. We were testosterone-stacked teenagers, invincibility confirmed in our own minds through our exploits on the running track and on the rugby pitch. Dad agreed to a challenge and a short sprint was set up on the road outside the holiday house. We lined up and Mum shouted, 'Ready, steady, go' – and Dad won! Our last Olympic 100 metre champion, Linford Christie, always maintained that he went on the 'B' of bang. If only he had elected not to go on the 'p' of 'pop', a performance-enhancing pill, his standing and sporting legacy would be somewhat higher. Well, that summer's day, Dad went on the 'y' of steady. He retired from all competitive sport immediately after that race and, despite our protestations, declined to make it the best of three. A contemporary view of such a situation could be seen as harsh treatment of impressionable offspring and that the little darlings should be allowed to win to maintain self-esteem and self-worth. This is absolute tosh in my book. If you don't know what it is like to lose and hurt over it, you will never be hungry enough to really want to win.

The road miles were passing. We ticked off Dalbeattie and returned to a southerly heading, quickly knocking off Palnackie, and then what i'd dreaded happened. At about 20 miles out, just short of Auchencairn, I picked up a puncture on my back wheel. The tyre softened and a quick look over my shoulder confirmed I had a flat. I pulled over, dismounted and looked helplessly at the back wheel. Helen pulled up beside me and without any fuss got her tool kit out and set about taking the tyre off. It was not easy; we struggled and struggled but the damn tyre would not pop off the rim. Shona, bless her, who had been waiting ahead, sussed something was up and came back down the road to see what was happening. She pulled up beside Helen and I – Ian had just carried on into the distance – and I immediately thought of getting the spare bike out of the boot of the car. My man Alastair McKendrick had thought it all through and out of the kindness of his heart had loaned me a spare road bike. It lay folded and bagged in the boot of the car and I started to rip the gear out of the boot to get at the bike carrier bag wedged in under all sorts of layers of kit and food.

Erik, who had been an absolute ace during the sailing leg, had come down unbeknown to me to join in for the last few miles to the finish. Right at that moment he pulled up and got out of his car. Quickly spotting the mood of the moment, and the bike in bits, he looked me in the eye and in his inimitable dry style imparted the words, 'Well, Christopher Columbus, is it not time you were on your way?' It broke the tension and I let out a belly-laugh, the first laugh for a few hours. Just at that moment, Helen yelped with delight as the tyre had popped off the wheel rim and we were in business. The puncture repaired, Helen and Shona zoomed off in the car to catch up with Ian. I finished off the repair job and pumped the tyre hard. After a snack and a drink I was on my bike and going again, determined to make up for lost time. Almost immediately I could feel a difference in the power of my pedalling. Gone was the rhythm and drive that had been with me for the last few hours and here was a new feeling of heavy legs and lack of inner strength. It was an ominous feeling and one that I did not like at all.

The final 10 miles to Kirkcudbright were hard and I did completely lose it at one point. I had just come off the back of two really hard hills and was coasting down to the bottom of a long straight that bottomed out before an incline that took the road up and up and away from me. I let a negative thought break in right at the wrong moment and in that split second I was defeated. Without even thinking or protesting, I pulled up, unclipped from the pedals and rested my elbows on the handlebars. At the precise moment I dropped my head onto the backs of my forearms and surrendered to the hill, Erik pulled up beside me, just as he had done at the puncture spot. He wound down his window, leaned across and chipped in with 'What do you think you are doing? Get a move on.' The comment really pierced me to the core and I was furious with him, angry that he did not understand where I was and how I was scraping the very bottom of the barrel. As defeat hit me, plus the apparent confirmation of that from Erik, the double whammy twisted my gut and I screamed back at him in an absolute rage, 'Sorry to keep you – you bastard!' I was furious with him. If Erik had got out of the car at that moment and been standing by my side, I could not have vouched for my actions. I am sure to this day that I would have punched him square in the face. I clipped in and got back on the bike and started on the hill, seething with rage that Erik did not get it; he just did not get it, I kept telling myself. This time, with mind back in gear, I was 100% certain that I would be coasting down the other side of the hill in no time at all just to prove to Erik he was wrong. That hill hurt.

It was after the whole event had been completed that I was chatting through the experience with my good friend, Curly Mills. Curly is a bit of a thinker and is never short on views or opinions. The chat was all about survival and decision-making processes when tired, scared and in danger. I told him how disappointed I had been with myself over recent years because my mind was not as strong or focussed as it had been in earlier life. Is the mind like muscle? Does it need exercise and testing in such pressure zones to keep it up to the job of keeping you going? Get the mind in gear and the body follows. Curly pointed out that the mind is the ultimate self-preservation tool in the body's kit-bag. The mind recognises that the body cannot do the things that a younger model could or would want to do. The mind will let the body go to failure stages through fatigue and then start to shut systems down, depending on messages from muscle, lungs and heart. A fixed or bloody-minded tunnel vision approach will get the best competitor further. That is often the difference between athletes who win and those who have no gold medals. However, Curly brought me to the conclusion that the mind was in tune with the ageing process and was the ultimate decider on what goes on and what does not. Clearly, I was focussed to get the job done and I was not as fit as perhaps I should have been, and I was 48 years young. The mind, Curly maintained, was the final arbiter on how far I could push myself and I should accept it as a fail-safe fuse box. Just as well I had not thought this through before the trip or else I would have been expecting my self-preservation automatic response and might have let it kick in earlier. Armed with this, I could now set about managing these sequences. I suppose the ultimate arbiter is the heart. Override the fuse and the whole thing can blow!

Dundrennan came and went and my map was plastered with 'Danger Area' over to the right. It was the MOD firing range. All I knew was that there was 'danger' right here if I did not reach the others soon. I knew that I must be getting close to the last hill on this never-ending road to Kirkcudbright, for my map told me so. Surely I must see Shona, Ian and Helen soon. I had fallen well behind at the puncture but was surprised that I had not caught up with them by now. I pleaded that it would be soon, and it was. I heaved up Grange Hill and started a slight downhill freewheeling and there they were waiting for me in an opening to a field gate. Helen, Ian, Shona and Erik were standing there waiting for me. Ian and Helen were in their freshly-donned, bright pink Parkinson's T-shirts, a change from their cycling colours.

As I came to stop at the top of the final hill, an overwhelming sense of finality, or was it achievement, came over me. I gently squeezed the brakes and came to a stop beside Shona who was standing by the open boot of the car. I unclipped and put my foot down and suddenly gulped a breath and gasped for air. It was that feeling when you swallow water and it feels as if it has gone down the wrong way. I gasped again and slumped over the handlebars, struggling for air but nothing was going down. It was all too much and I dissolved into floods of gasping, gagging tears. I could not stop. For the first time in the whole trip I was completely out of control. Shona grabbed my asthma inhaler from a bag and thrust it into my hand. I took a couple of puffs but the tears kept coming. Having had the security of the inhaler, I caught my breath and composed myself. I had taken myself over the edge and, in all the mad physical effort and focus of beating these bloody hills and headwind, fatigue, emotions and the stress of the whole trip had just overtaken me. The build-up, the busy period of work before the off, the first day storm, trawling the jib over the side, massive, steep breaking waves off Islay, St Kilda in a storm, the crash gybe, the damage and disappointment of heading for Stromness, Muckle Flugga, the Lerwick hangover and enforced stay, dodging the shipping traffic, North Sea speed and the final dropping of the broken and beaten mainsail off Blyth. It was all behind me but the building pressure had just been released in a flood of emotion and fatigue. This was new territory for me; I had never before dissolved into such a bubbling mess and it was uncomfortable. Being a stoic sort of chap, not prone to too much high emotion, the breakdown surprised me but, more alarmingly, it had exposed me as a person. Right now, here in a lay-by just short of Kirkcudbright it was of no real worry as I was amongst family and Erik, who had been my constant at sea and on shore. Looking back it was probably quite good to get the wobbler out of the way and exorcise it from my system. Hell of a bad show if I was to do it in public.

Realising that I was in a right state, my self-control mechanisms kicked in and I regained control of myself. After some mouthfuls of water and a bite on a chocolate bar, I was back in command. I guzzled down the rest of the chocolate bar and the sugars immediately kicked in, or so it felt. Ian handed me a bright pink Parkinson's T-shirt and said, 'Better get this done then, son.' My mind re-focussed on what was still to be done. I blotted the tears from my eyes with my cycling gloves and turned to the job in hand – the circumnavigation of Scotland was still to be done. We had to get to the finish which was giving me more concern than I dared think. I was now worried that I was not strong enough to hold it together at the church gates in St Mary's Street, Kirkcudbright. Would I be hit with a chin wobbler? Would I be OK?

The 'Parkinson's pink trio' coasting back down to sea level (Courtesy of Erik Archer)

Left: Kirkcudbright at last!
(Courtesy of Erik Archer)

Below: The last few yards
(Courtesy of Erik Archer)

Sunday 1st May - Kirkcudbright

- 998nm

- 163 miles

- 18 days, 2hrs 5 min

The Rankin and Collins clans together at the end of it all (Courtesy of Erik Archer)

The cycle on from 'that' lay-by was a delight. The sun shone and the chat was light and chirpy. We slid down the hill from Mutehill and Kirkcudbright Bay opened up to our left. Along the flat sea-level road we coasted until we came to the sign on the right of the road that really did mean it was nearly all over. 'Kirkcudbright – Artists' Town'. That was it, we were back in Kirkcudbright. Behind me were the puncture and hills, the gales and faulty gear, the emotions and disappointments, along with that morning of self-doubt off Stromness. Yes, I was going to be the first person to circumnavigate Scotland by boat and bike.

Ian and Helen fell in behind as we pulled into St Mary's Street and I could see a group of people standing in the road well ahead. Ian and Helen dropped further back and I coasted forwards. I was now picking out faces in the crowd that had gathered at the church gates. I could make out my Mum and then saw my eldest daughter Jennifer standing there in the sunshine. She had come down all the way from Aberdeen University to see her old man complete his madcap scheme. She looked so grown-up. That sounds corny but it was the thought that flashed through my mind at that moment. I also thought her poor little sister Katrina would be stuck in school right now. My Dad's sister, Aunt Harriet, my (now late) Uncle Charlie Collins, Derek and Mairi came into view, along with a sea of faces and all were waving and smiling in my direction. I swung past the crowd, only for a commotion of yells and shouts to go up and I realised that a finish tape had been strung up between the church gates. 'Typical', I thought, 'navigate all the way round Scotland and I miss the turning into the church gates'. A quick U-turn was called for so I pulled round and broke the finishing tape to cheers and clapping. My immediate thought was, 'Don't get all soft here boy and no trembling bottom lip'. The outburst at the top of the last hill had unsettled me and I knew that I was so tired, all used up, and that I might not be in total control of my emotions. The lip stayed firm, thank goodness.

The people gathered at the church gates gave me a rousing welcome, cheering and clapping. It was over. I unclipped and steadied my foot on the ground. My Mum was there and I gave her a huge hug, or was it her giving me a huge hug? Shona, Ian, Helen and Derek were there right beside me. I recall feeling hot in the bright sunshine and then a stream of unfamiliar faces pushed up and shook hands and slapped me on the back. 'Thank you, thank you,' I repeated again and again as these well-wishers made contact. 'Damn, no press', I thought, wanting to capitalise on the moment. But then a photographer pushed forward and soon had a group pulled together for the celebratory shot that would adorn the local paper. Some of the unknown faces were from the Parkinson's Disease Society and they soon had a big banner pulled out and strung across behind us while we all stood grinning at the camera. My mind was still 'hurting on the hill' and it needed to catch up with what was now, the present. I was still, motionless, stress-free, no rocking or bracing myself at sea, thinking of what might break, pushing for speed or waiting for the alarm. My legs were still, no more rotation and exertion, my heart was not pounding and I was not considering where I should set myself the next target to meet and move on from. I had eaten the whole elephant. Danger was over, worry was over, I had got

Job Done

here and the trip was done, over, completed. I had done it. A wave of satisfaction swamped me and I gave a big cheesy grin. My chin started to wobble and my eyes filled up. But no, there was still some control and resource in the tank to hold myself together. I turned to my brother Ian and muttered under my breath, 'Now, where is the beer?'

The crowd started to disperse and Shona was quietly tidying up behind me as she had done on so many times over the whole episode. That was that then; I had done it – well, not all of it. 'Two out of three was not bad', I thought to myself:

1. Become the first person to circumnavigate Scotland, by boat and bike – done.

2. Raise awareness and money for Parkinson's Disease Society and Ocean Youth Trust Scotland; £13,000 and masses of press coverage – done.

3. Set a non-stop world record – no, but that may well be for another day in another way.

12

SPEED, SLEEP AND RECORDS

The trip was a logistical challenge and, in effect, a project management job with myself as client, principal and auditor. Here are some comments and observations on its key characteristics.

During the whole trip I logged every six hours my position, speed, average speed, course, barometric pressure, sleep and sail plan. Such a record allowed me to keep track of and make comparisons on progress, also giving me some running averages. Other than it being a vital record for any subsequent verification by the WSSRC, it also kept me updated on my running boat speed. The best single six-hour distance covered was 49 miles, giving an average speed of 8.2 knots and the best 24-hour run was 180 miles, giving a fairly respectable average speed of 7.5 knots. That particular run was done fetching north-west from Barra Head to St Kilda. At the other end of the 'six-hour' league table, I struggled to make 7 miles at an average of 1.2 knots as I slipped out of Stromness at 06.00 hours after a stressful two days carrying out repairs. That particular 24-hour run is pretty gruesome reading as over one full day I only covered 85 miles at an average speed of a paltry 3.5 knots. All of this was in very light winds but it was perhaps a good way to ease back into the notion of being at sea after the wipeout. The sail down the North Sea was fairly uneventful, other than the wrecking of the mainsail near Blyth. Speed was remarkably level at or around 5.5–6.7 knots for most of the way south over the 330-mile leg. I remain frustrated by the bald statistics that came out from the trip. What do I remember with the most fondness? A run of six six-hour segments at average speeds of 6.7, 7.8, 8.2, 6.3, 7.7 and 7.2 knots, an average of 7.3 knots, which included the magical night and early morning sail out and round St Kilda.

In total the trip took 18 days 2 hours 5 minutes. Of that total elapsed time, 6 days 23 hours 58 minutes were taken to cover the 998 nautical miles at an average of 5.9 knots. My target had been 9 days so I was well within target. Of course the voyage was interrupted with unplanned stopovers that added a further 9 days 4 hours 56 minutes to the trip. The cycle leg of 163 miles was covered in 21 hours 11 minutes but that did include a four-hour recovery stop just short of Gretna. Including that much-needed, if not vital, stop, average bike speed was 7.7 miles per hour. Taking out the 4 hours 8 minutes stop, the bike leg and average rolling speed was a pretty mediocre 9.5 miles per hour, not exactly Tour de France speed and below my target of 10 miles per hour. Clearly I did not have enough training miles under my tyres and that showed. Was I suffering from the reaction to the painkillers taken back at Blyth? I don't know, but certainly the deep fatigue and general 'empty' feeling at times during the cycling leg was a surprise to me and one that I thought I would be able to breeze through. Perhaps it was Old Father Time giving me a message after all.

I have also reflected on the gear failure that ended the whole challenge. Sailing accidents are, it is well-recorded, a consequence of a series of events that build to a catastrophic finale. At times they are caused by something quite innocuous or just a plain simple or silly mistake. In my situation off Rona, failure developed from a series of events, starting with something innocuous but critical, the definition of a weakest link in the form of a small shear pin. One little shear pin the size of half a match stick had crumbled and from that resulted a buckled boom, torn Genoa, broken mainsail fitments, smashing of three deck blocks, loss of a satellite telephone, two nights in Stromness, seven days in Lerwick, an expensive piece of Shetland knitwear for my wife, Shona and, of course, the end of a dream. Could I have made an effective repair if I had spent time over the winter pulling the boat apart and putting it back together again so that I had an intimate knowledge of her workings? Maybe, maybe not. I do not really think, even armed with the most intimate knowledge of the self-steering mechanism, I would have ventured down into the bowels of the boat in a Force 8 gale to attend to the steering gear in an enclosed and suffocating space. I think not, so should I discard the repair option that still nags away in my mind? It is clear to me that if ever another voyage of this sort is tried in the future it will be on a boat of which I have a more complete engineering knowledge, far more than I knew of *Pegasus*. One issue absolutely clear in my mind is that I would make no assumptions whatsoever that others have covered things for me. The lads at Beneteau had offered to do a full check-up and they charged for their services. Should I have double-checked their work? All so easy to question in retrospect. The failure of the shear pin put me in the most dangerous position of the whole trip when I was forced to leave the safety of the cockpit to make good the unfurled Genoa and to make safe the mainsail, each activity being prone to further complications and exposure to danger. I agree that accidents at sea are a consequence of a series of events, innocuous to begin with but with a habit of growing arms and legs with too much ease and speed. All I know is that checking if this small part needs replacing is an element of the overall service of autopilot systems, which was not carried out. Do I remain angry and frustrated by that? Yes!

The other key indicator for this trip were the sleep management issues that threw out some interesting, if not worrying, figures. Did the lack of sleep bring about a failure in my decision-making process prior to the big wipeout? Should I have assessed the potential risks to the steering system and reefed down to a small jib? Should I have taken the helm more often to reduce wear and tear, especially in the corkscrewing waves prior to the wipeout? These are all 'what-ifs' and I am sure, on reflection, that I did contribute to the failure of the steering. But, after all, self-steering is there to take over when needed! Sleep is like fuel for the body and, like food, the body needed to get its fair share. I read endless Internet reports on sleep management from around the professional sailing world and some papers written for shift workers at sea and, in particular, from the United States Navy. Accidents were more likely at the end of a shift and clearly linked to sleep deprivation and its effects on decision-making, risk-taking and rational processing of data and surrounding circumstances. My average sleep per 24-hour period, after having been at sea for a day, was 3.5 hours, with the highest total being 4 hours and the worst 1 hour in 24. The 1-hour period was recorded over the 24 hours leading up to my arrival at Stromness. It was on the back of an uninterrupted 12-hour session at the wheel motoring to Stromness and after a long, hard, night sail from St Kilda on to North Rona.

At the start I was most definitely stressed as a result of the totally manic previous few months at work. That, coupled with the anxieties surrounding departure and the severe pasting I took over the first few hours, led me to deplete energy levels more than I had expected so early on in the trip. The beat out west across the Solway Firth into the gale was hard, but Fiona was absolutely right to say 'Go'. The reward from all that effort was a blast northwards to St Kilda. Were we too ambitious to take the wind speeds that were forecast? The wind at the time of the steering failure was not at levels that were causing me or, more importantly, *Pegasus*, any real difficulty. The seas were building but were rolling in behind us and all was in control and balanced. Even with the commotion and big waves off Rona there was never a single moment that I thought *Pegasus* was not capable of the sea and wave conditions. We were down to two reefs and small headsail; ideally a third reef would have taken some pressure off the autohelm but, having seen the residue of the failed shear pin, no amount of sail-set management could have avoided the failure. So, yes, I am content that with the luxury of hindsight we had set off at the right time, we had taken the right navigation and sail-setting options, but I had not managed my sleep as well as I might. I did well to persevere and get the job done and the shear pin, well, the shear pin was an avoidable accident waiting to happen.

The dream of a world record or, as this was to be the first attempt at establishing the route as an official WSSRC passage, a 'performance certificate' also deserves some comment. The basis of an unsupported non-stop passage is simply that. It is unsupported by any outside influence and there are no stopovers. I blew it on both counts. So the performance certificate was not on the cards but John Reed at WSSRC was still willing to record the voyage as a 'supported attempt performance certificate'. If the passage was attempted a second time and my time of just over 18 days was beaten, then the time would stand as a fully-fledged world record. For a supported attempt performance certificate to stand, £900 of the £1,500 application fee paid up-front would be applied to the administration of reconciling my logbooks and timed records. I elected not to take the option of the 'supported passage' and took the refund. I regret that decision but at the time I was down a few thousand pounds and facing the process of insurance claims, a rather large and almost punitive excess on the insurance taken out for the trip and the bill for the lost satellite phone. Knowing an insurance claim is not over until the cheque is banked, there were some potentially serious financial implications if the extensive repair bills were not covered. Adding a further wad to the bill was too much to bear and the decision was made not to proceed with the verification process. So there is no framed certificate on the mantelpiece to show for the voyage. There is, however, a video diary, a book and memories of my days at sea and on the road.

My journey had taken me to all corners of our country: Galloway, St Kilda, Muckle Flugga and the entire eastern coastline. I had seen the sun come up from the east, go over my head, set in the west and, without breaking with nature and the elements, seen it rise again in the east. Through that I had experienced our latitude on this globe. In my time I have also communed with our space on this earth by running on our hills, sailing on our lochs and playing in our rivers. I have lived and worked in our biggest cities and smallest rural towns so I have been lucky enough to see many views of Scotland that many have not had the opportunity to see.

All that done, I cannot help but feel as a nation we are biding our time when we consider what there is at our disposal. We have natural resources and potential wealth. I have seen, felt and tasted our elements. I have been smashed by powerful surging waves and toyed with by their gentle ripple on a seashore. I have surrendered to the pounding forces of our wind and ghosted along by the energy of the slightest zephyr. I have been pulled and pushed by angry boiling tides and had them as my friend when they helped push my bow up and past obstructive headlands. I have seen racing torrents of rivers and the high and valley-locked latent hydroelectric energy lying silent behind hillside dams. I have seen oil rigs in the North Sea sucking energy out of the earth, each of them in our waters. Who can deny we have resources in the water, in the skies and in our ground that could, with our Scots aptitude for design and engineering excellence, allow us to be master of our own future? I may not be well-tutored enough to be in a position to answer the complexities of arguments for and against economic self-determination, but with such wealth around us, the notion of such a choice gathers momentum in my mind. If pushed to make my position clear, I may only be able to satisfy the question over my position by the flag I would fly. If I ever made another attempt to do the trip, non-stop for the record books, it would be a Saltire.

Acknowledgements

Every single person, including those who would not want to be named, who donated towards Ocean Youth Trust Scotland and the Parkinson's Disease Society. Without the help and support of the following people I would not have passed 'go'. Thanks to:

- Shona Rankin, for letting me go and supporting me every inch of the way
- Jennifer and Katrina Rankin for putting up with their Dad's antics
- Ian and Helen Rankin for seeing me over the last miles
- David Warnock, for putting *Pegasus* in the water
- Erik Archer, Shore Manager
- Gordon McGeorge, Shore Manager
- Fiona Campbell, Skye Weather. Weather planning
- Sue McKichan, Marketing Matters. PR
- Andrea Tofta, Senior Media Officer Parkinson's Disease Society. PR
- Iain Taylor, Ezone Interactive Web Support. Web and e-mail support
- Nick Fleming. Ocean Youth Trust Scotland. Charts, EPIRIB safety kit
- Ocean Youth Trust delivery crew: Brian, Andy, Jim, Laurie, David
- Chris Limb, Sunbird Ardrossan. Pre-departure preparation of *Pegasus*
- Chris Dogson, Sunbird Ardrossan. Race readying of *Pegasus*
- Chris Owen, Owen Sails. Sails and discounted supply of new sail
- Dimension Polyant Sailcloth Technology. Discounted sail material

- Alastair McKendrick, Perth City Cycles. *Sponsor* and supplier of bike and cycling advice

- Dr Chris Idzikowski, Edinburgh Sleep Clinic. Advice on sleep management

- Mike Purdy, Cambridge Neurotechnology Ltd. Supply of sleep monitoring equipment

- Dr Peter Copp, GP Plus Edinburgh. Medical supplies

- Dr Ewan Crawford, NHS Lothian. Standby medical support

- Black and Lizars, Davidsons Mains, Edinburgh. Supply of constant wear contact lenses

- Derek Collins, Kirkcudbright

- Rab Thomson, Kirkcudbright Harbourmaster

- Peter Roberts, Kirkcudbright Marina

- John Aitken, Kirkcudbright

- Keith Newman, Kirkcudbright

- RNLI, Kirkcudbright

- RNLI, Stromness

- Coastguard: Liverpool, Belfast, Clyde, Stornoway, Shetland, Aberdeen, Forth, Northumberland

- Andy Steven and the VisitShetland office, Lerwick. Office, e-mail support and supply of images

- Barbara Foulkes and the VisitOrkney office, Kirkwall.

- Linda Lane-Thornton, Royal Blyth Sailing Club. Blyth shore support

- Peter Lederer, Gleneagles Hotel. Supply of fundraising prizes

- Titan Webhosting Services. Free Internet and e-mail account

- C-Map. Supply of electronic charts

- Autograph Signage Solutions. Boat graphics

- Trek Bikes. Cycling equipment

- John Reed World Speed Sailing Record Council

- Martin Waterhouse, Graphics

- Erik Archer Supply of Images

Appendix I

Solo Round Scotland Logbook

Summary

Start	End	Start	End	Sailing	Cycling	Transit	In port	Elapsed	Distance	Average speed
		(date/time)				(day.hr.min)			(nm/miles*)	(knots/mph**)
Balcary Point	Stromness	13/04/2006 12.11	16/04/2006 18.52	03.06.41		03.06.41		03.06.41	508	6.6
Stromness	Repairs	16/04/2006 18.52	19/04/2006 06.15				02.11.23			
Stromness	Lerwick	19/04/2006 06.15	20/04/2006 20.10	01.13.55		01.13.55		01.13.55	180	4.7
Lerwick	Weather stop	20/04/2006 20.10	27/04/2006 13.20				06.17.10			
Lerwick	Blyth	27/04/2006 13.20	29/04/2006 16.42	02.03.22		02.03.22		02.03.22	310	6.0
Blyth	Transition	29/04/2006 16.42	30/04/2006 17.05				01.00.23			
Blyth	Kirkcudbright	30/04/2006 17.05	01/05/2006 14.16		00.21.11	00.21.11		00.21.11	163*	7.7*
Total				06.23.58	00.21.11	07.21.09	09.04.56	18.02.05	1161	6.1
Average speed				5.9	7.7				6.1	

* 1 nautical mile (nm) = 1.852 kilometres = 1.1508 miles

** 1 knot = 1.15077945 miles per hour

Daily log

Date	Day	Time (hr/min)	Location	Log reading (nm)	6 hr distance (nm)	6 hr Average speed (knots)	24 hr distance (nm)	24 hr Average speed (knots)	Sleepover last 6 hrs (hr/min)	Sleepover last 24 hrs (hr/min)
13th	1	12.11	Kirkcudbright	0	-	-	-	-		06.25
		18.00	Luce Bay	31	31	5.2	-	-	01.00	06.40
		24.00	Mull of Galloway	62	31	5.2	-	-	00.15	07.10
14th	2	06.00	Mull of Kintyre	100	38	6.3	-	-	00.30	02.45
		12.00	Islay	136	36	6.0	136	5.7	01.00	03.00
		18.00	Skerryvore	162	26	4.3	131	5.5	01.15	03.33
		24.00	S Barra Head	202	40	6.7	140	5.8	01.00	04.15
15th	3	06.00	S St Kilda	249	47	7.8	149	6.2	01.00	05.15
		12.00	N St Kilda	298	49	8.2	162	6.8	02.00	05.00
		18.00	N Flannan Isles	336	38	6.3	174	7.3	01.00	05.15
		24.00	W Rona Isle	382	46	7.7	180	7.5	01.15	05.15
16th	4	06.00	N Cape Wrath	425	43	7.2	176	7.3	01.00	04.00
		12.00	Sule Skerry	463	38	6.3	165	6.9	00.45	03.00
		18.00	Hoy Sound	503	40	6.7	167	7.0	00	01.45
		18.52	Stromness	508	5	4.9	126	5.3	00	00.45
19th	7	06.15	Stromness	508	-	-	-	-	00	06.00
		12.00	Ness Head	515	7	1.2	-	-	06.00	06.00
		18.00	N of Westray	535	20	3.3	-	-	00.15	06.15
		24.00	Turbot Bank	557	22	3.7	-	-	01.15	07.30

188

20th	8	06.00	Ve Skerries	593	36	6.0	85	3.5	01.10	02.40
		12.00	Muckle Flugga	640	47	7.8	125	5.2	00.45	03.25
		18.00	Whalsay	674	34	5.7	139	5.8	00.30	03.40
		20.10	Lerwick	688	14	7.0	131	6.6	00	02.25
27th	15	13.20	Lerwick	688	-	-	-	-	00	07.00
		18.00	Sumburgh Head	718	30	5.0	-	-	00	07.00
		24.00	Dutch Bank	751	33	5.5	-	-	00.15	02.00
28th	16	06.00	E John O'Groats	784	33	5.5	-	-	00.45	02.15
		12.00	E Kinnaird Head	819	35	5.8	131	5.5	01.30	03.00
		18.00	E Aberdeen	859	40	6.7	141	5.9	01.15	04.15
		24.00	E Dundee	894	35	5.8	143	6.0	01.30	05.30
29th	17	06.00	E Forth Estuary	928	34	5.7	144	6.0	01.30	05.45
		12.00	Farne Islands	968	40	6.7	149	6.2	01.00	05.15
		16.42	Blyth	998	30	6.3	139	6.1	00	04.00
30th	18	17.05	Blyth	998	-	-	-	-	-	-
1st	19	14.16	Kirkcudbright	1161	-	-	163	7.7	-	-

* 1 nautical mile (nm) = 1.852 kilometres = 1.1508 miles;

** 1 knot = 1.15077945 miles per hour

Appendix II

Specifications of *Pegasus* and navigational aids

Specifications

Sails: (Owen Sails, Oban)

- Dacron fully battened mainsail
- Pentex lightweight 150% No.1 Genoa
- CXG Carbon 140% No.2 Genoa
- Dacron No.3 cruising headsail
- Dacron blade jib
- Dacron storm jib
- Asymmetric spinnaker

Hull and rigging:

- Overall length 50 feet 9 inches
- Length of waterline 45 feet 5 inches
- Beam 14 feet 8 inches
- Draft 5 feet 11 inches
- Weight 28,659 lbs
- Engine 100 hp Yanmar
- Mast height 63 feet 7 inches
- Designer, Farr Yacht Designs
- Builders, Beneteau France

Navigational aids

Pegasus had a full set of paper charts aboard for the trip, along with three independent GPS navigation systems. On the water navigation was maintained on C-map cartography running on a Raymarine RL80c plotter at the navigation table in the saloon and a RL70c repeater plotter at the port wheel. In addition *Pegasus* was equipped with:

- At each steering wheel: Raymarine ST80 Master View; Speed, depth, log, S6000 autopilot. RL70c Plotter at port wheel and ST80 wind analogue reader
- Navigation table: RL80 Plotter

- VHF: Simrad DSC radio
- Weather receiver: Navtex 6Plus
- Power: Panda generator
- C-Maps: C224 Scotland West, C220 Shetland Orkneys and Western Scotland, C214 Harwich to Shetland
- Admiralty Charts (Portfolio supplied by Ocean Youth Trust Scotland)
- Ordnance Survey maps: 1:50,000 scale sheets 4, 81, 83, 84, 85, 87, 86.

Appendix III

Charities at work

Ocean Youth Trust Scotland

Ocean Youth Trust Scotland (OYTS) is a charity devoted to inspiring positive change in young people through the challenge of *Adventure under Sail©*. It evolved from the original Ocean Youth Club, a UK-wide organisation established in 1960 by Chris Ellis and the Rev. Chris Courtauld. Ocean Youth Club disbanded in 1999, and a total of 6 regional, independent Trusts were then formed around the UK. Although the original objectives have changed very little over the last 50 years (using the unique challenge of a residential voyage on a large sailing vessel to encourage young people from all walks of life to gain confidence, take responsibility and work together as a team), the Scottish-based Trust has undergone significant development in its short life.

Established as an independent Scottish charity in 1999 with one vessel, three staff, a handful of volunteers and an annual capacity for working with 400 young people. OYTS has grown significantly in 10 years. It owns and operates three sail training vessels, employs 14 staff and is supported by 240 members and 140 volunteers with a capacity to work with 1200 young people annually. All three of the Trust's vessels have been provided by the amazing generosity of Patrons Curly and Barbara Mills. *Alba Venturer* is a custom-designed 70' ketch rigged Oyster built for OYTS in 1998. *Alba Explorer* and *Alba Endeavour*, both ex round-the-world race yachts entered service with the Trust in 2007 and 2008 respectively. All three vessels accommodate 12 young people and six sea staff, and are equipped and maintained to a very high standard.

OYTS aims to provide a safe, unique and extremely effective environment for the personal development of young people aged 12–24. Although the benefits to young people are very wide and varied it aims to deliver the following specific outcomes on every voyage in line with the Scottish Government's Curriculum for Excellence:

- Self-confidence
- Responsibility and respect
- Ability to learn from experience
- Ability to work with others

There is also an emphasis on literacy and numeracy, communication, technology and skills for work and life.

Each voyage is tailored to the to the needs and abilities of the young people onboard and designed to deliver a challenging and educational experience in a fun, supportive atmosphere where young people are empowered to take on responsibility and make decisions at every opportunity. Sailing a large vessel is hard work both mentally and physically requiring everyone onboard to participate fully in every aspect of running the vessel from cooking, cleaning and maintenance to sail handling, passage planning and navigation. All these activities create almost unlimited opportunities for achievement on many levels. For many young people, achievements during their time onboard, and the resulting increase in self-confidence provide a turning point in their lives. Participation in voyages can also lead to nationally-recognised qualifications, from the Duke of Edinburgh's Award Scheme, the John Muir Award and the Royal Yachting Association.

The Trust's sailing programme consists mainly of five to seven day residential voyages around the beautiful coastline and islands of Scotland, its vessels regularly taking part in the Tall Ships Races and longer expedition voyages to Iceland and Norway. Over the last few years OYTS has developed close links with the sailing community in Iceland who do not currently have their own sail training vessel. As Scotland's only national sail training charity, the Trust is in a unique position in providing services to very diverse groups of young people from all over Scotland and beyond. Our organisation is open to all young people regardless of ability, race, religion or financial means. Aboard our vessels, young people, staff and volunteers from a wide range of backgrounds come together to form a very close-knit team where everyone has an important role to play. In essence a micro community is formed where individual strengths are valued, weaknesses are supported and discrimination of any kind is challenged.

We recognise great value in the positive relationships formed between young people and our staff and volunteers during a voyage. Living and working together in such a demanding and close environment requires a high degree of interaction. Barriers are broken down very quickly, with everyone on board learning to trust and respect one another within the first couple of days. For many young people, a voyage with OYT Scotland is their first opportunity to meet and get to know people from different backgrounds, with differing opinions and beliefs. Being able to understand the needs and backgrounds of others, and value and respect diversity (rather than feel threatened by it) is yet another important benefit of the sail training experience.

OYT Scotland is very proud of its strong volunteer base. It employs a small staff team and depends heavily on volunteers for continued successful operations both ashore and afloat. Volunteers contribute over 50,000 hours annually towards the objectives of the Trust. Even costed at the minimum wage this equates to £250,000 worth of voluntary work every year, however the value of the Trust's dedicated and committed volunteers cannot be justified in financial terms. The energy and enthusiasm they bring is boundless and infectious and would be simply unsustainable by a full-time sea staff. Our volunteers really do reflect the entire cross-section of Scottish society. The rich diversity and wealth of life experience they bring is immensely beneficial to the young people who sail with the Trust.

The Trust demands a very high level of competency from its volunteer sea staff, requiring comprehensive training in youthwork, seamanship and safety. This in turn, requires a significant commitment from our volunteers, over and above the time spent actually delivering our voyage programme to young people. The Trust has developed a strong culture of training and development over the year and delivers a comprehensive training programme for its volunteers. With an annual turnover of nearly £750K, OYTS, like any other charity, faces a constant challenge to raise funds. Sources of funding include Scottish Government grants, corporate donations, grants from trusts and foundations and donations from individuals, and of course fundraising challenges such as Alan's Solo Round Scotland Challenge. On behalf of all the young people who benefit from *Adventure under Sail©*, the Trust is extremely grateful for all the support it receives.

www.oytscotland.org.uk

PARKINSON'S DISEASE SOCIETY

Parkinson's disease is caused by the loss of brain cells that produce dopamine, a chemical which allows messages to be sent to the parts of the brain that co-ordinate movement. It is a progressive neurological condition, affecting movements such as talking, walking, swallowing and writing. The condition can also cause mood changes, bowel problems and difficulties sleeping. There are approximately 120,000 people living with Parkinson's in the UK. Each year about 10,000 people are diagnosed. The risk of developing the condition increases with age, however, one in 20 people will be under the age of 40 when diagnosed.

The Parkinson's Disease Society was set up by Mali Jenkins in 1969. Her sister, Sarah, was diagnosed with Parkinson's during the 1960s. Mali had presumed that there would be patient associations to help people affected by Parkinson's, but searches found that no such society existed. There was also virtually no non-medical literature about Parkinson's. Determined to find out what she could about Parkinson's, Mali began an investigation. It was from this research that the idea of starting a society grew. By late 1967, Mali had set up an exploratory steering group of neurologists, solicitors, relatives, friends and supporters. Mali progressed plans that eventually led to the Parkinson's Disease Society being granted charitable status on 26 February 1969. The Parkinson's Disease Society is now the leading charity dedicated to supporting everyone affected with Parkinson's in the UK. In 2009, the charity marked its 40th anniversary year. The Parkinson's Disease Society has come a long way in the last four decades. We campaign for a better quality of life for people with Parkinson's and provide expert information on all aspects of living with the condition. Our pioneering research is transforming treatment and taking us closer to a cure. We have a network of over 330 branches and support groups across the UK. These groups offer an opportunity for people with Parkinson's and their families an opportunity to get in touch with others living with the condition. Branches and support groups are run and organised by volunteers, many of whom are living with Parkinson's.

The Parkinson's Disease Society has staff working across the UK to provide high quality support for people with Parkinson's. This includes providing benefits advice, emotional support and links to other local services. We work with local health trusts and social care providers to influence and support the ongoing development of appropriate services in the area. We also provide expert education and training to professionals working with people with Parkinson's. The Parkinson's Disease Society provides up-to-date and expert information, advice and support on all aspects of living with Parkinson's. We produce a wide range of free publications, information sheets and audiovisual materials.

The Parkinson's Disease Society aims to raise awareness of Parkinson's amongst the general public, and encourage greater understanding of the effects of the condition on people's lives. The Parkinson's Disease Society holds a Parkinson's Awareness Week every year in April. In 1989 we pioneered the first Parkinson's Disease Nurse Specialist. These nurses offer a targeted service to greatly improve the quality of care available for people with Parkinson's. Since then we have invested over £8million in funding these nurses. There are now around 250 Parkinson's Disease Nurse Specialists working across the UK, but we still need more. We believe all people with Parkinson's should have access to high-quality and integrated health and social care services delivered by professionals with a good understanding of the condition wherever they live across the UK. We work hard to campaign and influence Government policy and the development of high-quality services at a local and national level.

The Parkinson's Disease Society is the 11th biggest voluntary funder of medical research in the UK. We have invested more than £40 million since we were founded in 1969 in all aspects of Parkinson's including cutting-edge science such as genetics and stem cell research. Today's treatments can help relieve most symptoms during the early stages of Parkinson's, but they do not stop, slow down or reverse the progression of the condition. The Parkinson's Disease Society is focussing more strongly than ever on finding the ultimate breakthrough – a cure for Parkinson's. Building on existing discoveries and exploring innovative areas of research, we are continuing to support the UK's most talented researchers and to work closely with the world's experts in Parkinson's.

The Parkinson's Disease Society is totally dependent on voluntary donations to carry out its work. We organise fundraising events and activities across the UK, including running events, overseas treks and prize draws. We also raise funds from trusts and grant-giving institutions and companies. We are also supported by the amazing generosity of fundraisers who organise their own and numerous individuals' own fundraising events. The PDS website features comprehensive news, information and advice for everyone affected by Parkinson's. The site has a very active discussion forum where people living with Parkinson's can share their experiences.

Our freephone helpline, which provides help and advice to all people affected by Parkinson's, can be reached by calling 0808 800 0303, Monday–Friday 9.30 am–9 pm and Saturday 9.30 am–5.30 pm.

For more information about the Parkinson's Disease Society, visit our website at www.parkinsons.org.uk

Parkinson's Disease Society

BIBLIOGRAPHY

Bathurst, B. (1999) *The Lighthouse Stevensons*. HarperCollins, London.

Centre nautique des Glénans (1972) *The New Glenans Sailing Manual*. Trans. 1978, David & Charles, Newton Abbot.

Fairweather, N. (2002) *Coasting Around Scotland*. Cualann Press, Dunfermline.

Gordon, S. (1995) *Highways and Byways in the West Highlands*. Birlinn, Edinburgh.

Haswell-Smith, H. (1999) *An Island Odyssey*, Canongate Books, Edinburgh.

Haswell-Smith, H. (2004) *The Scottish Islands*. 3rd edn., Canongate Books, Edinburgh.

Jeukendrup, A. (2002) *High-performance Cycling*. Human Kinetics, Champaign IL.

Johnson, S. and Boswell, J. (1996) *Journey to The Hebrides.* Ed. I. McGowan, Canongate Books, Edinburgh.

Knox Johnston, R. (2004) *A World of My Own*. Adlard Coles Nautical, London.

Lloyd-Jones, R. (2008) *Argonauts of the Western Isles*. 2nd edn., Whittles Publishing, Scotland.

Martin, M. (1999) *A Description of the Western Isles Circa 1695*. Birlinn, Edinburgh.

Nicholson, C. (2006) *Rock Lighthouses of Britain*. Whittles Publishing, Scotland.

Pennant, T. (2000) *A Tour in Scotland 1769.* Birlinn, Edinburgh.

Reeds Almanac 2005. Adlard Coles, London.

Scott, W. (1998) *The Voyage of the Pharos*. Scottish Library Association, Hamilton.

Slocum, J. (2000) *Sailing Alone Around the World*. Phoenix Press, London.

Wilson, B. (2008) *Blazing Paddles*. 3rd edn., Two Ravens Press, Ullapool.